The Impact of Feedback in Higher Education

Michael Henderson · Rola Ajjawi ·
David Boud · Elizabeth Molloy
Editors

The Impact of Feedback in Higher Education

Improving Assessment Outcomes for Learners

Editors
Michael Henderson
Faculty of Education
Monash University
Melbourne, VIC, Australia

David Boud
Centre for Research in Assessment
and Digital Learning
Deakin University
Geelong, VIC, Australia

University of Technology Sydney
Ultimo, Australia

Middlesex University
London, UK

Rola Ajjawi
Centre for Research in Assessment
and Digital Learning
Deakin University
Geelong, VIC, Australia

Elizabeth Molloy
Department of Medical Education
University of Melbourne
Parkville, VIC, Australia

ISBN 978-3-030-25111-6   ISBN 978-3-030-25112-3   (eBook)
https://doi.org/10.1007/978-3-030-25112-3

© The Editor(s) (if applicable) and The Author(s), under exclusive licence to Springer Nature
Switzerland AG 2019
This work is subject to copyright. All rights are solely and exclusively licensed by the Publisher, whether
the whole or part of the material is concerned, specifically the rights of translation, reprinting, reuse
of illustrations, recitation, broadcasting, reproduction on microfilms or in any other physical way, and
transmission or information storage and retrieval, electronic adaptation, computer software, or by
similar or dissimilar methodology now known or hereafter developed.
The use of general descriptive names, registered names, trademarks, service marks, etc. in this
publication does not imply, even in the absence of a specific statement, that such names are exempt
from the relevant protective laws and regulations and therefore free for general use.
The publisher, the authors and the editors are safe to assume that the advice and information in this
book are believed to be true and accurate at the date of publication. Neither the publisher nor the
authors or the editors give a warranty, express or implied, with respect to the material contained herein
or for any errors or omissions that may have been made. The publisher remains neutral with regard to
jurisdictional claims in published maps and institutional affiliations.

Cover image: © MirageC/Getty

This Palgrave Macmillan imprint is published by the registered company Springer Nature Switzerland AG
The registered company address is: Gewerbestrasse 11, 6330 Cham, Switzerland

Contents

Part I Feedback That Makes a Difference

1 Why Focus on Feedback Impact? 3
*Michael Henderson, Rola Ajjawi, David Boud
and Elizabeth Molloy*

2 Identifying Feedback That Has Impact 15
*Michael Henderson, Rola Ajjawi, David Boud
and Elizabeth Molloy*

Part II Expanding Notions of Feedback Impact

**3 Beware the Simple Impact Measure: Learning
from the Parallels with Student Engagement** 37
*Joanna Tai, Phillip Dawson, Margaret Bearman
and Rola Ajjawi*

vi   Contents

4   Learners' Feedback Literacy and the Longer Term:
     Developing Capacity for Impact   51
     David Carless

5   Re-conceptualizing Feedback Through
     a Sociocultural Lens   67
     Rachelle Esterhazy

6   Attending to Emotion in Feedback   83
     Elizabeth Molloy, Christy Noble and Rola Ajjawi

7   Embracing Errors for Learning: Intrapersonal
     and Interpersonal Factors in Feedback Provision
     and Processing in Dyadic Interactions   107
     Jochem E. J. Aben, Filitsa Dingyloudi,
     Anneke C. Timmermans and Jan-Willem Strijbos

Part III   Pedagogies of Feedback Impact

8   Operationalising Dialogic Feedback to Develop
     Students' Evaluative Judgement and Enactment
     of Feedback   129
     Edd Pitt

9   Turning Self-Assessment into Self-Feedback   147
     Ernesto Panadero, Anastasiya Lipnevich and Jaclyn Broadbent

10   How Debriefing Can Inform Feedback:
     Practices That Make a Difference   165
     Margaret Bearman, Walter Eppich and Debra Nestel

11   Impact of Personalized Feedback: The Case
     of Coaching and Learning Change Plans   189
     Jocelyn M. Lockyer, Heather A. Armson, Karen D. Könings,
     Marygrace Zetkulic and Joan Sargeant

Contents   vii

Part IV   Visibility of Impact

12   **Identifying the Impact of Feedback Over Time and at Scale: Opportunities for Learning Analytics**   207
Tracii Ryan, Dragan Gašević and Michael Henderson

13   **Facilitating Students' Use of Feedback: Capturing and Tracking Impact Using Digital Tools**   225
Naomi Winstone

Part V   Implications for Research and Practice

14   **Improving Feedback Research in Naturalistic Settings**   245
Rola Ajjawi, David Boud, Michael Henderson and Elizabeth Molloy

15   **Designing Feedback for Impact**   267
Michael Henderson, Elizabeth Molloy, Rola Ajjawi and David Boud

Index   287

Notes on Contributors

Jochem E. J. Aben is a Ph.D. student at the Faculty of Behavioural and Social Sciences at the University of Groningen in the Netherlands. His Ph.D. project is about the relationships between intrapersonal factors as well as interpersonal factors, and feedback provision and feedback processing. Jochem's research interests are in writing processes, text quality, feedback provision and feedback processing.

Rola Ajjawi is Associate Professor in Educational Research at the Centre for Research in Assessment and Digital Learning (CRADLE) at Deakin University. She leads a program of research centred on professional practice and workplace learning with an interest in feedback with a particular interest in sociocultural and sociomaterial approaches to learning. She is Deputy Editor of the journal Medical Education.

Heather A. Armson, M.D. is a Professor in the Department of Family Medicine and Assistant Dean focused on Personalized Learning with the Office of Continuing Medical Education and Professional Development, Cumming School of Medicine, University of Calgary. She is an academic family physician and teaches learners across the

x **Notes on Contributors**

educational spectrum. Her research interests include exploration of the translation of knowledge into practice including the role of feedback and coaching in facilitating this process.

Margaret Bearman is an Associate Professor with the Centre for Research in Assessment and Digital Learning (CRADLE) at Deakin University. Margaret's interests include: assessment and feedback; simulation and digital technologies; sociomateriality; and educational workforce development. Her methodological expertise includes qualitative and quantitative research designs, as well as evidence synthesis.

David Boud is Professor and Foundation Director of the Centre for Research in Assessment and Digital Learning, Deakin University, Research Professor of Work and Learning at Middlesex University and Emeritus Professor at the University of Technology, Sydney. He has been a pioneer in developing learning-centred approaches to assessment across the disciplines, particularly in student self-assessment, building assessment skills for long-term learning and new approaches to feedback. He is an Australian Learning and Teaching Senior Fellow.

Jaclyn Broadbent is Associate Head of School (Teaching and Learning) in Psychology and a Research Fellow at the Centre for Research in Assessment and Digital Learning (CRADLE) at Deakin University, and a Senior Fellow of the Higher Education Academy. Jaclyn's research focuses on self-regulated learning as well as the development, evaluation and translation of effective teaching strategies to ensure student success. Jaclyn has won several awards for her teaching, including an Australian Award for University Teaching and Deakin University Teacher of the Year. Website: www.jaclynbroadbent.com.

David Carless is a Professor in the Faculty of Education, University of Hong Kong. His signature publication is the book *Excellence in University Assessment: Learning from Award-Winning Practice* (2015, Routledge). His current research focuses on disciplinary differences in feedback processes and the development of feedback literacy. He is a Principal Fellow of the Higher Education Academy and was the winner of a University Outstanding Teaching Award in 2016. His latest book published by Routledge is Winstone, N. & Carless, D. (2019).

Designing Effective Feedback Processes in Higher Education: A Learning-Focused Approach. He tweets about feedback research and practice @CarlessDavid.

Phillip Dawson is an Associate Professor and the Associate Director of the Centre for Research in Assessment and Digital Learning (CRADLE) at Deakin University. His research interests include feedback, particularly feedback literacy and academic integrity. He has a background in higher education.

Filitsa Dingyloudi is an Assistant Professor in the Faculty of Behavioural and Social Sciences at the University of Groningen in the Netherlands. She obtained her doctoral degree in Educational Sciences from the LMU Munich, Germany, in 2017. Her research primarily focuses on learning communities of students and professionals in educational settings, peer feedback, value creation and mixed methods—both at a conceptual and an empirical level.

Walter Eppich, M.D., Ph.D. is a pediatric emergency physician and Associate Professor Pediatrics and Medical Education at Northwestern University Feinberg School of Medicine, where he directs the Feinberg Academy of Medical Educators. In 2018, Walter completed a Ph.D. in Medical Education from Maastricht University. His research involves qualitative methodologies, healthcare debriefing and teamwork in extreme environments. He studies how talk within teams influences learning and performance. Walter has co-authored over 60 peer-reviewed articles and book chapters. In 2018, he completed a field campaign to Antarctica to study teamwork in extreme environments.

Rachelle Esterhazy is a Research Fellow at the Department of Education, University of Oslo in Norway. She holds a Ph.D. on the topic of feedback in higher education. Besides feedback, her research interest covers various topics in higher education, such as assessment, student learning, peer review of teaching and educational design.

Dragan Gašević is Professor of Learning Analytics in the Faculty of Education and Adjunct Professor in the Faculty of Information Technology at Monash University. A computer scientist by training and skills, Dragan considers himself a learning analyst developing computational methods that can shape next-generation learning and software technologies and advance our understanding of information seeking, sense-making, and self-regulated and social learning.

Michael Henderson is an Associate Professor in the Faculty of Education at Monash University. Michael is a founding member of the Digital Education Research group and is Director of Graduate Studies. Michael's research focuses on instructional design, often in connection with digital technologies. Unique to his profile is that his research spans early childhood, schools, universities and professional learning contexts. Over the last decade, he has increasingly become interested in the pivotal role of feedback and seeks to improve research, policy and practice to leverage it for better learning outcomes.

Karen D. Könings, Ph.D. is an Associate Professor at the School of Health Professions Education at Maastricht University, The Netherlands, and an Honorary Professor at the University of East Anglia, UK. Her research focuses on feedback in the context of workplace-based learning. Additionally, a central topic in her work is the involvement of learners in participatory design of education, to better account for the different perspectives of students, teachers and educational designers, as well as ensuring upwards and bidirectional feedback that foster staff development.

Anastasiya Lipnevich is an Associate Professor of Educational Psychology and a Director of Faculty Research Development at Queens College and the Graduate Center of the City University of New York, USA. She also holds a number of visiting professorship at universities across the world (e.g. New Zealand, Singapore, Germany, Belarus). Her research interests include (1) feedback and formative assessment in a variety of contexts (e.g. secondary education, higher education, MOOCs); (2) psychosocial characteristics (e.g. emotions, attitudes, coping) and their links to meaningful educational outcomes; (3) personality and socio-emotional variables and their relations to feedback receptivity.

Jocelyn M. Lockyer, Ph.D. is Professor Emerita and Adjunct Professor, Department of Community Health Sciences, Cumming School of Medicine, University of Calgary. She previously served as Associate

Dean, Continuing Professional Development and as Senior Associate Dean, Education at the Cumming School of Medicine where she supervised Masters and Ph.D. students. Jocelyn's research has included the evaluation and impact of short courses, multisource feedback and assessment and feedback. She is currently examining the impact of assessment activities undertaken by Canadian specialist physicians as well as modifications to the R2C2 model to enable its use after clinical encounters.

Elizabeth Molloy is Professor of Work Integrated Learning in the Department of Medical Education, School of Medicine at the University of Melbourne, and Academic Director of interprofessional education and practice in the Faculty of Medicine, Dentistry and Health Sciences. Her research focusses on feedback, workplace learning and teacher development.

Debra Nestel is Professor of Simulation Education in Healthcare, Monash University, and Professor of Surgical Education, Department of Surgery, University of Melbourne, Australia. Debra is Editor in Chief, Advances in Simulation, and program lead for award courses in surgical education, surgical science and clinical simulation. Debra leads a national faculty development program for simulation practitioners—NHET-Sim (www.nhet-sim.edu.au) and a virtual network in simulated patient methodology (http://www.simulatedpatientnetwork.org/). Debra has published over 200 peer-reviewed papers in health professions education, edited books on simulated patient methodology, healthcare simulation (2017), surgical education and research methods for healthcare simulation.

Christy Noble is a Principal Medical Education Officer and Principal Allied Health Research Fellow at Gold Coast Health, Queensland, Australia. She holds Academic Title roles as Senior Lecturer in School of Medicine, Griffith University, and School of Pharmacy, the University of Queensland. Her research focuses on feedback, research capacity development, interprofessional learning and workplace learning in healthcare settings.

Ernesto Panadero is Ramon y Cajal Researcher at the Faculty of Psychology, at Universidad Autónoma de Madrid (Spain), and Honorary Professor at the Centre for Research in Assessment and

xiv   **Notes on Contributors**

Digital Learning, at Deakin University (Australia). His research focuses on several areas—first, the understanding and promotion of self-regulated learning. Second, formative assessment practices exploring their effects on learning. Third, the relationship between self-regulated learning and the use of formative assessment (self-assessment, peer assessment and formative uses of feedback). His research on educational assessment also explores the psychological correlates of self-assessment and peer assessment (e.g. interpersonal and social variables).

Edd Pitt is the Programme Director for the Post Graduate Certificate in Higher Education and Senior Lecturer in Higher Education and Academic Practice at the University of Kent, UK. Edd has recently been collaborating with Academics in the UK and Australia. His principal research field is assessment and feedback with a particular focus upon student's emotional processing during feedback situations. His current research agenda explores UK undergraduate students' experiences and use of dialogic feedback.

Tracii Ryan is a Research Fellow in the Faculty of Education at Monash University and in the Melbourne Centre for the Study of Higher Education at the University of Melbourne. Tracii has research expertise relating to assessment feedback, along with the motivations, outcomes and individual differences associated with social media and educational technologies.

Joan Sargeant, Ph.D. is Professor (post-retirement), Medical Education, Faculty of Medicine, Dalhousie University, Halifax. She is past-Head, Division of Medical Education and has been engaged in medical education across the continuum as an educator, researcher and administrator. Her research program is particularly interested in understanding the role external data and feedback play in learner development across undergraduate, postgraduate and continuing education, and in promoting continuous learning, and with an international team, has developed the R2C2 feedback and coaching model.

Jan-Willem Strijbos is a Full Professor of the Department of Educational Sciences at the University of Groningen in the Netherlands. He obtained the Ph.D. degree (with honours) from the Open University of the

Netherlands in 2004. His research focuses on design, implementation and effectiveness of interactive learning practices—collaborative learning, peer assessment and feedback, learning communities—in physical and virtual settings. He has edited two special issues on "formative peer assessment and peer feedback" (*Learning and Instruction*, 2010; *European Journal of Psychology of Education*, 2018).

Joanna Tai is Research Fellow at the Centre for Research in Assessment and Digital Learning (CRADLE) at Deakin University. Her research interests include student perspectives on learning and assessment, peer-assisted learning, feedback and assessment literacy, developing capacity for evaluative judgement and research synthesis. She has a background in health professions education.

Anneke C. Timmermans is an Assistant Professor at the Faculty of Behavioural and Social Sciences of Groningen University in the Netherlands. She received her Ph.D. in 2012 at the University of Groningen. Her research interests are in interpersonal expectations, the transition from primary to secondary schools in tracked educational systems, multilevel modelling, and the validity and reliability of school performance indicators. In 2016, Anneke received an Early Career Researcher Award from the *British Journal of Educational Psychology* for the paper "Accurate, inaccurate, or biased teacher expectations: Do Dutch teachers differ in their expectations at the end of primary education?"

Naomi Winstone is a Senior Lecturer and Head of the Department of Higher Education at the University of Surrey, UK. Naomi holds B.Sc., M.Sc. and Ph.D. degrees in Psychology and has extensive experience of academic leadership, having held the positions of Director of Learning and Teaching and Associate Dean (Learning and Teaching) at the University of Surrey. Naomi is a cognitive psychologist, specialising in learning behaviour and engagement with education. Her research focuses on the processing and implementation of feedback. Naomi is a Senior Fellow of the Higher Education Academy and a National Teaching Fellow.

Marygrace Zetkulic, M.D. is general internist and clinician educator. She is Assistant Professor of medicine at Hackensack-Meridian School of Medicine at Seton Hall and serves as program director of Internal

xvi   **Notes on Contributors**

Medicine Residency. Feedback and coaching became her primary research interest after experiencing how practising internists struggled to incorporate data into improved performance and how little internal medicine residents took away from their assessments.

List of Figures

Fig. 4.1	3P model of the learner experience of feedback	53
Fig. 5.1	Three-layer model of feedback practices in a course unit (Esterhazy, 2019)	73
Fig. 7.1	Conceptual model for the processes of providing and processing feedback and the assumed dynamic interplay with intra- and interpersonal factors	114
Fig. 13.1	FEATS dashboard	234
Fig. 13.2	Self-reported current and ideal feedback use	236

List of Tables

Table 10.1	Debriefing pedagogies and OSAD (London Handbook for Debriefing, n.d., pg 13)	180
Table 13.1	Features of FEATS and intended purpose with regard to the impact of engagement with feedback	232
Table 13.2	Changes in perceptions of feedback use	235

Part I

Feedback That Makes a Difference

1

Why Focus on Feedback Impact?

Michael Henderson, Rola Ajjawi, David Boud and Elizabeth Molloy

Introduction

Feedback is a topic of hot debate in universities. Everyone agrees that it is important. However, students report a lot of dissatisfaction: they don't get what they want from the comments they receive on their work and they don't find it timely. Teaching staff find it burdensome, are concerned

---

M. Henderson (✉)
Faculty of Education, Monash University, Melbourne, VIC, Australia
e-mail: michael.henderson@monash.edu

R. Ajjawi · D. Boud
Centre for Research in Assessment and Digital Learning (CRADLE),
Deakin University, Geelong, VIC, Australia
e-mail: rola.ajjawi@deakin.edu.au

D. Boud
University of Technology Sydney, Ultimo, NSW, Australia
e-mail: david.boud@deakin.edu.au

Middlesex University, London, UK

© The Author(s) 2019
M. Henderson et al. (eds.), *The Impact of Feedback in Higher Education*,
https://doi.org/10.1007/978-3-030-25112-3_1

that students do not engage with it and wonder whether the effort they put in is worthwhile.

Prompted by concerns from institutions that they are being criticised about their feedback practices, this has led to an explosion of literature about feedback in recent years. While some of these publications are of the "how to do it better" kind, there has been a heartening increase in scholars looking more closely at feedback, undertaking studies about it and generally questioning what it is for and how can it be done more effectively.

The more telling work has focused on critiquing the idea of feedback as we presently know it. Is the way we have been thinking about feedback useful? Is it compatible with the ways feedback is thought of in other disciplines? This has led to a revolution of feedback thinking which has shifted the focus from the quality and timing of the comments educators provide to students about their work, to how students become feedback aware and utilise more effectively the information they receive or help generate.

Feedback is seen as a process that makes a difference to what students do. It does not stop when students' work is returned to them. Without student action, we cannot meaningfully use the term feedback.

This shift of thinking from a teaching-centred process to a learning-centred one, means we have to look to new ways of thinking about the quality of feedback. No longer should we be solely concerned with the quality of comments made by teachers, but whether these comments, and indeed comments or information from other sources, lead to a positive influence on student learning. Instead of only focusing on the quality of the teacher's input, we need to consider the quality of the whole process, including the active role of students. The focus must be on: Does it make a difference, and how does it make a difference?

These concerns about identifying the impact of feedback, and how it may be fostered to make a difference to student learning have led to this book.

E. Molloy
Department of Medical Education, School of Medicine,
The University of Melbourne, Parkville, VIC, Australia
e-mail: elizabeth.molloy@unimelb.edu.au

1 Why Focus on Feedback Impact?   5

This book offers the field a new understanding of how we might conceptualise, design for and evaluate the impact of feedback in higher education. While there has been a growing interest in feedback research, there has not been a coherent focus on the impact of feedback on improving outcomes or learning strategies. Clearly, teachers cannot simply provide information and "hope for the best" but, instead, need to carefully design it to have impact on future performance. Importantly, they also need to find ways to understand and measure that impact in order to best support student learning as well as instructional designs. Without this critical bit of information, all feedback no matter how well-intentioned or carefully designed needs to be treated with caution.

The Development of This Book

In this book, leading international researchers across diverse disciplines explore the notion of feedback impact and offer promising directions for both research and practice.

The 28 contributors are drawn from eight nations. They include many of the most influential researchers in the field as well as newly emerging leaders. The contributors in this book have been invited because of their reputation and proven scholarship in the field, and importantly, because their combined contributions promise a coherent but broad scope of methodological and disciplinary contexts that address the distinctive focus of this book.

The editors selectively invited contributors for what they might add to the book. During the writing process, the editors and contributors engaged in several cycles of feedback. Initially, the contributors developed abstracts in response to a description of the purpose of the manuscript and the key conceptual, methodological and practice challenges. The editors then provided comments and recommendations to each writing team with the aim of maintaining a strong focus on the book's central goal as well as to better ensure key issues are covered.

As a second stage, the contributors worked their ideas into brief papers of around 3000 words. These were then organised into a compendium shared with all authors. At least one author from each writing team then attended a three-day "Feedback that makes a difference" symposium in Prato, Italy. Every participant had read every brief paper prior to the symposium which was then characterised as intellectually robust conversation about the key issues, challenges and opportunities for research and teaching.

Each writing team had the rare experience to engage in a rich dialogue with about their work with a diverse range of scholars in the field. In addition, the participants, including the editors, were able to spend an extended period of time enhancing the coherence and conceptual strength of the book, from vigorously debating definitions through to compiling diverse challenges and opportunities in research and practice. These conversations helped develop a coherent vision throughout the book, but also greatly informed the concluding chapters on research and practice.

Subsequent to the symposium, the contributors reworked their brief papers into full chapters. These were then sent to two other writing teams for peer review. The authors then received two sets of peer-reviewed comments and edits, as well as overarching guidance from one of the editors. The authors then worked with one of the editors in developing their final manuscript.

Structure of This Book

The book has fourteen chapters (not including this one) organised into five parts.

Part I—Feedback That Makes a Difference

This part identifies the critical issues which this book addresses. It brings together the most current thinking and offers new insight into the significant challenges in the field, in terms of research and practice, including policy.

Chapter 2—Identifying Feedback That Has Impact

By Michael Henderson, Rola Ajjawi, David Boud and Elizabeth Molloy

This chapter offers new insight regarding the theoretical, methodological and practical concerns relating to feedback in higher education. It begins with the construction of a new definition of feedback. We explain how feedback is a learner-centred process in which impact is a core feature. The chapter then explores the reasons why identifying, let alone measuring, impact is problematic. We briefly revisit the contingent nature of educational research into cause and effect, and question the implications for feedback processes that are likely to be experienced by individuals in different ways with different effects over different timescales. It is here we then discuss some ways we conceive the various forms of feedback effect including the intentional and unintentional, immediate and delayed, cognitive, affective, motivational, relational and social.

Part II—Expanding Notions of Feedback Impact

The Part II includes chapters that extend current thinking about what we mean by "making a difference" or impact. The dominant conception of feedback is that it should improve student grade outcomes and that it is largely a cognitive process. However, through the chapters in this part we establish that in addition to learning outcomes, we need to also consider the way in which learning strategy, engagement and affect should also be considered as factors that influence outcome as well as being outcomes in themselves.

Chapter 3—Beware the Simple Impact Measure: Learning from the Parallels with Student Engagement

By Joanna Tai, Phillip Dawson, Margaret Bearman and Rola Ajjawi

This chapter argues that researchers must look beyond narrow and simple notions of feedback impact in educational practice. It draws comparisons with what has occurred within student engagement research. This illustrates the challenges of researching a phenomenon that lacks conceptual clarity and hence gives rise to a range of contradictory measures, which promote misaligned research designs, and a focus on what is easy to measure. When feedback is acknowledged as a complex, social process, then the notion of impact itself changes.

Chapter 4—Learners' Feedback Literacy and the Longer Term: Developing Capacity for Impact

By David Carless

The main focus of this chapter is to analyse implications for short-term and long-term impacts of feedback by drawing on a qualitative longitudinal inquiry into four learners' experiences of feedback during a five-year undergraduate programme. The student experience of feedback is conceptualised by a 3P Model comprising presage, process and product factors. Learner feedback literacy is a key element spanning these three interactive cycles of the learner experience. Key findings from the study are learners' wishes for stronger partnerships between teachers and learners in feedback processes and evidence of challenges and possibilities for learner uptake of feedback. The main implications discuss ways of developing practical forms of feedback dialogue and future longitudinal research possibilities.

Chapter 5—Re-conceptualizing Feedback Through a Sociocultural Lens

By Rachelle Esterhazy

This chapter outlines a re-conceptualisation of feedback from a sociocultural perspective. Feedback is conceptualised as a social practice that is enacted together by teachers and students, and that is deeply embedded in the sociocultural context of the given course unit. Whether feedback has an impact depends from this perspective on whether students, teachers and their sociocultural environment interact in productive ways. A three-layer model of feedback practices is presented to describe the relations between the knowledge domain, the course design and the concrete feedback encounters. Based on this model, the chapter outlines practical challenges that might inhibit feedback practices from being productive and how we may plan for productive feedback practices in our course units.

Chapter 6—Attending to Emotion in Feedback

By Elizabeth Molloy, Christy Noble and Rola Ajjawi

The feedback literature has a habit of treating emotion as a form of interference. Therefore, many guidelines for improving practice are geared towards reducing learners' emotions so that messages can "get through" and take root. In this chapter, we present a case for a re-orientation of how we conceive the role of emotion in feedback. We use a social cognitive theory of emotional regulation, to help illuminate the affective dimensions of feedback processes. The theory focuses on students' perceptions of control over themselves and their circumstances, and the values that underpin their appraisal of their situation. Drawing on a case study, we illustrate how we may help learners to acknowledge the primacy of relationships in feedback and to recognise and work with emotions.

Chapter 7—Embracing Errors for Learning: Intrapersonal and Interpersonal Factors in Feedback Provision and Processing in Dyadic Interactions

By Jochem E. J. Aben, Filitsa Dingyloudi, Anneke C. Timmermans and Jan-Willem Strijbos

Previous feedback models in education (1) overlook that intrapersonal factors (i.e. factors describing one's personality) as well as interpersonal factors (i.e. factors describing the relationship between people) simultaneously affect feedback provision and feedback processing, and (2) only implicitly assume that the feedback sender and feedback recipient deal with error identification and error making during feedback processes. This chapter provides a model that conceptualises the concurrent interplay between intrapersonal and interpersonal factors and feedback provision and feed-

10 M. Henderson et al.

back processing in dyadic interactions, while taking as a starting point the assumption that errors, if identified and acted upon, offer a potential to revise one's own performance. As such, the model embraces the theoretical complexity of interpersonal communication, as well as the importance of errors for learning.

Part III—Pedagogies of Feedback Impact

The Part III is that of pedagogies of impact. In this part, we have sought out chapters that build on the previous and offer empirically supported arguments of key strategies and principles that have been shown to improve the impact of feedback. These chapters do not represent all possible strategies. However, they do reinforce key messages such as the agency of the learner and demonstrate the variety of ways that impact can be achieved across disciplines and other contexts.

Chapter 8—Operationalising Dialogic Feedback to Develop Students' Evaluative Judgement and Enactment of Feedback

By Edd Pitt

This chapter explores how UK-based film, comedy, drama and music performance lecturers demonstrate the possibilities of differing educational practices that pursue, through dialogic interactions, the development of students' evaluative judgement. It discusses the classroom culture that lecturers create and the learning potential of feedback dialogue which affords students the opportunity to learn from their mistakes in formative situations. The dialogic interactions surrounding professional exemplars and live exemplars of students' work in progress are discussed. In particular, the pedagogical initiatives of comedy buddies, scriptwriters' forum and speed dating feedback are introduced as ways of practically embedding dialogic peer feedback to potentially develop students' evaluative judgement and feedback enactment. Conclusively, it considers how we might measure the potential impact of such educational approaches over time.

Chapter 9—Turning Self-Assessment into Self-Feedback

By Ernesto Panadero, Anastasiya Lipnevich and Jaclyn Broadbent

This chapter proposes moving our conceptualisation of self-assessment to that of self-feedback, in which the final goal is for students to produce and search for feedback to close the gap between their current and desired performance. We propose six main venues to achieve self-feedback: (a) making the implicit aspects of self-assessment explicit to correct for self-bias, (b) shifting from scoring accuracy to content accuracy, (c) using a developmental approach: the power of practice/expertise, (d) connecting self-feedback and self-regulated learning, (e) exploring the role of individual characteristics and interpersonal variables, and (f) anchoring self-feedback to evaluative judgement: changing the view from task-specific to long-term learning. Additionally, the impact of self-feedback on learning is analysed.

Chapter 10—How Debriefing Can Inform Feedback: Practices That Make a Difference

By Margaret Bearman, Walter Eppich and Debra Nestel

"Debriefings" are the developmental conversations that take place after real or simulated work. A specialised form of feedback, debriefing has a substantial evidence base, particularly in healthcare simulation. This chapter explores how the healthcare simulation debriefing can inform feedback in higher education. The impact of debriefing may stem from: (1) its embedded nature with the entire learning activity and (2) the development of a culture which encourages learner-centred values, productive tensions and lifelong development. Valuable debriefing approaches that improve learning are identified and analysed, alongside their implication for feedback practices.

12 M. Henderson et al.

Chapter 11—Impact of Personalized Feedback: The Case of Coaching and Learning Change Plans

By Jocelyn M. Lockyer, Heather A. Armson, Karen D. Könings, Marygrace Zetkulic and Joan Sargeant

This chapter describes an empirically derived model for impactful feedback discussions. The R2C2 model has four phases: educators build the relationship (R) between educator and learner, gain learner reactions (R) to the feedback which can be used to determine the potential for change and development, and explore and ensure a mutual understanding of the content (C) in order to coach for change (C) to co-create achievable learning change plans that can be monitored to ensure learner progress. Two mechanisms, in particular, coaching and learning change plans, support learner acceptance and use of the feedback. The chapter concludes with suggestions for future application and research in health professions education and higher education.

Part IV—Visibility of Impact

The Part IV in the book addresses a significant challenge that of making the impact within a feedback process to be more visible. While all of the previous chapters offer insight into how we can design for impact, these chapters propose ways in which digital technologies may be used to track the impact or changes over time, by the individual learner or at a broader systems level.

Chapter 12—Identifying the Impact of Feedback Over Time and at Scale: Opportunities for Learning Analytics

By Tracii Ryan, Dragan Gašević and Michael Henderson

In contemporary higher education, learner behaviour is increasingly traced by digital systems. As such, there is a strong potential for data mining over time to track and represent learner actions in the context of their assessment performance. This chapter explores how learning analytics can assist educators to design impactful feedback processes and help learners identify the impact of feedback information, both across time and at scale. In doing so, it offers current examples of how learning analytics could guide educational designs and be employed to support learners to direct their own learning and study habits. This chapter also highlights how learning analytics can help understand and optimise learning and the environments in which the learning occurs.

Chapter 13—Facilitating Students' Use of Feedback: Capturing and Tracking Impact Using Digital Tools

By Naomi Winstone

This chapter explores the potential for digital tools to capture and track the impact of feedback. Advocating a shift from transmission-focused to learning-focused feedback processes, the chapter surfaces challenges inherent to visualising the impact of feedback processes and then reviews uses of learning analytics to illuminate students' responses to feedback. The potential to capture the digital footprint of students' interactions with feedback is discussed with reference to an e-portfolio system with a learning analytics dashboard. In this example, students were able to synthesise multiple feedback exchanges, visualise their key strengths and areas for development and record and monitor actions on the basis of feedback information. Winstone argues that it is important for feedback impact to be visible to students as well as educators.

Part V—Implications for Research and Practice

The Part V concludes the book. It brings together key issues raised in previous chapters and draws on the broader interdisciplinary literature of assessment and feedback to offer challenges, implications and "next steps" for research and practice relating to effective feedback.

Chapter 14—Improving Feedback Research in Naturalistic Settings

By Rola Ajjawi, David Boud, Michael Henderson and Elizabeth Molloy

This chapter discusses researching feedback inputs and processes to examine effects. Specifically, we promote a research agenda that contributes an understanding of how feedback works, for particular learners, in particular circumstances through research designs that take account of theory, occur in naturalistic settings and focus on students' sense-making and actions. We draw attention to categories of research on effects of feedback: (a) task-related performance/work; (b) meta-learning processes such as self-regulation; and (c) identity effects such as orienting students to the professionals they wish to become. We also discuss the difficulties in eliciting effects, attributing effects to particular feedback practices and the importance of exploring how effects are achieved and at what points in time, rather than simply looking for outcomes.

Chapter 15—Designing Feedback for Impact

By Michael Henderson, Elizabeth Molloy, Rola Ajjawi and David Boud

This chapter focuses on influences, affordances and challenges for teachers in designing for (and identifying) feedback impact. We propose four key questions that need to be asked: Do learners know the purpose of feedback and their role(s) in it? Can learners make sense of the information? Can learners take action? What effects should we be looking for? We then explore strategies that have been shown to be valuable in designing feedback that makes a difference. These are organised according to three important considerations: creating opportunities for effective feedback; developing learner and teacher capacities; and looking for effects. We finish the chapter by taking a step back and considering the implications at the programme and institutional levels in cultivating feedback that make a difference.

2

Identifying Feedback That Has Impact

Michael Henderson, Rola Ajjawi, David Boud and Elizabeth Molloy

Introduction

Feedback Is Important But There Is a Gap

Feedback is critical for effectively promoting learning. Without feedback, learners are limited in how they can make judgements as to their progress, and how they can change their future performance. Feedback is the lynchpin to learners' effective decision making, and the basis of improved learning outcomes. The value of feedback is tied with its assumed connection to an improved future condition, in other words—impact. However, while there is a growing body of research regarding feedback design, such as the potential of diverse sources (e.g. peers, automated systems), modes

---

M. Henderson (✉)
Faculty of Education, Monash University, Melbourne, VIC, Australia
e-mail: michael.henderson@monash.edu

R. Ajjawi · D. Boud
Centre for Research in Assessment and Digital Learning (CRADLE),
Deakin University, Geelong, VIC, Australia
e-mail: rola.ajjawi@deakin.edu.au

© The Author(s) 2019
M. Henderson et al. (eds.), *The Impact of Feedback in Higher Education*,
https://doi.org/10.1007/978-3-030-25112-3_2

The Structure of This Chapter

This chapter has two sections. The first section outlines how we conceive feedback. We explain how feedback is a learner-centred process in which impact is a core feature. In doing so we aim to reveal some of the complexities of feedback processes which then provides a context for the remainder of the chapter. In the second section of this chapter we explore the reasons why identifying, let alone measuring, impact is problematic. We briefly revisit the contingent nature of educational research into cause and effect and question the implications for feedback processes that are likely to be experienced by individuals in different ways with different effects over different timescales. It is here we then discuss some ways we conceive the various forms of feedback effect. The chapter concludes with a reminder that in the current climate of evidence-based policy and practice, there is an urgent need for research to inform students, educators, higher education institutions and industry partners about how they might identify impact and understand it in connection with feedback processes as a whole.

D. Boud
University of Technology Sydney, Ultimo, NSW, Australia
e-mail: david.boud@deakin.edu.au

Middlesex University, London, UK

E. Molloy
Department of Medical Education, School of Medicine,
The University of Melbourne, Parkville, VIC, Australia
e-mail: elizabeth.molloy@unimelb.edu.au

Feedback Must Have Impact

What Do We Mean by Feedback?

Our starting point is that the common conception of feedback—that it is something that is done by educators and given to learners, an act that is commonly described as "giving comments"—is in fact a misconception. Both academics and learners often assume that feedback is a one-way flow of information, which happens after assessment submission and is isolated from any other event, and worse, that the role of feedback is less about improving future performance but merely serves to justify the grade. In contrast, leading researchers in the field argue that feedback is not a simple input. Building on the works of Boud and Molloy (2013) and Carless (2015), we argue that feedback is usefully defined **as processes where the learner makes sense of performance-relevant information to promote their learning**. Here, we purposely position feedback as a process, or a series of processes, and not simply an event involving the transmission of information or input. In addition, learners are understood to be active participants in this process, which does not necessarily involve academics at all. In this definition, we talk about making sense of information; however, we do not presuppose this is necessarily a rational or conscious process. Indeed, we conceive the possibilities of the sense-making process from a variety of frames including social constructivist and sociocultural learning. For example, the notion of entanglement between the individual and their environment within a sociocultural frame offers further challenges to understanding sense-making and impact.

A further critical element of this definition is that we explicitly tie impact or effect to the feedback process. The purpose of assessment feedback is to result in improved learning strategies or performance. The improved outcome is an impact of feedback. However, we purposefully conceive impact in a broad way. We use the terms impact and effect interchangeably and by which we mean that the learner's condition is somehow changed as part of the feedback process. Therefore, we seek to explore the effects that occur in the feedback process and how they support or hinder improved learning strategies or performance.

We Are Focused on Assessment Feedback

Feedback is a term used across many fields and in a variety of ways. However, here we are focused on feedback processes surrounding assessment, particularly in the context of higher education. This includes any systematically organised or structured approach to collecting evidence of performance, whether it is diagnostic, formative or summative in nature. There are many occasions of informal or casual feedback processes, but these are beyond our present consideration. As is demonstrated throughout this book, the enactments of assessment feedback can surface in many different ways, from the all-too-familiar comments at the end of an essay, to peer feedback prior to submission of work, to face-to-face performance conversations in work integrated learning contexts. However, while assessment designs are important, we argue that they are only one part of the complex context in which feedback processes occur.

Impact Is a Necessary Characteristic of Feedback

In contexts other than education, such as engineering or biology, feedback is not understood as an input but rather a process within a system. For instance, if a blood vessel is damaged, platelets cling to the injured site and release chemicals that attract more platelets, eventually forming a clot. In this system, feedback regulates or optimises the output. In this example, we can see that impact is a necessary component of the feedback loop. Applying this metaphor to education, feedback can be usefully understood as a process in which information about a learner's performance somehow influences their future capabilities or actions. With this in mind, any information without effect is not feedback, just information.

This understanding of feedback is not new. An early reference to feedback as a mechanism of learning can be found in Wiener's treatment of cybernetics in his 1950 treatise on *The Human Use of Human Beings*. He draws on a range of examples from engineering, computing and biology to make the point that feedback is a process "of being able to adjust future conduct by past performance" (Wiener, 1989, p. 33) and that "effective behavior must be informed by some sort of feedback process" (p. 58).

2 Identifying Feedback That Has Impact   19

Wiener's conception of feedback inherently involves a dialogue between action and effect. In doing so, he takes great pains to be clear that this includes regulation of simple behaviour but is also the basis of what he calls "policy-feedback" that can inform new courses of action:

> Feedback may be as simple as that of the common reflex, or it may be a higher order feedback, in which past experience is used not only to regulate specific movements, but also whole policies of behavior. Such a policy-feedback may, and often does, appear to be what we know under one aspect as a conditioned reflex, and under another as learning. (p. 33)

The point is that feedback is not just information about performance but it is a process in which that information is somehow used to influence subsequent performance. This is true whether we are looking at simple engineering models of feedback or more complex processes of learning. Nevertheless, there is a danger in assuming overly deterministic and simple direct connections between the performance information and impact. For example, the same performance information can result in different outcomes by learners, which highlights among other things, the complexity of learner individuality, their sense-making processes and the contexts in which they operate.

This raises a serious challenge for educators and educational institutions who are committed to effective feedback. They can no longer simply provide information and "hope for the best" but instead need to (a) design it in anticipation of its impact on future performance and (b) find ways to understand or measure that impact to optimise learner outcomes. If learners are not benefiting from engagement in feedback processes, the conditions can be reconfigured until such effects are observed. However, there is a danger here of focussing too much on the teacher or institution. Feedback need not be instigated or managed by the educator. Indeed, as described in the next section, we conceive the learner to have agency in the process, including the potential to identify their own goals, criteria and even generate their own evaluative information to inform their future constructions and actions. It is possible that the educator may not be directly involved at all.

Feedback Is a Learner-Centred Process

In higher education, policy and practices surrounding feedback tend to be framed as teacher-centred—that is something that an educator does to learners. Worse, the construct of feedback is often unshackled from that of teaching and understood to be a labour of accountability or an act of beneficence on the part of a lecturer for which learners should be grateful. Teacher-centred perspectives emphasise the role of academics in "giving feedback" while failing to adequately recognise learners' active role in the process of their own learning. It is an indictment on the higher education system that, for many learners, the experience of teacher-led feedback is underwhelming or negative. In many cases, learners are effectively left to their own devices, ill-equipped to seek, interpret or act upon evaluative information.

The shift from a teacher-centred perspective to one focused on learning provides a valuable opportunity to reposition the teacher as just one possible source of evaluative information. Feedback processes can, and often do, involve a variety of agents, particularly in the performance information generation. These may include family members, friends, automated systems (e.g. simple spell checkers, writing assistants such as Grammarly, code compilers), social networks, peers, educators, client/patient/consumer (in the case of work-based learning) and, of course, the learner. These various sources of feedback information may be as a result of the learner themselves, or through the careful design of the educator. While we argue that feedback needs to be conceived as student-centred, the educator can, and usually does, have a significant role in shaping the feedback processes. The educator may have designed the assessment that elicits and shapes the performance, but also can—and we argue should—orchestrate opportunities for learners to engage with a variety of sources and types of information designed to develop their evaluative judgement, that is decisions about the quality of their work (Tai, Ajjawi, Boud, Dawson, & Panadero, 2018). Finally, the educator also has an important role in designing ways for the learner to evaluate what they have learned through a subsequent performance. Regardless of whether it is by teacher design or through learner agency, it is likely several agents have been utilised any one assessment event which includes researching, building/drafting and submission or performance. While there is a strong body of literature that deals with peer feedback designs, the role and impact of the broader feedback networks are less clear (Dawson et al., 2018).

Arguably, learning is a process over which educators have no direct control. It is not a simple process of transmission. The learner needs to be actively involved in attending to the stimulus or relationship or environment and engaging in a complex process of meaning making. In many conceptions of learning, the social environment is understood to have an important role in shaping the experiences of learners and simultaneously providing a mechanism to test and evaluate new ideas, which may then result in modified or new conceptions of the world. It is worth noting that these conceptions may be incomplete, inaccurate or contradictory and are often fluid, changing and influenced by other active schema or changes in context. From this perspective, learning is a process of knowledge construction rather than reproduction and it emphasises the central role of the learner and context.

Sense-Making and Feedback Literacy Are Important for Feedback to Make a Difference

This brings into focus the issue of learner capacity to seek or generate, make sense of and use performance information. While the quality of the feedback information cannot be forgotten, unless learners can identify, interpret and act upon it then the feedback process is thwarted. The presence of evaluative information in any format does not necessarily mean that feedback has occurred. Nicol (2010) notes that from a social constructivist perspective, if learners are to consciously influence future actions, performance information needs to stimulate an "inner dialogue" in which learners are "actively decoding feedback information, internalising it, comparing it against their own work, to make judgements about its quality and ultimately to make improvements in future work" (p. 503). Ultimately, learners need to make sense of the information in order to act upon it. However, we suggest that the act of sense-making is much more than simply being able to comprehend the feedback information.

A prerequisite for students taking an active role in feedback as Nicol suggests is that they have an appreciation of the purpose of feedback processes and how they can operate to their benefit. The taken-for-granted assumption in student evaluation surveys that feedback consists of what teachers do undermines the development of a stronger student role in the process. Carless and Boud (2018) have called for the development of what they have termed "feedback literacy". That is, "an understanding of what feedback is and how it can be managed effectively; capacities and dispositions to make productive use of feedback; and appreciation of the roles of teachers and themselves in these processes" (p. 1316). They take the view that in order for feedback to do its job, students need to have a deeper appreciation of how feedback can work if they are to make the most of the opportunities that their courses provide, and that this needs to be scaffolded throughout courses, starting in first year units.

Identifying Impact Is Not Easy

We have described feedback as processes in which learners make sense of information about their work in order to improve learning strategies and future performance. We have purposely made explicit the notion of impact as a critical and necessary component of feedback. However, the effects that occur in the feedback process are largely internal to the learner and may not directly manifest in subsequent actions. This creates a dilemma for anyone trying to understand the effectiveness of feedback: How can we know that feedback has occurred unless we can see some evidence of its effects? Designing feedback for impact, and in particular, evidencing that impact, is problematic. It is perhaps a symptom of this difficulty that feedback initiatives and research often focus on front-end design, but assume or simply omit any concerted effort to define or evidence impact.

The Problem of Cause and Effect in Educational Research, Practice and Policy

At the most simple level, feedback relating to a task should result in a learner being able to perform that task more effectively in the future. It is conceivable that when the tasks are simple skill or knowledge acquisition then we may be able to track the influence of the evaluative information on future performance. However, higher education and professional learning contexts normally involve more complex learning tasks. Identifying the nature of impact is problematic, not least, because subsequent performances that allow learners to enact their understanding of the feedback information are usually delayed (if not absent) are in response to different conditions and measured by different criteria.

In addition, at a more fundamental level, ascribing clear causality of feedback impact, outside of experimental conditions, is near impossible. The problem of causality in education research has been well documented. In his book on *Causation in Educational Research*, Morrison (2009) points out that "one can soon become stuck in a quagmire of uncertainty, multiplicity of considerations, and unsureness of the relations between causes and effects" (p. 4). There are so many variables to take into account, for example the curriculum design, the assessment design, pedagogy, context, and learner agency. Indeed, the role of individual conditions, including beliefs, motivation, prior experience and emotion, is well-recognised modifiers in causation (Maxwell, 2004). Regardless of the cause–effect model being applied or the methods in measuring it, Gorard (2002) concludes that we are unable to detect cause–effect directly. It is in this context that we need to be cautious in our search for impact and attributing change to the feedback process. Nevertheless, this does not mean to suggest that we should not try to identify or measure impact. Simply, that some caution needs to be made in the strength of causal claims.

The Problem of Sequence—And Its Implication for Locating Effect

Fundamental to most conceptions of cause–effect is that it is temporal, that is cause is followed by effect. In the case of feedback, we might assume there is (1) a performance by the learner (e.g. essay), followed by (2) the generation of performance information from different sources (either by the learner or others), then (3) sense-making including forming evaluative judgements, and which may finally result in (4) some form of effect or change. Given the purpose of feedback is to result in improved performance it is also reasonable to argue that the learner should also engage in a subsequent performance to enact and test their new understanding, and thereby also beginning the cycle again.

This description of a feedback process is seductively simple, but also highly problematic. There is a danger of assuming that the elements of performance, generation, sense-making and effect are linear and that each only occur once within a single cycle. In contrast, each element is likely to be more complex and fluid in how it is experienced.

Each stage does not necessarily occur in a specific order. It is possible for learners to move back and forth between stages. For example, from a single performance, learners may engage in several iterations of generation and sense-making. It is possible that a learner may produce a draft of an assignment from which the educator generates evaluative information for the learner. After attempting to make sense of that information, the learner might then also seek other sources of evaluative information using the same draft assignment. In this example, the learner has moved back and forth between the stages of generation and sense-making. It is likely that this is not an uncommon experience for students—often in any one assessment there is a history of evaluative information being generated from several sources (e.g. educator, family, peers, automated systems, self) all of whom would potentially be representing different values or understanding of the success criteria. These multiple instances of evaluative information can interact, adding to, or even confounding the sense-making process. This causes a problem for us in trying to identify and understand effect, which, in this example, is no longer a simple product of a linear sequence.

2 Identifying Feedback That Has Impact   25

A further complication is that the movement between stages may not be apparent, and indeed, the very distinction between stages may need to be questioned. For instance, the internal process of effect is likely to be fluid—shifting whenever the learner engages in sense-making but also when they engage in performance. As an example, a learner can engage in a subsequent performance, drawing on their new understanding. However, in enacting that performance the learner will be actively creating new meanings. This is particularly true for learners who have well developed evaluative judgement and are constantly monitoring and regulating their ongoing performance.

Subsequent Performance May Not Represent an Effect of Feedback

A key problem in determining feedback impact is that sense-making and effects such as emotion and identity are largely internal processes and therefore particularly hard for us to measure or observe directly. A simple response to this dilemma has been to suggest that learners need to engage in subsequent performance utilising the same knowledge or skills. This can aid the learner to test out their new understanding and continue their learning journey. A subsequent performance also can provide the educator or "other" with a better understanding of the effect their feedback information or design.

However, subsequent performance may not actually represent the particular effect(s) of the feedback process that it is meant to be evidencing. For example, subsequent performances are often conducted at a later time and in response to different task requirements and thereby likely to be drawing on more than just the understanding developed from the first performance. In addition, there may be a variety of effects arising from the initial feedback process that are not evident in the subsequent performance. This may be simply because it is not called for by the assigned task, or it may be because the effect is harder to observe, such as emotional, motivational, relational or other changes.

A further complication is that in the process of preparing the assessment, such as researching, drafting, editing, discussing ideas and writing the learner constructs a history of actions that constitute the learner's experience of the performance as a whole. In other words, the assessment process may involve a number of feedback loops, interacting with each other and impacting on the learner. In treating the final assessment submission (essay, test, oral performance, action, etc.) as the whole of the performance, it may result in the generation of evaluative information that is partial and less relevant than we might otherwise assume.

Clearly, we need to be circumspect in treating the subsequent performance as a manifestation of effect. While we argue that a logical and valuable feedback design is to ensure there is a subsequent opportunity for learners to enact their new understanding, we need to be careful assuming that the subsequent performance is connected to any particular event. This creates an interesting challenge for evidence-based policy and practice, as well as feedback research attempting to identify effect.

The Different Forms of Feedback Impact

We conceive impact as essentially any changed state within the learner as a result of the feedback process. The nature of that change could be related to their thinking processes, emotions, relationships, work strategies, identity and more. In addition, a single feedback loop may result in more than one effect, which may in turn interact and together influence future performance. The diverse forms of impact, and the potential ways in which they may combine, are multifarious. However, in better understanding impact within a feedback loop, we are more likely to better understand how to improve feedback outcomes. Here, we describe a number of ways we conceive feedback impact.

Impact is not just a learning outcome. We have already pointed out that subsequent performance may not be an accurate or complete representation of the feedback impact. A student may be able to meet the learning outcomes of a unit without this being attributable to feedback. Grades or formal measures of achievement are poor representations of particular performance and are very unlikely to represent the whole of a feedback effect. While it is desirable that an assessment feedback process should result in learners being able to perform better, there may be other

2 Identifying Feedback That Has Impact

effects involved, and desired, that are not reflected by the grade. The challenge here is to look beyond simple or familiar forms of measurement, such as grades and student satisfaction, to think about how we may usefully evidence the impact of feedback in more nuanced ways.

Impact may be cognitive. Learners may now have a better understanding of a concept or skill. Their knowledge may have been impacted. The feedback process may result in new schemas, reframing of a problem, or connecting ideas that were otherwise not associated or associated in partial or incorrect ways. However, the effect may also be in terms of their cognition itself, that is their thinking processes. This may include the way in which they attend to details, process information, form concepts, and how they store and retrieve memory. Therefore, in engaging with a feedback process, it is possible that learners may shift in not only what they think, but also how they think. This can be difficult to detect.

A particularly desirable form of cognitive effect would be in the area of metacognition, that is the way we think about thinking. It includes both an awareness of ones thinking processes and an ability to regulate or influence that process. For example, knowing when and how to use particular strategies for generating performance information, making sense of that information, or utilising newly acquired understandings in subsequence performances. It is arguably one of the greatest potential impacts of feedback—to improve learner capacity to effectively engage in the feedback process itself and to be able to judge what they can and cannot do; whether this is in relation to developing students' self-regulation of learning (development of goals, monitoring and action planning; Nicol, 2010) or in terms of the development of evaluative judgement (Boud, Ajjawi, Dawson, & Tai, 2018; Sadler, 1989).

Evaluative judgement is defined as "the capability to make decisions about the quality of work of oneself and others" (Tai et al., 2018), as such it involves metacognitive processes that need to be refined through the inputs of others, not just on the quality of a learner's work but on their ability to make it for themselves. Feedback is required to develop these capacities and feedback processes of this kind should be judged in terms of their effects on learners' self-judgements, not just improved work. How evaluative judgement is manifested around assessment activities and the role of feedback in this development process is not well understood.

Impact may be affective or motivational. The feedback process is often intimately connected with issues of motivation and affect (including emotion). An example may be how motivation and emotional resilience influences how a learner engages with a task. However, the impact of the feedback process can also surface in changes to the affective and motivational states of learners. For example, when learners perceive comments from educators as being critical it can lead to negative emotional reactions (Ryan & Henderson, 2017). When learners perceive feedback comments to be negative or upsetting it can have a detrimental effect on their self-esteem and perceived self-efficacy (Rowe, 2017; Sargeant, Mann, Sinclair, Van der Vleuten, & Metsemakers, 2008), they can also become demotivated and less likely to use those comments to improve (e.g. see Poulos & Mahony, 2008). It has also been found that in some cases, negative emotional responses can have long-term effects—hindering subsequent learning and potentially influencing career decisions (Crossman, 2007; Falchikov & Boud, 2007; Molloy, Borrell-Carrió, & Epstein, 2013). While we understand that emotion and motivation can be involved, the mechanisms that cause such effects and their consequence need to be further researched as it is likely that this relationship is more complex than a simple positive/negative emotional valence.

Impact may be relational. The relationship between the educator and the learner can influence the feedback experience. For example, Telio, Regehr, and Ajjawi (2016) found in their study that the credibility of the educator "not only affects a learner's engagement with a particular piece of feedback at the moment of delivery, but also has consequences for future engagement with (or avoidance of) further learning interactions with the supervisor" (p. 933). Therefore, learners' perceptions of the strength of the educational alliance (based on shared goals, activities and bond) influence immediate and subsequent feedback behaviours (Farrell, Bourgeois-Law, Ajjawi, & Regehr, 2017; Telio et al., 2016). In addition to credibility, issues of trust (Carless, 2009, 2013; Molloy et al., 2013) and perceived safety/ threat (Orsmond, Merry, & Reiling, 2005) have been shown to

2 Identifying Feedback That Has Impact   29

influence the way in which learners engage with the feedback process, including how they seek out, interpret and act on feedback comments. The relationship serves both as a mechanism for engagement with feedback and as a potential impact in the sense of strengthening of an educational bond, this being mutually constitutive.

Impact may change values, beliefs and identity. Different fields of inquiry define identity in different ways. From a social theory of learning, identity could be understood to be both how we perceive ourselves and how we are perceived, in relation to our competence and values within a community of practice (Wenger, 1998). Identity in this sense is defined socially; that is, it is produced through participation in a community and in relation to another. It is both internal and external to the individual. In feedback processes, the assessment performance is a form of practice and so is the way in which the learner may engage and react to feedback information. Through this practice, the learner both negotiates and reifies their identity which in turn influences future participation. Sutton and Gill (2010) note that "active participation in feedback discourse opens up the possibility of students acquiring a different voice, and provides opportunities for the construction, deconstruction and reconstruction of students' academic self-identities" (p. 11). Research highlights that feedback processes can have an impact on professional socialisation (Molloy, 2009; Ajjawi & Boud, 2018) and this needs to be explored in more depth.

Impact may be intentional or unintentional. This is perhaps obvious but the impact on the learner may be by design, but could also be unintended, unexpected and thereby potentially unnoticed. In the context of medical education and multi-source feedback, Sargeant et al. (2007) describe how feedback can have "low consequential validity", that is feedback with unintended or even detrimental consequences, such as decreased motivation, emotional distress and deteriorated performance. In Hattie's (2009) meta-analysis a third of feedback studies were found to have a detrimental effect on learning attainment. Why this is so and for whom, under which circumstances is less well known.

Impact may be delayed or have ripples. Both effect and subsequent performances may not occur in quick succession. The effect may evolve over time as the learner processes the information and comes to understand it in different ways. Similarly, subsequent performances, in other words the external manifestation of effect, may occur months later in different contexts. All of these pose serious difficulties for policy, practice and research approaches to locating effect.

Impact may be plural. We have already indicated that there is a potential, if not likelihood, of multiple effects occurring in (short and/or long) feedback loops. An example may be that a learner may improve in their knowledge of a concept while also strengthening their perceived self-efficacy. It is also logical then to assume that these multiple effects may interact and influence future performance. This raises an interesting problem for research that tries to identify and measure a particular form of effect and, in so doing, may not account such other effects, including interactive effects, that may influence future performance.

Different Forms of Impact for Different Parties and Purposes

People have stakes in looking for different effects and therefore necessarily look for certain outcomes in feedback processes. The above discussion has focused on impact on learners in order to improve learning strategies and future performance. However, the feedback processes in education are not necessarily benign. They can be value-laden, simultaneously serving different purposes and potentially compromised.

For example, institutions are situated within complicated governance environments including needing to demonstrate they meet the standards set by quality assurance agencies. In this context, there is often a focus on student satisfaction of the quality of their educational experience, including feedback. This has shaped the design of student satisfaction surveys that have become the basis of not only a reporting mechanism to quality assurance agencies but also are used to sustain university ranking systems, university marketing and even academic promotion. At the same time, the way in which feedback is often referred to in these contexts is a teacher-centred one, where feedback is an input rather than a process with an improved outcome. With this in mind, the high stakes and high visibility of the student satisfaction surveys reinforces a particular understanding of the teaching and learning process in higher education which is not conducive to stimulating effective feedback designs.

Another example of how university structures compromise feedback is the way in which many universities break subjects into relatively short sequences (e.g. semester, term and carousel models). This modularisation of units has been known to encourage bunching of assessment tasks at the end of the teaching period which makes it difficult for educators to provide feedback comments that connect to future assessments, particularly across programmes of study (Timmerman & Dijkstra, 2017; van der Vleuten et al., 2012).

Educators and educational/instructional designers also have value-laden, contingent and compromised approaches in their feedback designs. Assessment feedback can provide valuable information back to the educators and designers regarding the effectiveness of their planning and enactment, facilitating their continual improvement of their teaching/designs. This is desirable. It is a key concern of this book to further explore the ways in which we might understand impact to both improve the learner journey but also the teaching and designs of the educators/designers. However, it needs to be also noted that feedback designs are also often compromised. Educators often complain of not having enough time to do feedback well and not enough control over the ways in which feedback can be enacted. These perceived constraints have in turn been used to justify efficient but arguably ineffectual methods such as rubrics. A further example of educator compromise has been shown when educators shy away from providing comments that may result in potential negative student reactions. Sensitivity to student sensitivities and needs, such as those of emotion and motivation, is valuable. However, it can also result in strategies, such as the sandwiching, that have been characterised as mealy-mouthed.

Conclusion

Feedback is a set of processes in which learners make sense of evaluative information about their work to improve future performance. Impact is a necessary characteristic of effective feedback. We have framed impact as essentially any changed state within learners as a result of feedback processes. As we have discussed, identifying the processes that influence impact and its connection to subsequent performance continues to require research. Indeed, the nature of impact itself needs to be better understood. For instance, we have suggested that impact may be intentional/unintentional, immediate/delayed, cognitive, affective, motivational, relational, social (identity) and plural and intersecting. As a consequence, we argue that it is important to understand how, when and why feedback processes result in various forms of effect, and how those effects may then influence future performance.

References

Ajjawi, R., & Boud, D. (2018). Examining the nature and effects of feedback dialogue. *Assessment & Evaluation in Higher Education, 43*(7), 1106–1119. Retrieved from https://doi.org/10.1080/02602938.2018.1434128.

Boud, D., & Molloy, E. (2013). Rethinking models of feedback for learning: The challenge of design. *Assessment & Evaluation in Higher Education, 38*(6), 698–712.

Boud, D., Ajjawi, R., Dawson, P., & Tai, J. (Eds.). (2018). *Developing evaluative judgement in higher education: Assessment for knowing and producing quality work.* London: Routledge.

Carless, D. (2009). Trust, distrust and their impact on assessment reform. *Assessment & Evaluation in Higher Education, 34*(1), 79–89.

Carless, D. (2013). Trust and its role in facilitating dialogic feedback. In D. Boud & E. Molloy (Eds.), *Feedback in higher and professional education* (pp. 100–113). London: Routledge.

Carless, D. (2015). *Excellence in university assessment: Learning from award-winning practice.* London: Routledge.

Carless, D., & Boud, D. (2018, May 3). The development of student feedback literacy: Enabling uptake of feedback. *Assessment & Evaluation in Higher Education.* Published Online. https://doi.org/10.1080/02602938.2018.1463354.

Crossman, J. (2007). The role of relationships and emotions in student perceptions of learning and assessment. *Higher Education Research & Development*, *26*(3), 313–327.

Dawson, P., Boud, D., Henderson, M., Phillips, M., Molloy, E., & Ryan, T. (2018). What makes for effective feedback: Staff and student perspectives. *Assessment and Evaluation in Higher Education*. https://doi.org/10.1080/02602938.2018.1467877.

Falchikov, N., & Boud, D. (2007). Assessment and emotion: The impact of being assessed. In D. Boud & N. Falchikov (Eds.), *Rethinking assessment in higher education: Learning for the longer term* (pp. 144–155). Oxon: Routledge.

Farrell, L., Bourgeois-Law, G., Ajjawi, R., & Regehr, G. (2017). An autoethnographic exploration of the use of goal oriented feedback to enhance brief clinical teaching encounters. *Advances in Health Sciences Education, 22*(1), 91–104.

Gorard, S. (2002). The role of causal models in evidence-informed policy making and practice. *Evaluation & Research in Education, 16*(1), 51–65.

Hattie, J. (2009). *Visible learning: A synthesis of over 800 meta-analyses relating to achievement.* London: Routledge.

Maxwell, J. (2004). Causal explanation, qualitative research, and scientific inquiry in education. *Educational Researcher, 33*(2), 3–11. https://www.jstor.org/stable/3699970.

Molloy, E. (2009). Time to pause: Giving and receiving feedback in clinical education. In C. Delaney & E. Molloy (Eds.), *Clinical Education in the Health Professions: An Educator's Guide.* Chatswood, New South Wales: Elsevier Australia.

Molloy, E., Borrell-Carrió, F., & Epstein, R. (2013). The impact of emotions in feedback. In D. Boud & E. Molloy (Eds.), *Feedback in higher and professional education* (pp. 60–81). London: Routledge.

Morrison, K. (2009). *Causation in educational research.* London: Routledge.

Nicol, D. (2010). From monologue to dialogue: Improving written feedback processes in mass higher education. *Assessment & Evaluation in Higher Education, 35*(5), 501–517. https://doi.org/10.1080/02602931003786559.

Orsmond, P., Merry, S., & Reiling, K. (2005). Biology students' utilization of tutors' formative feedback: A qualitative interview study. *Assessment and Evaluation in Higher Education, 30,* 369–386.

Poulos, A., & Mahony, M. J. (2008). Effectiveness of feedback: The students' perspective. *Assessment & Evaluation in Higher Education, 33*(2), 143–154.

Rowe, A. D. (2017). Feelings about feedback: The role of emotions in assessment for learning. In D. Carless, S. Bridges, C. Chan, & R. Glofcheski (Eds.), *Scaling up assessment for learning in higher education: The enabling power of assessment*, pp. 159–172. Singapore: Springer.

Ryan, T., & Henderson, M. (2017). Feeling feedback: Students' emotional responses to educator feedback. *Assessment & Evaluation in Higher Education.* https://doi.org/10.1080/02602938.2017.1416456.

Sadler, D. R. (1989). Formative assessment and the design of instructional systems. *Instructional Science, 18*(2), 119–144. https://doi.org/10.1007/BF00117714.

Sargeant, J., Mann, K., Sinclair, D., Van der Vleuten, C., & Metsemakers, J. (2007). Challenges in multisource feedback: Intended and unintended outcomes. *Medical Education, 41*(6), 583–591. https://doi.org/10.1111/j.1365-2923.2007.02769.x.

Sargeant, J., Mann, K., Sinclair, D., Van der Vleuten, C., & Metsemakers, J. (2008). Understanding the influence of emotions and reflection upon multisource feedback acceptance and use. *Advances in Health Sciences Education, 13,* 275–288.

Sutton, P., & Gill, W. (2010). Engaging feedback: Meaning, identity and power. *Practitioner Research in Higher Education, 4*(1), 3–13.

Tai, J., Ajjawi, R., Boud, D., Dawson, P., & Panadero, E. (2018). Developing evaluative judgement: Enabling students to make decisions about the quality of work. *Higher Education, 76*(3), 467–481. https://doi.org/10.1007/s10734-017-0220-3.

Telio, S., Regehr, G., & Ajjawi, R. (2016). Feedback and the educational alliance: Examining credibility judgements and their consequences. *Medical Education, 50,* 933–942.

Timmerman, A. A., & Dijkstra, J. (2017). A practice approach to programmatic assessment design. *Advances in Health Sciences Education.* https://doi.org/10.1007/s10459-017-9756-3.

van der Vleuten, C. P., Schuwirth, L. W. T., Driessen, E. W., Dijkstra, J., Tigelaar, D., Baartman, L. K. J., & van Tartwijk, J. (2012). A model for programmatic assessment fit for purpose. *Medical Teacher, 34*(3), 205–214. https://doi.org/10.3109/0142159x.2012.652239.

Wenger, E. (1998). *Communities of practice: Learning, meaning, and identity.* Cambridge, MA: Cambridge University Press.

Wiener, N. (1989). *The human use of human beings: Cybernetics and society.* London: Free Association Books.

Part II
Expanding Notions of Feedback Impact

3

Beware the Simple Impact Measure: Learning from the Parallels with Student Engagement

Joanna Tai ⓘ, Phillip Dawson ⓘ, Margaret Bearman ⓘ and Rola Ajjawi ⓘ

Introduction

There are many potential impacts of feedback; a commonly desired impact is learning. Within this volume, and also elsewhere, in discussing and focussing on "feedback that has an impact", we are likely to be thinking of positive impacts such as improved work and self-efficacy. In measuring the impact of feedback, we hope that those measurements will provide information on learning. However, impact may not always be positive;

J. Tai (✉) · P. Dawson · M. Bearman · R. Ajjawi
Centre for Research in Assessment and Digital Learning (CRADLE),
Deakin University, Geelong, VIC, Australia
e-mail: Joanna.tai@deakin.edu.au

P. Dawson
e-mail: p.dawson@deakin.edu.au

M. Bearman
e-mail: margaret.bearman@deakin.edu.au

R. Ajjawi
e-mail: rola.ajjawi@deakin.edu.au

© The Author(s) 2019
M. Henderson et al. (eds.), *The Impact of Feedback in Higher Education*,
https://doi.org/10.1007/978-3-030-25112-3_3

any intervention might also result in unintended consequences. In this chapter, we seek to critique straightforward notions of impact in educational practice, as impacts may be difficult to measure, connections between input and output cannot be assumed, and we may not know to investigate impacts if we are unaware of them in the first place.

Measuring, assessing, or otherwise tracking learning is problematic. Most measures that might shed light on learning are proxies for measuring the internal and hence unknowable state that takes place within the student. Assessment tasks such as responding correctly to a multiple choice question, providing working for a particular maths problem or demonstrating a particular skill only provide evidence of a consequential output of learning, rather than measuring learning itself. By focussing on the impacts of feedback, researchers and practitioners are encouraged to look more broadly for evidence of learning, beyond what conventional assessments can substantiate.

We contend however that there may be dangers in taking a narrow view of impact. In particular, if care is not taken, too much energy will be expended on identifying and measuring easily identifiable impacts of feedback, such as an immediate improvement in performance on an assignment. Researchers and practitioners may therefore neglect or overlook aspects of impact which are more difficult to measure, across divergent tasks and the longer term. We support and illustrate our argument through the example of student engagement, a concept which, similar to feedback, holds an elevated position in higher education policy and practice, but also suffers from ambiguous use within the literature, and has been the subject of a multitude of investigations of varying focus and quality. In this chapter, we begin by outlining similarities between the positioning of engagement and feedback within higher education. We then elaborate on the current dilemmas of measurement within the realm of student engagement, at institutional and classroom levels. Finally, we explore what might be learned from such a case study, to ensure that feedback research and practice does not fall into the same traps, making suggestions to avoid simple solutions where the complex is more meaningful.

Parallels Between Feedback and Engagement

Feedback and engagement have many parallels. Both feedback and student engagement have been variously and continually (re)defined, and both are held as crucial to higher education. Both, by dint of being used in common parlance, seem to be accessible concepts for the average academic (and indeed layperson) and have a powerful plausibility in their common-sense use. They have also been subject to significant investigation, scrutiny and metricisation, at institutional levels and for individual classes.

The origins of the term feedback are said to come from engineering or computer science; prior to educational use, feedback was described in 1950 as "the control of a machine on the basis of its *actual* performance rather than its *expected* performance" (Wiener, 1967, p. 36). Its gradual adoption in education settings over the years has resulted in various understandings of what feedback entails, including its common English sense of "[i]nformation about reactions to a product, a person's performance of a task, etc. which is used as a basis for improvement" (Oxford Dictionaries, 2015). Within education, several shifts with conceptions of feedback have occurred over time, from feedback merely as an information artefact which can be transmitted to be taken on board passively by students (i.e. feedback as input), to more student-oriented shifts which privilege feedback processes and actively engage the students in making sense of the feedback. Others foreground the relational, cultural and contextual dimensions of feedback (Ajjawi, Molloy, Bearman, & Rees, 2017; Esterhazy & Damşa, 2017; Telio, Regehr, & Ajjawi, 2016). Some hold the notion that feedback only looks backwards towards the past, and therefore "feedforward" is also a necessary term to distinguish feedback that has advice for the future; others hold that feedback encompasses the entire notion and there is no need for "feedforward" as a separate item, since future action is a requirement of feedback. A further advance on the process-oriented approaches holds that feedback only occurs once action has been taken by the student; hence, impact (Boud & Molloy, 2013). In this conceptualisation, notions around students' feedback literacy are important, rather than just what the educator might be able to do or impose upon the student (Carless & Boud, 2018). Feedback is now conceptualised and implemented across the spectrum from teacher to student actions and from information provision to co-construction of meaning and understanding as a relational act. The potential impacts of feedback are already mutable, depending on the definition of feedback.

Similarly, engagement is frequently used as a common language term— e.g. one can be engaged to be married, be engaged in warfare or be engaged for an event. Engagement also exists as a concept within education, usually in a psychological sense, though uses have expanded in recent years. Azevedo (2015) reports that engagement has been used to describe many things. Definitions have developed also as the field has progressed: while it originally indicated primarily time-on-task, it firstly expanded as a psychological construct to include cognitive and affective components (Mandernach, 2015). Further work has then posited sociocultural dimensions of engagement (Kahu, 2013) and reconsidered engagement in a post-structuralist paradigm (Westman & Bergmark, 2018); however, all definitions continue to be used concomitantly. The fuzziness of the concept of engagement has also led to some criticisms about its utility (Vuori, 2014).

An important parallel is found in the intended "effects" of feedback and engagement. While the intended effect of feedback is learning, the key goal of student engagement is to promote student success (Kuh, 2001). Success itself has been variably defined and can be thought of as anything from completion of a degree, down to achievement on an individual learning task; furthermore, it may also be conceived of as improved learning and experiences of learning (Ifenthaler & Yau, 2018). It is described as an "amorphous" term with different meanings where getting through the day can be defined as success by a student (O'Shea & Delahunty, 2018). What success means within the engagement literature is also likely dependent on the original conceptualisation of engagement, and may therefore be difficult to measure with respect to sociocultural engagement or "belonging". These challenges strike us as similar to those found with measuring "learning" as a result of feedback. We usually use proxies for learning such as performance on a subsequent task; such performance might be measured immediately after a learning episode or in the longer term. Measurement might occur at various levels, from simple recall of knowledge to problem-solving and the application of learning to other situations. Feedback may also result in unintended learning, which manifests in ways not thought of or captured by any particular assessment.

The accessibility of both "feedback" and "engagement" means these terms are understood in one way or another by a wide range of individuals within higher education, with a variety of disciplinary backgrounds. Though shifts in conceptualisation of both "feedback" and "engagement" have occurred amongst scholars in their respective fields, this much broader population use both "feedback" and "engagement" in their everyday language as educators. This, in part, is also likely to account for the popularity of research and investigation in this area, beyond institutional drivers of performance, resulting in a number of operationalisations of these concepts and associated methods of investigation. Within this chapter, we have chosen not to privilege one conceptualisation of feedback nor engagement, choosing instead to illustrate and embrace the ongoing ambiguity. This allows therefore for many possibilities, rather than a singular definition that is likely to include and/or exclude certain forms of feedback impact, and constrain thinking and research around what could be considered as an effect of feedback.

Engagement: The Problems of Measurement

Having made a case for the parallels between engagement and feedback, we now turn to the problems of measurement in the student engagement literature. Engagement was first conceptualised and thus measured in terms of student behaviours, i.e. time-on-tasks or other discernible actions (Mandernach, 2015). It was then developed into a psychological construct involving cognition, behaviours and emotions (Fredricks, Blumenfeld, & Paris, 2004). Recent conceptualisations include sociocultural and holistic perspectives, where interactions with others, and aspects of identity can be examined (Kahu & Nelson, 2018). Student engagement has also leaned on psychological concepts of motivation, interest, self-efficacy and self-regulated learning (Kahu & Nelson, 2018). While this adds, it also muddies understandings, as these concepts each have their own literature, and own established research methodologies and methods.

In a systematic review of the literature on student engagement, we identified both a broad and confusing array of engagement measures as well as a poor alignment between the aims of the research, the conceptualisations of the phenomenon and the measures to hand (Tai, Ajjawi, Bearman, & Wiseman, 2018). Measures identified comprised self-report surveys, a test of knowledge, researcher or educator observations of students, interviews, focus groups, interactions with others and interactions with a learning management system (i.e. learning analytics). Within these categories, over 30 specific surveys or scales were referred to, including four related to online contexts. An additional 50 surveys were created by study authors without reference to previous research. 13 different observational methods were described. Interactional data collected included email responses, log ons and interactions with the website, learning management analytics, game analytics and audience response system data. Generally, these measures focussed on the process of engagement rather than the outcomes: where engagement resulted in a state of being, it was difficult to quantify. Instead, many studies focussed (consciously or otherwise) on the easy to measure, such as behaviours, concrete demonstrations of knowledge and surveys on behaviours or feelings of engagement.

Though there may not be a *single* appropriate way to measure engagement, it was clear within the review that there were a range of deficiencies in the alignment of the conceptualisation and execution of studies. These were usually related to an insufficient grounding in the extant literature, and the abundant use of easily obtainable data (such as self-report surveys completed by students or information about interactions with technology). Similar concerns may be applied to researching the impacts of feedback, as alignment of research aims and methods may be disrupted and confused by definitional/conceptual murkiness and incomplete or misaligned means of measurement.

Often technology was seen as a solution for engagement. However, it may also be that conceptualising engagement as a function of student behaviour was more amenable to measurement with technology. Early work in the field of learning analytics had a significant focus on engagement as a key construct being measured (Macfadyen & Dawson, 2010). However, what was often measured was quite rudimentary, for example, some tools operationalised engagement as a function of students logging in, completing assigned tasks, making forum posts and reading forum posts (Liu, Richards, Dawson, Froissard, & Atif, 2016). This view of engagement was driven by the data available, and the likely correlates with student success within that data, rather than any sophisticated conceptualisation of engagement.

This computerisation of engagement through learning analytics has parallels with feedback. Learning analytics has been driven by people with an understanding of technology and statistics, rather than deep domain knowledge about engagement. If the call for "effects" in feedback is made loudly, a similar phenomenon may happen to feedback: colonisation by researchers with a naïve understanding of feedback, access to a large set of data and quantitative approaches to find effects. They may be able to precisely measure differences in performance on a standardised test before and after feedback information was provided, while ignoring other influential but harder to quantify factors like overarching feedback designs and cultures. Their research designs might not be driven by what is known about feedback, but by what can be known from the data that is easily available.

Taken together, these ambiguous conceptualisations, and easy access to large-scale data and measurement instruments, may result in misalignment in research aims and methods, and promote a turn towards what is easily measured and the data that are easily obtained. Though the research on student engagement is substantial, it leaves a gap between its conclusions and the intentions behind student engagement, such as improving student learning, retention and success. It also illustrates the real challenges facing educators as they try to improve "engagement" within their classrooms.

Similar problems may befall research on feedback impact, and so we can learn what to do, or not to do, through considering what has occurred within engagement research. There have been suggestions that given the disparity within the field, that a better unifying framework, recognition of disparity, or abandonment of the term student engagement, be the three options available to researchers (Azevedo, 2015). We suggest a moderate approach, which explicitly recognises different research traditions, and therefore different aims, foci and outcomes. Work can then be situated within a tradition, and adhere to the standards for research and reporting within that tradition: a study focussing on sociomaterial impacts of

44   J. Tai et al.

feedback would have different aims and methodologies, compared to a study grounded in a cognitivist tradition. In the following section, we elaborate on the ways that choosing an underpinning theory, frame or perspective, and aligning aims with methods can promote research rigour in researching the effects of feedback.

Aligning Feedback Conceptions with Effects

Feedback research to date has largely recorded impact where it focusses on what is easy to measure. This may be grade associated with the unit of study, performance on a test, improvement in essay score, or more practically, adhering to medication protocols and psychomotor tasks (Hattie & Timperley, 2007; Kluger & Denisi, 1996). However, it seems likely that feedback is just as important in promoting things that are difficult to measure. For example, group work is a prime example of a topic that we know is important to learn, and where feedback has much to offer, but measurement is very challenging. Similarly, impact is also easiest to measure over the short term. What about learning skills that carry forward into future practice? Longer-term impacts may be very difficult to trace, but are nonetheless significant. Furthermore, and especially in the abovementioned reviews, feedback was previously conceptualised as information regarding performance. Novel conceptualisations of feedback bring new ways of thinking about impact. We now consider some of these possibilities using three recent conceptualisations that view feedback as a complex social process: educational alliance, feedback literacy, and feedback as a social practice. We examine each in turn to explore possibilities for identifying and researching impacts and effects. Then, we spend some time considering the potential negative impacts of feedback and how they might be studied.

What happens to the notion of impact when feedback is conceptualised as relational co-construction? The educational alliance borrows from the therapeutic alliance, where evidence suggests patients who perceive a strong therapeutic alliance with their health care provider achieve better health outcomes. The educational alliance therefore conceptualises feedback as a process of co-construction through shared goals and activities within the context of a strong bond between the educator and learner. Where learners perceive a strong educational alliance, they are more likely to engage in positive feedback behaviours leading to learning. Educators must work towards (re)establishing and leveraging an educational alliance with their learners (Ajjawi & Regehr, 2019). Preliminary research highlights that when learners perceive a strong educational alliance, they are more likely to act on the feedback and engage in positive feedback behaviours such as feedback seeking, disclosure and openness to feedback (Farrell, Bourgeois-Law, Ajjawi, & Regehr, 2017; Telio et al., 2016). However, the actions that are the consequence of the feedback remain challenging to measure even though it is possible to measure perceptions of the strength of the alliance which might mediate the action. Multiple data collection points are thus needed alongside perceptions of the educational alliance, such as follow-up interviews with participants asking about actions or document/performance analysis of subsequent work with think-aloud prompting discussion of the relevant sense-making and associated actions. Interactional analysis, which preserves context and focuses on the discursive role of feedback dialogue, can also be used. For example, feedback dialogue was found to prompt self-regulatory behaviours such as self-evaluation, monitoring of work and seeking of feedback (Ajjawi & Boud, 2017, 2018).

If the problems of feedback are conceptualised through the lens of feedback literacy (Carless & Boud, 2018), impact again looks different. Feedback literate learners know how to seek out feedback information, make sense of it, use it and manage emotions through the whole process. Students who are highly feedback literate become the owners of feedback impact, and have the power to selectively reject and disregard feedback information, or use it strategically for purposes other than learning. Feedback literate students overcome sub-optimal feedback practices by autonomously seeking supplementary feedback information. They can also effectively manage their emotions despite heavy and poorly communicated criticism. All of these practices make isolating the impact of a particular feedback intervention very difficult. However, researching students' feedback literacy trajectory may be possible, through methods that sample experiences over time, such as longitudinal audio diaries.

Going beyond what the student does as an individual, arguments have been made that, in contrast to individual cognitive processes, feedback is a *social* practice which is determined by a range of factors, including the social, political, cultural and material. So far, the theory of practice architectures has been used to understand why students might not take part in feedback processes despite the promotion of individual student agency (Jørgensen, 2018). Jørgensen (2018) even suggests that focussing on effects is incompatible with feedback as a co-construction process between two people and the idea of impacts is based within a behavioural/cognitive framework. However, what students do, or do not do, with feedback, is a type of effect, or impact: the endpoint does not have to be a particular piece of work. Esterhazy's (2017, 2018) sophisticated ethnography similarly eschews a straightforward or linear relationship between feedback "interventions" and student behaviours by seeking to observe what emerges through the interrelation of the individual and the affordances of the sociocultural milieu. This is not a simple input–output relationship, hence our assertion that researchers must pay attention to their conceptualisation of feedback and understandings of learning when thinking about the sorts of effects they would like to explore.

We must also consider the negative impacts of feedback and pay special attention to investigating and reporting on these: bias in published learning and teaching interventions may paint an overly optimistic picture of feedback effects (Dawson & Dawson, 2018). In extreme cases, students may fail, or leave study, influenced by feedback messages. Though we would like to think this only occurs where feedback was absent, and students found their efforts pointless, it is possible that there are unintended consequences of even the most well-intentioned intervention: a large-scale review found that 38% of feedback effects were indeed negative (Kluger & Denisi, 1996). In more moderate scenarios, feedback may lead to unintended learning and the perpetuation of practices that are less desirable. For example, feedback dialogue that focusses on essay structure and form may signal a valuing of set structures rather than creative thinking. Though it is hard to capture unintended effects, these may be better addressed through qualitative research methodologies where there is room for new possibilities to be introduced and discussed. One instance where these effects were captured was in a study by Urquhart, Rees, and Ker (2014) where they explored how students make sense of feedback through narrative enquiry. Here, in addition to learning about student processes of feedback sense-making, the authors identified the negative effects of feedback, such as the immediate and memorable emotional impacts. This was achieved through interview techniques that elicited stories from students, and analysis which focussed on personal narratives as a whole, and within these, on both positive and negative experiences. Investigations of negative impacts need not be complicated; however, they are likely to require more time and resources, such as incentives to recruit participants, conduct interviews, and transcribe and analyse complex data.

Conclusions: Beware of the Naive

Feedback research is at a crucial crossroads. We have argued that feedback impact research could take the example of student engagement research as a cautionary tale. Impact is a starting point, a way to consider how to move forward, rather than a solution in itself. While the low-hanging fruits might be easy to reach, feedback research should move beyond this, to investigate what matters in the interplay between processes and effects, rather than what is easy to measure. If we are not conscious of this, focussing on impact may lead to us privileging those things that can be measured rather than those things that are effective. Tacit impacts may also be important. Research on the impact of feedback must also be rigorous and well aligned from the conceptualisation of feedback and learning, to aims, research methodologies and means of data collection. This will ensure that conclusions about impact can be reasonably drawn from the research, and avoid the problems which student engagement research currently faces: criticisms from within and without regarding the utility and meaning of research in this area.

References

Ajjawi, R., & Boud, D. (2017). Researching feedback dialogue: An interactional analysis approach. *Assessment & Evaluation in Higher Education, 42*(2), 252–265. https://doi.org/10.1080/02602938.2015.1102863.

Ajjawi, R., & Boud, D. (2018). Examining the nature and effects of feedback dialogue. *Assessment & Evaluation in Higher Education, 43*(7), 1106–1119. https://doi.org/10.1080/02602938.2018.1434128.

Ajjawi, R., Molloy, E., Bearman, M., & Rees, C. E. (2017). Contextual influences on feedback practices: An ecological perspective. In D. Carless, S. Bridges, C. Chan, & R. Glofcheski (Eds.), *Scaling up assessment for learning in higher education* (Chapter 9, pp. 129–143). Singapore: Springer. http://link.springer.com/chapter/10.1007/978-981-10-3045-1_9.

Ajjawi, R., & Regehr, G. (2019). When I say ... feedback. *Medical Education, 53*(7), 652–654. https://doi.org/10.1111/medu.13746.

Azevedo, R. (2015). Defining and measuring engagement and learning in science: Conceptual, theoretical, methodological, and analytical issues. *Educational Psychologist, 50*(1), 84–94. https://doi.org/10.1080/00461520.2015.1004069.

Boud, D., & Molloy, E. (2013). Rethinking models of feedback for learning: The challenge of design. *Assessment & Evaluation in Higher Education, 38*(6), 698–712. https://doi.org/10.1080/02602938.2012.691462.

Carless, D., & Boud, D. (2018). The development of student feedback literacy: Enabling uptake of feedback. *Assessment & Evaluation in Higher Education,* 1315–1325. https://doi.org/10.1080/02602938.2018.1463354.

Dawson, P., & Dawson, S. L. (2018). Sharing successes and hiding failures: 'Reporting bias' in learning and teaching research. *Studies in Higher Education, 43*(8), 1405–1416. https://doi.org/10.1080/03075079.2016.1258052.

Esterhazy, R., & Damşa, C. (2017). Unpacking the feedback process: An analysis of undergraduate students' interactional meaning-making of feedback comments. *Studies in Higher Education,* 1–15. https://doi.org/10.1080/03075079.2017.1359249.

Esterhazy, R. (2018). What matters for productive feedback? Disciplinary practices and their relational dynamics. *Assessment & Evaluation in Higher Education, 43*(8), 1302–1314. https://doi.org/10.1080/02602938.2018.1463353.

Farrell, L., Bourgeois-Law, G., Ajjawi, R., & Regehr, G. (2017). An autoethnographic exploration of the use of goal oriented feedback to enhance brief clinical teaching encounters. *Advances in Health Sciences Education, 22*(1), 91–104. https://doi.org/10.1007/s10459-016-9686-5.

Fredricks, J. A., Blumenfeld, P. C., & Paris, A. H. (2004). School engagement: Potential of the concept, state of the evidence. *Review of Educational Research, 74*(1), 59–109. https://doi.org/10.3102/00346543074001059.

Hattie, J., & Timperley, H. (2007). The power of feedback. *Review of Educational Research, 77*(1), 81–112. https://doi.org/10.3102/003465430298487.

Ifenthaler, D., & Yau, J. Y.-K. (2018). Utilising learning analytics for study success in higher education: A systematic review. In M. Campbell, J. Willems, C. Adachi, D. Blake, I. Doherty, S. Krishnan, ... J. Tai (Eds.), *Open oceans: Learning without borders* (pp. 406–411). Geelong: ASCILITE. Retrieved from http://2018conference.ascilite.org/wp-content/uploads/2018/11/ASCILITE-2018-Proceedings-Pre-Conference-1.pdf.

Jørgensen, B. M. (2018). Investigating non-engagement with feedback in higher education as a social practice. *Assessment & Evaluation in Higher Education,* 1–13. https://doi.org/10.1080/02602938.2018.1525691.

Kahu, E. R. (2013). Framing student engagement in higher education. *Studies in Higher Education, 38*(5), 758–773. https://doi.org/10.1080/03075079.2011.598505.

Kahu, E. R., & Nelson, K. (2018). Student engagement in the educational interface: Understanding the mechanisms of student success. *Higher Education Research & Development, 37*(1), 58–71. https://doi.org/10.1080/07294360.2017.1344197.

Kluger, A. N., & Denisi, A. (1996). The effects of feedback interventions on performance: A historical review, a meta-analysis, and a preliminary feedback intervention theory. *Psychological Bulletin, 119*(2), 254–284.

Kuh, G. D. (2001). Assessing what really matters to student learning inside the national survey of student engagement. *Change: The Magazine of Higher Learning, 33*(3), 10–17. https://doi.org/10.1080/00091380109601795.

Liu, D. Y. T., Richards, D., Dawson, P., Froissard, J.-C., & Atif, A. (2016). Knowledge acquisition for learning analytics: Comparing teacher-derived, algorithm-derived, and hybrid models in the moodle engagement analytics plugin. In H. Ohwada & K. Yoshida (Eds.), *Knowledge management and acquisition for intelligent systems: 14th Pacific Rim Knowledge Acquisition Workshop, PKAW 2016* (pp. 183–197). Cham: Springer.

Macfadyen, L. P., & Dawson, S. (2010). Mining LMS data to develop an "early warning system" for educators: A proof of concept. *Computers & Education, 54*(2), 588–599. https://doi.org/10.1016/j.compedu.2009.09.008.

Mandernach, B. J. (2015). Assessment of student engagement in higher education: A synthesis of literature and assessment tools. *International Journal of Learning, Teaching and Educational Research, 12*(2), 1–14. Retrieved from http://www.ijlter.org/index.php/ijlter/article/view/367.

O'Shea, S., & Delahunty, J. (2018). Getting through the day and still having a smile on my face! How do students define success in the university learning environment? *Higher Education Research & Development, 37*(5), 1062–1075. https://doi.org/10.1080/07294360.2018.1463973.

Oxford Dictionaries. (2015). *Feedback.* Retrieved July 26, 2018, from https://en.oxforddictionaries.com/definition/feedback.

Tai, J., Ajjawi, R., Bearman, M., & Wiseman, P. J. (2018). Exploring the mismatch between conceptualisations and measures of student engagement. In *European Association for Research on Learning and Instruction: Special Interest Group 1 (EARLI-SIG1).* Assessment and Measurement, Helsinki.

Telio, S., Regehr, G., & Ajjawi, R. (2016). Feedback and the educational alliance: Examining credibility judgements and their consequences. *Medical Education, 50*(9), 933–942. https://doi.org/10.1111/medu.13063.

Urquhart, L. M., Rees, C. E., & Ker, J. S. (2014). Making sense of feedback experiences: A multi-school study of medical students' narratives. *Medical Education, 48*(2), 189–203. https://doi.org/10.1111/medu.12304.

Vuori, J. (2014, July). Student engagement: Buzzword of fuzzword? *Journal of Higher Education Policy and Management, 36,* 1–11. https://doi.org/10.1080/1360080X.2014.936094.

Westman, S., & Bergmark, U. (2018). Re-considering the ontoepistemology of student engagement in higher education. *Educational Philosophy and Theory, 1857,* 1–11. https://doi.org/10.1080/00131857.2018.1454309.

Wiener, N. (1967). *The human use of human beings: Cybernetics and society (first Avon).* New York: Avon Books.

4

Learners' Feedback Literacy and the Longer Term: Developing Capacity for Impact

David Carless

Introduction

The focus of the chapter is to analyse feedback impacts by drawing on a longitudinal inquiry into learners' experiences of feedback. The study involved a five-year investigation of four learners, pseudonyms Alicia, Candice, Eva and Philippa, taking a double degree in Arts and Education at the University of Hong Kong. Due to structural changes in the Hong Kong education system, learners now spend six years rather than seven in high school and an extra year at university, so a four-year Bachelor of Education degree is extended to five years. I interviewed the four learners eight times each over the course of their study to understand their experience of feedback: what feedback was useful or not; the extent to which it was monologic or dialogic; evidence of learner action in response to feedback; and its affective impact. The informants also shared documentary feedback evidence, principally examples of feedback which they perceived

D. Carless (✉)
University of Hong Kong, Hong Kong, China
e-mail: dcarless@hku.hk

© The Author(s) 2019
M. Henderson et al. (eds.), *The Impact of Feedback in Higher Education*,
https://doi.org/10.1007/978-3-030-25112-3_4

as striking, helpful or unhelpful. The main aim of the chapter is to illustrate how longer-term perspectives can contribute to research on feedback impact.

Despite the small sample, the approach is a fresh one and I have not been able to find any examples in the literature on feedback of this kind of longitudinal investigation of the learner experience. Through analysing learners' development over the longer term, insights about the outcomes of feedback processes are accumulated. In line with the orientation of this book, a recurrent probe was to identify the impact of feedback comments so I repeatedly asked the learners to provide examples of feedback that they had acted upon. The longitudinal dimension enabled a variety of short-term and longer-term learner uses of feedback to surface. The analysis in the chapter links these impacts to current thinking on feedback literacy: the know-how to interpret and use feedback. A key point is that without learner capacities and dispositions to engage with feedback, impacts are inevitably modest.

The theoretical orientation to the chapter is based on social constructivist learning theories (O'Donovan, Rust, & Price, 2016; Palincsar, 1998). Social constructivist feedback research takes the perspective that shared and individual interpretations are developed through dialogue, sense-making and co-construction between participants (Price, Handley, & Millar, 2011). Feedback predominantly in the form of teacher transmission of information to learners is insufficient to promote complex learning (Sadler, 2010). Feedback needs to be conceptualized as a dialogic process that involves co-ordinated teacher-learner and peer interaction as well as active learner engagement (Nicol, 2010). A major challenge for current feedback practices is that social constructivist processes are generally not being applied, and there is insufficient emphasis on the agency of learners in feedback processes (O'Donovan et al., 2016).

A 3P Model of Learners' Experiences of Feedback

Learners' constructions of feedback are bound up with their previous experiences, learning strategies and motivations. They are also impacted by how

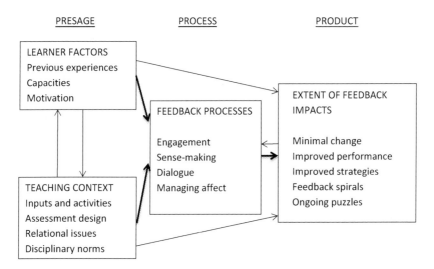

Fig. 4.1 3P model of the learner experience of feedback

teachers in different disciplines organize learning activities and assessment. This interplay between various prior and ongoing experiences resonates with Biggs' well-known 3P (presage, process, product) models of learning and teaching (Biggs, 1993, 1999). In Fig. 4.1, I adapt the model to depict the learner experience of feedback. The aim of the model is to describe both linear elements of progression from presage to process to product and interactive aspects that represent some of the temporal and developmental aspects of the learner experience over the duration of a programme.

The model describes three components of the learner feedback experience: presage or prior experiences; processes of engaging with feedback; and products, namely the likely outcomes and impact of the processes. Presage factors are of two main kinds: learner factors and the teaching context. Learner factors include previous feedback experiences; existing capacities to engage with feedback; and motivation to use feedback for ongoing improvement. The teaching context involves course design, teaching inputs, learning activities and assessment design. There are also relational factors, including the course atmosphere and the relationships between participants. Teaching and learning also take place within disciplinary cultures which have their own particular norms for how pedagogy, assessment and feedback are implemented.

The process-level factors focus on the learner response to feedback. They include the extent of engagement with feedback and making sense of feedback through interaction with text or others. These processes are envisaged as involving dialogues and co-construction resonating with the principles of social constructivism. As feedback often prompts emotional or attitudinal responses, managing the affective side of feedback is also a significant part of the process dimension.

The impacts of these feedback processes are varied according to learners' responses to inputs and experiences, and how teachers have designed courses, learning activities and assessment. A critical factor influencing impact is how well the presage and process factors are managed by teachers and learners. There is plenty of evidence in the literature of minimal impacts of feedback processes but with careful designs there are potentially positive outcomes. These include learners' improvements to both short-term performance and longer-term enhancement of learning strategies. Impacts are also envisaged as involving learning spirals where students make sense of and use feedback inputs over an extended time frame. Feedback spirals suggest temporal and iterative features in that insightful feedback frequently has a gradual, cumulative impact (Carless, 2019a). Feedback spirals involve a series of cycles building on engagement with previous feedback experiences and including struggling with ongoing puzzles that are not easily resolved. The airing of long-term impacts is hard to uncover except through longitudinal analysis of the learner experience.

The model also illustrates the individual nature of learner response to feedback in that each learner will have different prior experiences; will respond in a variety of ways in the process stage; and will derive different outcomes. The most powerful directions of effect in the model are marked by heavy arrows, and the lighter arrows indicate the interactive and cyclical nature of the model as a system. The potential impacts emerge in different ways from the interaction between various factors.

Learners' Experiences and the Longer Term

Alicia reported that in her first year of university study, she mainly tried to memorize material in similar ways to what she had done in high school. She was not particularly motivated to engage with feedback and did not report any significant feedback experiences. In other words, the presage learner factors were not particularly favourable for positive impacts of feedback. In her second year, she teamed up with some high-achieving classmates on a group project and learnt from them how to use criteria to self-evaluate work in progress, indicative of a social constructivist element of learning from interaction with peers. In her final year, Alicia provided an example that illustrated learner agency when she talked about reducing her bad habit of procrastination when preparing her assignments. Whereas procrastination had bedevilled her assignment preparation in the early years of her undergraduate study, by her final year she felt that this was one of the main enhancements she had made to her learning strategies. She was not directly informed by teacher feedback to avoid procrastination; the change arises from her reflections, agency and decision-making (Carless, 2019a). In this example, the product of Alicia's spiral engagement over the longer term is an enhanced learning strategy.

A prominent theme in Candice's case relates to a key presage teaching context factor: the importance of assessment design in promoting or inhibiting action on feedback. Candice was quite dismissive of any teacher comments that came at the end of courses as she perceived them to be of little use because it was too late for her to take action. She did not consider that she could transfer ideas across courses to different topics with different teachers. Instead, she favoured teacher approaches which involved a draft followed by a submission, or two interlinked assessment tasks with comments from the first informing the second. This example reiterates the importance of assessment designs which promote learner uptake of feedback (Carless et al., 2011; Zimbardi et al., 2017). It also reinforces thinking that teachers could reduce time spent on comments which are offered at times when learners cannot reasonably take them up (Boud & Molloy, 2013).

There was some evidence in the data of short-term and longer-term examples of learner action on feedback. Eva talked about how she received clear advice on a draft lesson plan and successfully acted on the feedback. She was appreciative of both the teacher comments and how she had opportunities to use them to revise her lesson plan. So the product of the feedback experience was improved performance. A critical view of this episode might, however, question the long-term benefits of this kind of teacher feedback followed by learner action in that they might be quite formulaic and behaviourist: the teacher advises and the learner corrects (Carless, 2019a). Boud and Molloy (2013) refer to these kinds of sequences as Feedback Mark 1: a task which demonstrates the current learner performance level, teacher provision of comments and a subsequent task in which a change in performance can be identified. A feedback loop is closed which is a positive outcome but there are also risks of reinforcing dependency on the teacher rather than developing capacities for learners to deploy internal feedback effectively (Carless, 2019a).

Philippa generally achieved excellent grades. Throughout her studies, she evidenced sophisticated learning strategies and a high degree of feedback literacy. In the first semester of her studies, she described a strategy of copying and pasting rubrics to the top of her essay drafts. She reported using this strategy throughout her studies so she could continuously self-evaluate work in progress against the stated requirements (Carless, 2019a). She thus evidences promising presage factors in self-monitoring capacities. She was also active in the process stage in sense-making and dialogue by frequently contacting teachers to try to understand assessment requirements and standards. Philippa was aware that she was exceptional in being motivated to engage teachers in dialogues around learning, improvement and the nature of quality work. She felt that there could be more dialogue about the process of feedback and understanding criteria. She also perceived that teachers could empathize more with learners' needs in relation to their imperative of achieving high grades. In sum, she wanted more partnership between teachers and learners so that both parties could better understand each other's perspectives.

Social Affective Impacts

There were also a number of social affective impacts which speak to both relational issues in the teaching context and managing affect as part of feedback processes. Candice found it frustrating when a teacher corrected in great detail the grammar and punctuation of her summative assignment. She did not feel that this was helpful because it focused too much on the mechanics of writing which she did not perceive as useful, particularly after the assessment cycle was completed. The content, manner and timing of this teacher feedback were not what she felt catered for her needs and preferences.

Eva often talked about relational aspects of feedback. A key presage factor was that she was initially overawed by entering a prestigious university, so in the first year of her study, she felt that she really needed praise and encouragement. She expressed a preference for positive feedback and sensitive teacher communication. After a few years, she learnt that her academic performance was good and she became confident that she could do well at university. So in the later years of her study, she became more open to critical comments because she wanted to improve further (Carless, 2019b). This seems to represent interplay between becoming accustomed to expectations, developing confidence and increased resilience.

Alicia highlighted the importance of a balance of praise and comments for improvement. She reported that teachers invariably provided this balance and she did not seem to experience any powerful emotional responses to feedback or assessment results. This was partly because she was quite a relaxed and laid-back student. On the one hand, she did not experience any negative emotional responses to feedback, but on the other hand she did not generally feel a strong motivation to strive for improvement. She appreciated teacher commitment and reported being more motivated if she could feel teacher investment of time and effort in providing feedback.

Philippa often expressed a desire for critical feedback that would help her achieve the high grades to which she aspired. High achievers are often relatively receptive to critical comments so as to contribute to their goal of continuous improvement. She was aware that the initial emotional reaction to feedback may not be optimal and that it is necessary to accept one's strengths and weaknesses, and be open to constructive critique.

Taking wider data into account than has been presented here, the learners hoped to experience some empathy and a sense that teachers were supportive in enabling them to achieve their goals. This might have been facilitated by a dialogic approach but instead the learners generally experienced feedback processes as a teacher monologue about their performance rather than a dialogue. When there were opportunities for oral interaction, Alicia, Candice and Eva were often reticent to approach teachers for reasons related to confidence, possible threats to self-esteem or lack of willpower to strive for continuous improvement. Only Philippa was eager to enter into sustained dialogues with teachers. Philippa's ideas around partnership converged with some of the data on affective factors from the other three students. All of them wanted to feel that teachers were on the same wavelength as them and had their best interests at heart. The broader evidence from the study suggests a need for enhanced teacher-learner partnerships in feedback processes (Carless, 2019b). Partnership feedback approaches could involve communication about the role of feedback in improving work or writing strategies; discussion of the timing of feedback to maximize impact; and sharing of strategies for dealing with emotional challenges, including staff sharing their experiences of peer review and rejections of their outputs or research grant applications.

The Role of Learners' Feedback Literacy

Learners' feedback literacy denotes the understandings, capacities and dispositions required to make sense of feedback comments and use them for enhancement purposes (Carless & Boud, 2018). Presage factors play significant roles in the development of learner feedback literacy. Learners need capacities to appreciate feedback processes and see their value. They also need motivation to summon the volition to work with feedback as a tool for improvement. Learner engagement with feedback in the shorter and longer term is likely to be enhanced through processes where they have agency and opportunities to act on feedback. Unless comments make sense to learners within their existing belief systems and priorities, they may not engage with them. Furthermore, unless there are opportunities for uptake, there may be limited motivation to do more than pay lip service to comments.

The most striking element of learner feedback literacy revealed by the data was Philippa's cue-seeking behaviours. She strived to understand teachers' expectations in relation to assessment tasks and would readily enter into co-constructed dialogues with them to understand more deeply their specific requirements. When there were two assignments for a course, she would clarify with the teachers the feedback on the first task to inform her preparation of the second one. Throughout the five-year period, she talked about her struggles to identify what each individual teacher was looking for in the course assignments. This seems to represent a long-term form of spiral engagement that was challenging because quality is hard to define and articulate. It was an ongoing puzzle that was never fully resolved (Carless, 2019a).

One of the few other overt strategies suggesting feedback literacy was reported by Candice. She kept a file of her assignments and made some notes about what feedback she could use for improvement. She would return to the file when she was working on assignments and remind herself of some key issues (Carless, 2019a). This was a promising strategy which involved Candice storing and accessing previous work and comments, and accessing them to inform her current work in progress. The strategy involved appreciating the value of previous feedback, accessing it and taking action (cf. Carless & Boud, 2018). She worked on the strategy individually without sharing it or getting support from teachers or peers, and eventually she abandoned it. By mid-way through her studies, she was satisfied with her level of performance and lost the volition to strive for further improvement (Carless, 2019b).

Alicia did not seem to evidence significant development of feedback literacy but in her final year, she reported increased willingness to seek guidance from teachers. Whereas in the first few years of the programme she was reticent to approach teachers because of lack of confidence, towards the end of her study she was more willing to initiate dialogue with teachers about assessment expectations. A specific driver for Alicia's change was her desire to achieve an upper second-class degree. By her final year, she was near the borderline of upper second-class honours, and so was determined to maximize her potential for achieving high grades. Approaching the teachers for guidance seemed to be a useful strategy at this stage of her study.

For Eva, the main development of her feedback literacy was in relation to managing affect. She experienced quite a lot of anxiety in her early years at receiving critical comments which might demoralize her. By the end of her study, instead of agonizing over criticism she was able to look at it in a more positive way within an improvement mentality. Similar to Alicia, the role of honours classification in striving to achieve upper second-class honours was significant in accepting critical comments that could help her improve.

The spiral development of aspects of learner feedback literacy seemed to arise from a gradual internalization of a combination of inputs, including working on assignments; interaction with teachers and their comments; peer learning; and learners' own reflections. To promote the development of learner feedback literacy, teachers need to design curriculum and assessment in ways which enable students to make academic judgements, involve themselves in dialogue with peers and work with feedback for the purposes of improving performance and learning strategies.

Implications

The analysis suggests both implications for practice and for longitudinal research.

Implications for Practice

Course and assessment design can in various ways inhibit or enhance the impact of feedback processes. A significant teacher role lies in designing curriculum and assessment in ways which can promote learner feedback literacy (Carless & Boud, 2018). A useful teacher strategy to encourage learner use of feedback is to design assessment in ways which facilitate iterative cycles of processing, making sense of and using feedback. When assessment tasks are designed to build on earlier tasks, and the links in a sequence are made explicit, learners are more likely to draw on feedback from preceding tasks (Zimbardi et al., 2017). There are also specific assessment task types which promote feedback interactions between learners, such as group projects or collaborative writing tasks, such as wikis.

Programme-based approaches, such as e-portfolios, carry significant potential to enable learners to work with feedback over a period of time, and make connections between diverse assessment and feedback experiences. E-portfolios encourage learners to refine work iteratively over time; use a range of internal and external feedback; and act progressively on feedback insights. E-portfolios enable learners to store, retrieve and use comments, prompting the revisiting and uptake of feedback (Fung, 2016). The curation process of e-portfolio development facilitates learners providing, receiving and working with feedback from teachers and peers (Clarke & Boud, 2018). Learners can demonstrate to themselves and others that medium-term feedback loops are being addressed. Digitally enabled feedback storage tackles a problem that learners often find it difficult to track and act on the diverse feedback information that they receive. The digital use of feedback can serve to activate the development of learner feedback literacy by focusing them on the need to revisit and use feedback messages.

Dialogues of different forms are at the heart of the development of learner feedback literacy, yet dialogue is sometimes seen as an impractical aspiration within massified higher education (Nicol, 2010). To support the development of their feedback literacy, learners need sustained opportunities for their voice to be heard in communication with others through an active presence in feedback dialogues (Steen-Utheim & Wittek, 2017). A user-friendly means of stimulating dialogue within written feedback processes involves learners using an interactive coversheet to state what kind of feedback they would prefer (Bloxham & Campbell, 2010). This strategy repositions feedback as something solicited by learners and enables a more co-constructed feedback process in line with the principles of social constructivism. Perhaps an even better interactive coversheet strategy is to invite learners to state what feedback they are acting upon (Barton, McAleer, & Ajjawi, 2016; Winstone & Carless, 2019). This reinforces the need for action on previous comments that have been received and supports the development of learners' feedback literacy by encouraging them to revisit and use previous feedback.

Implications for Longitudinal Research

A key implication of the chapter is that feedback research benefits from longer-term perspectives. A longitudinal approach enables a deeper understanding of the learner response to feedback than that produced by cross-sectional designs. Longitudinal inquiry encourages learners to articulate how they have used feedback or not, providing some insight into the impact of feedback. Repeated interviewing enables the researcher to differentiate between one-off statements and those that are reiterated on multiple occasions. Being able to revisit themes from earlier interviews is also advantageous and can facilitate understanding of how and why learners change over time. Sometimes informants referred to recent experiences, but when they went back to events from previous years it was an indication that these occurrences had been stored in long-term memory and were probably more significant.

There are also a number of ways in which the longitudinal approach could have collected more evidence of impact, additional to learners' self-reports. It would be feasible to document more closely the process of learners acting on comments, for example, through inviting them to submit samples of assignments which evidenced uptake of feedback. It would also be possible to undertake a closer examination of assignment products, including comparison of learners' academic writing over time. Future longitudinal research could utilize additional strategies, such as think-aloud data about how learners are revising assignments in relation to feedback, or learner auto-ethnographies of how they respond to feedback over time. Multimodal longitudinal journaling encourages learners to collect and record artefacts to document their experiences (Gourlay & Oliver, 2018) and could be adapted for use in feedback research. Reflection logs are another means of involving learners in documenting their experiences and use of feedback over a period of time (Steen-Utheim & Hopfenbeck, 2019). In sum, different kinds of longitudinal inquiry carry significant potential as research designs to trace impacts of feedback.

Conclusion

A key theme in this chapter is that feedback research and practice might profitably be focused on learner development over the longer term. The short-term closing of feedback loops sometimes involves relatively superficial impacts of feedback without developing learners' capacities for independent learning. Longer-term progress in improving performance or adjusting learning strategies often involves spiral forms of learning in which students revisit and reflect on previous feedback experiences. Dialogue based on social constructivist principles is an important process stage, including peer feedback, inner self-reflections and practical forms of interaction with teachers. The 3P model exemplifies the interaction between presage, process and product aspects of the learner experience of feedback. The model opens up a number of avenues for further research. Future longitudinal inquiry across different disciplines and contexts might enable validation or refinement of key presage, process and product factors.

References

Barton, K., Schofield, S., McAleer, S., & Ajjawi, R. (2016). Translating evidence-based guidelines to improve feedback practices: The interact case study. *BMC Medical Education, 16*(1), 53–64. https://doi.org/10.1186/s12909-016-0562-z.

Biggs, J. (1993). From theory to practice: A cognitive systems approach. *Higher Education Research and Development, 12,* 73–86. https://doi.org/10.1080/0729436930120107.

Biggs, J. (1999). *Teaching for quality learning at university: What the student does.* Buckingham: SRHE and Open University Press.

Bloxham, S., & Campbell, L. (2010). Generating dialogue in assessment feedback: Exploring the use of interactive cover sheets. *Assessment & Evaluation in Higher Education, 35*(3), 291–300. https://doi.org/10.1080/02602931003650045.

Boud, D., & Molloy, E. (2013). Rethinking models of feedback for learning: The challenge of design. *Assessment & Evaluation in Higher Education, 38*(6), 698–712. https://doi.org/10.1080/02602938.2012.691462.

Carless, D. (2019a). Feedback loops and the longer-term: Towards feedback spirals. *Assessment and Evaluation in Higher Education, 44*(5), 705–714. https://doi.org/10.1080/02602938.2018.1531108.

Carless, D. (2019b, forthcoming). A longitudinal inquiry into students' experiences of feedback: A need for teacher-student partnerships. *Higher Education Research and Development.*

Carless, D., & Boud, D. (2018). The development of student feedback literacy: Enabling uptake of feedback. *Assessment & Evaluation in Higher Education, 43*(8), 1315–1325. https://doi.org/10.1080/02602938.2018.1463354.

Carless, D., Salter, D., Yang, M., & Lam, J. (2011). Developing sustainable feedback practices. *Studies in Higher Education, 36*(4), 395–407. https://doi.org/10.1080/03075071003642449.

Clarke, J., & Boud, D. (2018). Refocusing portfolio assessment: Curating for feedback and portrayal. *Innovations in Education and Teaching International, 55*(4), 479–486. https://doi.org/10.1080/14703297.2016.1250664.

Fung, D. (2016). *A connected curriculum for higher education.* London: UCL Press.

Gourlay, L., & Oliver, M. (2018). *Student engagement in the digital university: Sociomaterial assemblages.* London: Routledge.

Nicol, D. (2010). From monologue to dialogue: Improving written feedback processes in mass higher education. *Assessment & Evaluation in Higher Education, 35*(5), 501–517. https://doi.org/10.1080/02602931003786559.

O'Donovan, B., Rust, C., & Price, M. (2016). A scholarly approach to solving the feedback dilemma in practice. *Assessment & Evaluation in Higher Education, 41*(6), 938–949. https://doi.org/10.1080/02602938.2015.1052774.

Palincsar, A. S. (1998). Social constructivist perspectives on teaching and learning. *Annual Review of Psychology, 49*(1), 345–375. https://doi.org/10.1146/annurev.psych.49.1.345.

Price, M., Handley, K., & Millar, J. (2011). Feedback: Focusing attention on engagement. *Studies in Higher Education, 36*(8), 879–896. https://doi.org/10.1080/03075079.2010.483513.

Sadler, D. R. (2010). Beyond feedback: Developing student capability in complex appraisal. *Assessment & Evaluation in Higher Education, 35*(5), 535–550. https://doi.org/10.1080/02602930903541015.

Steen-Utheim, A., & Hopfenbeck, T. (2019). To do or not to do with feedback: A study of undergraduate students' engagement within a portfolio assessment design. *Assessment & Evaluation in Higher Education, 44*(1), 80–96. https://doi.org/10.1080/02602938.2018.1476669.

Steen-Utheim, A., & Wittek, A. (2017). Dialogic feedback and the potentialities for student learning. *Learning, Culture and Social Interaction, 15,* 18–30. https://doi.org/10.1016/j.lcsi.2017.06.002.

Winstone, N., & Carless, D. (2019). *Designing effective feedback processes in higher education: A learning-focused approach.* London: Routledge.

Zimbardi, K., Colthorpe, K., Dekker, A., Engstrom, C., Bugarcic, A., Worthy, P., … Long, P. (2017). Are they using my feedback? The extent of students' feedback use has a large impact on subsequent academic performance. *Assessment & Evaluation in Higher Education, 42*(4), 625–644. https://doi.org/10.1080/02602938.2016.1174187.

5

Re-conceptualizing Feedback Through a Sociocultural Lens

Rachelle Esterhazy ⓘ

Introduction

Many higher education teachers put much effort into giving feedback, but experience shows that students often do not engage with the feedback as intended. This leads to a gap between the intended and experienced impact of feedback. This "feedback dilemma" (Scott, 2014) has preoccupied the work of many researchers over the last decades who have attempted to find those aspects of feedback that are most relevant for it to make a difference in student learning. The most common approaches are focused on identifying the best ways of formulating feedback comments, how to deliver these comments, what kind of students are most likely to make use of feedback, and what characteristics are inherent to teachers providing good feedback (Jonsson, 2012; Winstone, Nash, Parker, & Rowntree, 2017). Many of these studies are characterized by a narrow focus on isolated aspects of feedback and a limited attention to the specific higher education environment in which feedback takes place.

R. Esterhazy (✉)
University of Oslo, Oslo, Norway
e-mail: rachelle.esterhazy@iped.uio.no

© The Author(s) 2019
M. Henderson et al. (eds.), *The Impact of Feedback in Higher Education*,
https://doi.org/10.1007/978-3-030-25112-3_5

In this chapter, I present an alternative conceptualization of feedback as a social practice that is made up of complex relations and deeply embedded in its sociocultural context. The main aim is to illustrate how such an alternative way of thinking of feedback helps us understand the abovementioned feedback dilemma and potential ways out of it. Drawing on sociocultural theories on human activity and learning (Säljö, 2005; Vygotsky, 1978; Wertsch, 1991), I present a three-layer feedback model developed through a series of empirical studies (Esterhazy, 2018, 2019; Esterhazy & Damşa, 2019). Throughout this chapter, I will draw on examples from my empirical work to illustrate aspects of the model and how it contributes to our understanding of what matters for feedback that has an impact on student learning.

Reconsidering "Feedback Impact" from a Sociocultural Perspective

To begin with, taking a sociocultural perspective requires us to reconsider what it means for feedback to have an impact. The term "impact" evokes the idea of a linear relationship between feedback (as the subject that impacts) and student achievement (as the object that is impacted on). Closely related to this idea is usually the assumption that it is possible to find an ideal one-size-fits-all type of feedback that will lead to impact independent of the context, the discipline or the individuals involved. This assumption may be called reductionist and creates a regrettable limitation for our understanding of the complex processes and relations involved in feedback. Indeed, the idea that feedback can be reduced to isolated elements that can be studied and optimized has regularly led to puzzling contradictions in the literature. Studies might show that certain delivery modes, timing or focus of feedback are effective, while other studies come to the opposite conclusion when conducted in different contexts (Shute, 2008). Research that is explicitly or implicitly operating with such reductionist assumptions might generate important findings about impactful feedback, but will always be faced with considerable limitations concerning its capacities to address the complex relations that make up the higher education context in which feedback occurs.

Aiming to overcome these shortcomings, I employ a sociocultural lens to re-conceptualize feedback from a more context-sensitive perspective (Säljö, 2005; Vygotsky, 1978; Wertsch, 1991). Instead of trying to find a one-size-fits-all solution, the focus here lays on unpacking the relations and processes that are at play when feedback takes place, and on providing new ideas for what it means for feedback to have an impact.

At the core of this conceptual framework is the notion of "feedback practices," i.e., the processes, relations and interactions that take place when students and teachers are providing and engaging with feedback information on student work (Esterhazy, 2019). This notion avoids the implication of linearity and directs the focus to what students and teachers do when engaged with feedback. For feedback practices in a course unit to be *productive*, i.e., to have an impact on student learning, it requires much more than just providing pieces of feedback information to students that make a positive change in their achievement. It requires the involved individuals to generate evaluative judgments about a piece of work, share this information, make sense of it and then use it to improve the given work (Esterhazy & Damşa, 2019). These actions are deeply intertwined with the standards and the implicit rules and conventions of the given discipline and institution. In other words, feedback practices are deeply embedded in their sociocultural context and whether they are productive depends on a myriad of relations and processes that make up this context.

To understand the wider implications of this way of conceptualizing feedback, it is necessary to take one step back and to understand the basic assumptions about human activity and learning that are inherent to sociocultural theories.

Zooming Out into the Landscape of Sociocultural Theories

In this conceptualization of feedback, I draw mainly on sociocultural perspectives on human activity and learning as originated in the work by Vygotsky (1978) and developed further by Wertsch (1991) and Säljö (2005). While having many similarities, it is important to distinguish sociocultural perspectives from socio-constructivist theories of learning.

Both give the "social" a central role in their understanding of knowledge and learning. However, how they address the social plays out in different ways in the two theoretical perspectives.

Socio-constructivist theories have a focus on the different ways knowledge is constructed, in particular how the learner moves towards increasingly more adequate levels of knowledge by interaction with the world (Packer & Goicoechea, 2000). That means learning is seen as construction and reorganization of internal knowledge structures that result from the social interaction of the learner with the environment.

Sociocultural learning theories, on the other hand, have a focus on social participation, activity and the relationships between participants and the environment (Packer & Goicoechea, 2000). Learning is believed to develop historically through changes at the sociocultural level that are intertwined with the development of the individual. From this postulate follows that all human activity—including learning—is inherently relational and situated in the sociocultural context and its social practices (Vygotsky, 1978; Wertsch, 1991). Social practices are "ways of doing" that people share in communities (Säljö, 2005). Every person is part of many social practices at the same time and everything in our sociocultural (and to an extent also physical) environment is structured by these practices. That is to say, how a person acts and sees the world is dependent on the social practices he or she is part of.

Another core assumption in the sociocultural perspective is that humans do not act in a direct way in the physical and social world; instead, action is always mediated by cultural tools (Vygotsky, 1978; Wertsch, 1991). Cultural tools refer to material and intellectual resources relevant for the enactment of a practice. In the university context, such tools might be the chairs in a lecture room, textbooks, student assignments, or scientific concepts. These tools have developed over time and, as such, incorporate the collective knowledge, norms, and values of the social practices from which they have developed.

Social practices also entail certain social conventions and rules related to how these tools are commonly used and what actions and routines people usually engage in when enacting a practice. Whenever people come together in a social encounter, their (inter)actions are shaped by the social practices at play and the cultural tools and conventions that come with them (Wertsch, 1991). At the same time, these (inter)actions are never enacted in the same way and through every enactment of a social practice its tools and conventions are reinterpreted and given a new meaning by the involved people.

In line with these ideas, institutional contexts such as a university course unit may be thought of as a set of social practices, including their tools and conventions that the course participants need to make sense of while being enrolled in the course unit. Higher education is a particularly complex context because it encompasses many different disciplines characterized by idiosyncratic social practices that have developed over many centuries (Trowler, 2012). These disciplines and their social practices frame the way teaching and learning, but also feedback, take place in a given course unit.

Feedback as Social Practices: A Three-Layer Model

The above-described premises of the sociocultural perspective suggest that feedback can be conceptualized as social practices that are situated in the specific sociocultural context of the given course unit. Feedback practices involve a wide range of relations, processes, and actions that take place during feedback encounters between students, teachers, and the tools in the unit. Feedback practices are considered to be productive, i.e., they lead to student learning, when these feedback encounters include processes of generating, making meaning of, and acting upon information about the quality of student performances (Esterhazy, 2019). If such processes do not—or only partly—occur, for example, when teachers provide feedback comments but students do not engage with them, the feedback practices in the course unit can consequently not be considered productive. That is, they do not have the desired impact on student learning.

A sociocultural view suggests further that whether feedback practices are productive is dependent on the epistemic and social relations at play in the given course context. Epistemic relations refer to the different ways knowledge is organized and generated in the course unit and the wider knowledge domain. Social relations refer to the different contacts between teachers, students, and materials that are arranged in pedagogical designs and that emerge during the semester (Esterhazy, 2019).

Feedback practices in a course unit can be visualized by a model that depicts the different social and epistemic relations within and across three layers: the feedback encounter layer, the course design layer, and the knowledge domain layer (see Fig. 5.1). This model is primarily an analytical representation of the complexity of feedback practices and is not intended to depict one-to-one reality or causal relationships. It implies that feedback practices comprise concrete enactments in the form of feedback encounters in which course participants "do feedback" during the course unit (top layer), but they are also characterized by more abstract structures in the form of the course design (middle layer) and the knowledge domain (bottom layer) that are sustained over time and beyond concrete instances of enactment. The relations that are relevant for how feedback practices look like in a course unit are depicted as lines between different elements—in each layer, different elements and the relations between them become relevant. In the following section, I will illustrate with the help of empirical examples how these three layers are relevant to understanding feedback practices in a course unit and what makes them productive.

Feedback Encounter Layer

Feedback practices are always enacted through "feedback encounters" in which students, teachers, and knowledge resources in the environment come together and "do feedback" (Esterhazy, 2018). Examples of such knowledge resources are assessment criteria, standards of academic writing or scientific concepts from the knowledge domain, but also the concrete feedback comments provided by teachers or peers. How students and teachers interact with each other and with such knowledge resources shapes the way in which feedback practices emerge "on the ground" (Esterhazy & Damşa, 2019). For example, a student group that is discussing a written feedback comment from their teacher on a group assignment is enacting a concrete feedback encounter. Whether the students succeed and whether their discussion will eventually lead to a positive improvement in their assignment (and develop their underlying understanding)

5 Re-conceptualizing Feedback Through a Sociocultural Lens 73

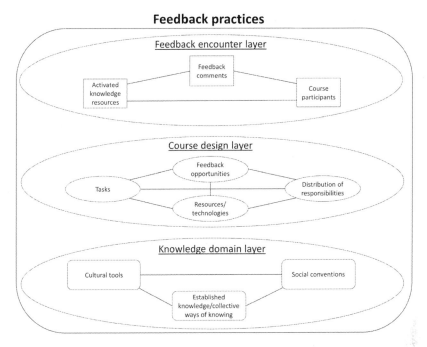

Fig. 5.1 Three-layer model of feedback practices in a course unit (Esterhazy, 2019)

is dependent on their interactions in this encounter. Do they build constructively on each other's suggestions? Do they take the time to look up information in their textbooks when uncertain? Do they approach their teacher to clarify something they are uncertain about? Only some of these interactions will lead to successful understanding of the comment and an appropriate strategy to integrate it in the assignment, while others will not. This illustrates that it is not the quality of the individual feedback comment alone that will determine whether feedback will have an impact on this situation. Rather, it is a myriad of emerging interactions and relations that will shape how students may or may not learn during this feedback encounter.

The student group who is engaging in such a productive feedback encounter can thus be seen as moving along a "meaning-making trajectory" toward a more complete understanding of the problem the feedback comment is addressing (Esterhazy & Damşa, 2019). To successfully move along this trajectory, the students need to make meaning not only of the comment itself, but also of how it relates to the knowledge content of their knowledge domain, of the standards and assessment criteria used in this particular course unit and of many more aspects. This example illustrates how important it is for productive feedback practices that students have the possibility to interact with each other and with relevant knowledge resources in order to make meaning of feedback comments and to make productive use of them in their work.

Course Design Layer

Feedback practices are also formed by the social and epistemic relations that teachers envision between different elements in their course design, for example, between the course participants, the tasks, and the knowledge resources. These elements are arranged by the teacher during the course design process, thereby generating sets of relations that will create different affordances and constraints as to which activities are likely to emerge during the semester. Teachers arrange these course elements in different ways depending on the activities they intend their students to engage in during the course (Goodyear, 2015). This assumption implies that teachers who want to include feedback in their course units have to plan relations between course elements in such ways that will create opportunities for generating, making meaning of, and using information on the quality of student work (i.e., feedback opportunities). As such, the envisioned relations in the course design layer constitute a structure with different feedback opportunities that may (or may not) be realized as actual feedback encounters once the course unit starts unfolding in situ during the semester.

That the envisioned relations in the course designs matter for what kind of feedback encounters may emerge is illustrated by two different examples. Taking a course design from a biology course unit, the responsible teacher envisioned his students to work on many separate tasks over the whole semester. In addition, he planned explicit and pre-scheduled feedback opportunities (both written comments and oral feedback) linked to each of these tasks. This design generated an iterative task organization

5 Re-conceptualizing Feedback Through a Sociocultural Lens   75

and a clear distribution of responsibilities in which students at all times knew when, where, and how they were to receive formative comments on their work. This organization led to students engaging in frequent and highly structured feedback encounters during the semester. These structured feedback encounters had a positive impact on the continuity in which students worked on their assignments and on their experience of being able to predict and influence their final grade.

Another example is a software engineering course unit, in which the teacher organized his tasks in a more cumulative manner, so that students were to work on one large project over the whole semester. Feedback opportunities, in this case, were planned with a more impromptu character, as they were intended to occur ad hoc in weekly course activities, in which students were able to ask for guidance and feedback from teaching assistants when needed. This design created a completely different set-up for the students who had to take more responsibility in deciding when, how, and where they needed comments on their work. This organization led to students engaging in feedback encounters that were of a more informal character and that had less clear starting and end points. These kinds of ad hoc feedback opportunities had a positive impact on the students' feeling of agency and their ability to decide themselves what kind of feedback they required at what point in time to progress successfully in their project work.

These two examples show that in each course design the feedback encounters that eventually emerged were of very different kind and demanded different actions and skills from students. This illustrates that feedback practices and whether they are productive is not only related to teachers' decisions about format and timing of feedback in itself, but also to the ways tasks, responsibilities and resources are arranged in the overall course design. These scenarios also illustrate that productive feedback cannot be simply added to an existing course design. Instead, feedback opportunities should be seen as integral parts of designs that can be incorporated by re-arranging responsibilities, tasks, and resources in different ways.

Knowledge Domain Layer

Finally, feedback practices are formed by the social and epistemic relations in the knowledge domain layer, which is spanning contexts and time. Every knowledge domain, or discipline, is characterized by specific cultural tools (e.g., different concepts, methods, equipment) and social conventions (e.g., typical ways of searching information, typical ways of interacting between students and teachers). According to the sociocultural perspective presented above, these cultural tools and conventions are imbued with—and shaped by—the given domain's knowledge, norms, and values that have developed over time. These tools and conventions from the given knowledge domain shape feedback practices in two ways: First, they influence the ways teachers arrange course elements that might generate feedback opportunities (in the course design layer) and, second, they influence how the course participants interact within each concrete feedback encounter (in the feedback encounter layer). This idea implies that all (inter)actions that individuals engage in while planning or engaging with feedback are always situated in the knowledge domain and cannot be studied without taking into account the tools and conventions of the domain they are embedded in (Säljö, 2005).

A concrete example of how the knowledge domain shapes the feedback practices in a course unit is the way in which the unfolding interactions within a feedback encounter are mediated by intellectual tools (such as scientific concepts and standards from the domain) and material tools (such as the lecture rooms, laptops, or textbooks). A written feedback comment on a group assignment might mention a relevant scientific concept from the domain (e.g., "statistical linear relationship") that opens up a space for rich discussions within a student group and, eventually, leads them along the meaning-making trajectory to productive changes in their group assignment (Esterhazy & Damşa, 2019). Another example might be material tools that are typical for the specific knowledge domain, such as a laptop connected to a white board in a software engineering lecture room. The presence of such a tool might for instance generate new interaction possibilities for a teaching assistant who can add a practical demonstration to her oral feedback comment that may help students get a deeper understanding of the issue at hand (Esterhazy, 2018). The fact that the teaching assistant and her students are sitting together around a white board in a lecture room is in itself a result of the course planning by the teacher beforehand (e.g., he hired the assistant, booked the room). This example illustrates how the availability of these domain-specific tools (i.e., the laptop and white board) has shaped both the emerging interactions in the feedback encounter layer as well as the planned relations in the course design layer.

What are the Implications of the Sociocultural Perspective for Productive Feedback Practices?

The main aim of this chapter was to illustrate how a sociocultural perspective on feedback helps us understand why feedback may not have the kind of impact that teachers intended it to have, and how this feedback dilemma might be addressed in practice. The three-layer model of feedback practices has provided new ideas about where to look for the core issues of the feedback dilemma. It raises the question whether it is really enough to focus our research efforts only on what makes individual feedback comments or teachers' communication strategies more impactful than others? While such insights might be important for our understanding of good feedback delivery, the sociocultural perspective suggests that we need to study these isolated aspects as part of a larger, complex set of relations that make up the specific course context we are studying.

The notion of feedback practices always being enacted in interaction between students, teachers and their environment suggests that neither students or teachers should be solely blamed for a situation in which feedback does not have impact as intended. That is, what kinds of impact feedback practices have is never fully controllable by the teacher, nor should it be seen as the sole responsibility of the learner. Instead, a sociocultural conceptualization of feedback suggests that the feedback dilemma can only be overcome, if we pay more attention to how epistemic and social relations between course participants, pedagogical designs, and the knowledge domain can be brought together in productive ways.

When feedback practices in a course unit are not productive, that is, when they do not lead to impact on student learning as intended by the teacher, this might be explained by a number of practical challenges. Some of these challenges that were observed in the empirical examples used in this chapter include:

- Too little time and space planned in the course design, which keeps students from making meaning of the received feedback comments (i.e., inhibits their move along the meaning-making trajectory).
- Unclear distributions of responsibilities with regard to feedback encounters that leave students uncertain of what is expected of them and makes them thereby likely to remain passive.
- Teacher reference to specific concepts or tools from the knowledge domain during a feedback encounter that the students are unfamiliar with, while the teacher might not realize these tools or concepts as domain-specific and therefore does not make the conventions around them more explicit.
- Unavailability of knowledge resources that would be necessary for students to understand and make use of the provided comments during a feedback encounter.

How to Plan for Productive Feedback Practices in Your Course Unit

Based on these considerations, several practical implications are suggested with regard to what teachers should pay attention to when planning for productive feedback practices in their course units.

First, the institutional conditions in the study program, such as expertise of teaching staff or availability of rooms and technologies, are relevant when planning for feedback in a course unit. These institutional conditions cannot simply be isolated and improved, but should be seen as part of an intricate set of relations in which changes have wide-reaching and often unpredictable consequences. If teachers want to develop productive feedback practices in their course unit, it is therefore not enough just to think about how they might provide more or better feedback comments.

5 Re-conceptualizing Feedback Through a Sociocultural Lens   79

Instead, they should take a step back and consider how different arrangements of tasks and responsibilities in their course designs might create feedback opportunities in which students are likely to make judgments about and use of the feedback information they receive. To achieve this, teachers have to be aware of the different logics that come with certain task organizations and how these relate to the potential opportunities to engage with feedback in the course. In this regard, it is relevant to think of sequencing of tasks when planning for productive feedback. For example, if a course design requires students to work on a task early on during the semester in order to be able to solve a follow-up task later on, this task sequence will make it more relevant and motivating for students to make use of the feedback comments provided on the first tasks. This illustrates that different sequences of tasks generate different needs and motivation for students to engage with feedback.

Second, when planning for productive feedback practices, it is also important to incorporate relevant knowledge resources in the course designs, which are needed for students to make meaning and act upon the information they engage with during feedback encounters. Such resources are also important for students to be able to make their own judgments about the quality of their work. To that end, teachers need to carefully decide what knowledge content and activities they want students to engage in the different tasks; and to predict what prior knowledge can be expected among the student cohorts. Based on these preparations, it then becomes possible to envision different kinds of feedback opportunities that have different purposes. Examples could be oral feedback opportunities on early drafts of student assignments that serve the purpose of encouraging students to explore new ideas and literature; or peer feedback opportunities close to the final submission deadline which serve the purpose of letting students judge examples of other assignments, thereby motivating them to engage with the relevant assessment criteria. Depending on the purpose, the same set-up could be also offered the other way around with peer feedback early on to help students grasp the standards and conventions they are expected to follow in their assignment, and oral feedback opportunities later on to enable students to address specific concerns.

Whichever kind of feedback opportunities are eventually envisioned for a specific course unit, it then becomes important to identify what knowledge resources are necessary for students to successfully engage in the different opportunities. Moreover, this also entails that teachers should become more aware of the feedback opportunities they could generate by including technologies or knowledge resources that have "feedback potential" and that can provide students with information about the quality of their work without the teachers having to give feedback comments themselves. Examples of such knowledge resources could be the use of rubrics and exemplars, but also the use of online resources in which students might seek and share information about what constitutes good quality in the given domain (e.g., discussion fora where professionals discuss best practices).

Finally, planning course designs with feedback opportunities in itself is not enough to generate productive feedback practices. Students also need guidance and encouragement to navigate the provided feedback opportunities and how to make use of the provided feedback information in their learning. In this regard, it is helpful to plan for learning activities and work formats (e.g., group work) that encourage dialogue and shared meaning-making of feedback. While students should be informed about the roles they are expected to take in a feedback encounter, it is also important to provide flexibility to negotiate the roles that are most productive at any given time.

Conclusion

In this chapter, I have illustrated how conceptualizing feedback through a sociocultural lens may shed new light on what it means for feedback to be productive, that is, to have an impact on student learning. Rather than looking only for qualities of good feedback comments or effective communication strategies by teachers, the here presented three-layer model suggests considering feedback as social practices that are achieved in interaction between teachers, students, and the given course environment. The assumption that feedback practices are deeply intertwined with the knowledge domains they take place in strengthens the idea that feedback is a powerful pedagogical strategy that can help students gain access to the practices and discourses of their disciplines. To tap into the full pedagogi-

5 Re-conceptualizing Feedback Through a Sociocultural Lens   81

cal potential of feedback, however, it is necessary to become aware of how even small adjustments, such as changing locations or timing of a course activity, might have far-reaching implications for the ways students might engage with the feedback information they receive. Whether feedback has an impact on student learning, thus, is dependent on the delicate network of relations that characterize our course designs, the wider knowledge domain and the interactions we engage in on a day-to-day basis.

References

Esterhazy, R. (2018). What matters for productive feedback? Disciplinary practices and their relational dynamics. *Assessment & Evaluation in Higher Education, 43*(8), 1302–1314. https://doi.org/10.1080/02602938.2018.1463353.

Esterhazy, R. (2019). *Productive feedback practices in higher education. Investigating social and epistemic relations in two undergraduate courses* (Doctoral thesis). University of Oslo, Oslo, Norway.

Esterhazy, R., & Damşa, C. (2019). Unpacking the feedback process: An analysis of undergraduate students' interactional meaning-making of feedback comments. *Studies in Higher Education, 44*(2), 1–15. https://doi.org/10.1080/03075079.2017.1359249.

Goodyear, P. (2015). Teaching as design. *HERDSA Review of Higher Education, 2,* 27–50.

Jonsson, A. (2012). Facilitating productive use of feedback in higher education. *Active Learning in Higher Education, 14*(1), 63–76. https://doi.org/10.1177/1469787412467125.

Packer, M. J., & Goicoechea, J. (2000). Sociocultural and constructivist theories of learning: Ontology not just epistemology. *Educational Psychologist, 35*(4), 227–241. https://doi.org/10.1207/S15326985EP3504_02.

Säljö, R. (2005). *Lärande och kulturella redskap: om lärprocesser och det kollektiva minnet* [Learners and cultural tools: On learning processes and the collective mind]. Stockholm, Sweden: Norstedts akademiska förlag.

Scott, S. V. (2014). Practising what we preach: Towards a student-centred definition of feedback. *Teaching in Higher Education, 19*(1), 49–57. https://doi.org/10.1080/13562517.2013.827639.

Shute, V. J. (2008). Focus on formative feedback. *Review of Educational Research, 78*(1), 153–189. https://doi.org/10.3102/0034654307313795.

Trowler, P. (2012). Disciplines and academic practices. In P. Trowler, M. Saunders, & V. Bamber (Eds.), *Tribes and territories in the 21st-century: Rethinking the significance of disciplines in higher education* (pp. 30–38). Abingdon: Routledge.

Vygotsky, L. S. (1978). *Mind in society: The development of higher psychological processes.* Cambridge, MA: Harvard University Press.

Wertsch, J. V. (1991). *Voices of the mind: A sociocultural approach to mediated action* (1st paperback ed.). Cambridge, MA: Harvard University Press.

Winstone, N. E., Nash, R. A., Parker, M., & Rowntree, J. (2017). Supporting learners' agentic engagement with feedback: A systematic review and a taxonomy of recipience processes. *Educational Psychologist, 52*(1), 17–37. https://doi.org/10.1080/00461520.2016.1207538.

6

Attending to Emotion in Feedback

Elizabeth Molloy⬤, Christy Noble⬤ and Rola Ajjawi⬤

Introduction

The issue of emotion in feedback for learners and educators is often dismissed or addressed clumsily through compensatory feedback delivery approaches, where educators attempt to disguise learner criticism within layers of praise. Such an approach is typified by the "feedback sandwich" model where the educator is encouraged to provide stratified

---

E. Molloy (✉)
Department of Medical Education, School of Medicine,
The University of Melbourne, Parkville, VIC, Australia
e-mail: elizabeth.molloy@unimelb.edu.au

C. Noble
Medical Education Unit and Allied Health, Gold Coast Health,
Southport, QLD, Australia
e-mail: christy.noble@health.qld.gov.au

R. Ajjawi
Centre for Research in Assessment and Digital Learning (CRADLE),
Deakin University, Geelong, VIC, Australia
e-mail: rola.ajjawi@deakin.edu.au

© The Author(s) 2019
M. Henderson et al. (eds.), *The Impact of Feedback in Higher Education*,
https://doi.org/10.1007/978-3-030-25112-3_6

information—positive, negative and then positive—as a means to improve learner performance whilst preserving the learner's emotional stability. Like many in the field, we question the assumptions underpinning these models which fundamentally position teachers at the centre of feedback and challenge the utility of such models in helping set up feedback conversations which have developmental effects on emotions and learning.

There are many reasons why feedback is seen as "an emotional business" (Molloy et al., 2019). One reason cited is the uni-directional nature of feedback information from teacher to learner (Molloy, Borello, & Epstein, 2013). This sense of being "against the ropes" and waiting for another to impose a judgement are often less palatable when the "delivery" of information is unsolicited. In the literature, we read about examples of feedback encounters where learners' agency has been reduced through the interaction. Another key explanatory mechanism posed for why learners find feedback "hard to take" is that the incoming data presents a threat to the learner's work, or perceptive skills and/or, by extension, identity. The negative ramifications of "hard hitting" feedback encounters can be felt by learners well beyond the exchange itself and have been shown to influence future feedback behaviours, relationships and career paths (Ende, Pomerantz, & Erickson, 1995; Urquhart, Rees, & Ker, 2014). In the light of these perceived risks, there has been a strong precedent in the feedback field to mitigate emotion within feedback encounters, as if emotion is noise that needs to be muted so that the "real message" gets through to the recipient.

In this chapter, we argue for a re-orientation of how we view the role of emotion in feedback. First, we explore the literature around the social-affective dimensions of feedback and the mechanisms by which feedback processes can validate, build on or challenge learner identities. We use Pekrun's (2006) Control-Value Theory (CVT) to help shed light on the affective dimensions of feedback processes, including outputs. In the second part of the chapter, we present a research case study (Noble et al., 2019), where a feedback literacy programme was designed and delivered within the healthcare setting to improve health professional students' ability to understand, engage with and generate feedback. We present the design features of this programme and the effects reported by students after having opportunities to engage with workplace feedback. We propose

6 Attending to Emotion in Feedback 85

that part of helping learners to become feedback ready *is to help them to recognise and work with emotions*. We also highlight that designing feedback processes so that the conversations have effects (traceable outputs relating to performance, knowledge, values and identities) necessarily positions feedback as a forward-facing mechanism with a fundamental orientation towards improvement. This re-orientation in itself, a departure from the "what went wrong" discourse, may have an impact on the emotions of both learner and "other" within feedback processes. We aim to build a picture of the complexity of feedback and the primacy of relationships and emotion within these processes.

What is Emotion and How Does it Influence Feedback Practices?

There is no unifying definition of emotion, rather multiple discourses frame emotion as physiological, sociocultural, psychological or skill-based (McNaughton, 2013). Emotions are associated with a specific event or moment, real or imagined, e.g. feeling sad about losing a ring, unlike affect which is an umbrella term for reflective neurophysiological state, e.g. being irritable in mood (McConnell & Eva, 2015). Emotions have inward and external manifestations, in that they relate to cognitive and dispositional elements. For example, emotions influence decision-making and dispositions to act. Moreover, "emotions drive attention, which in turn drives learning, memory and problem-solving behaviour. Without emotional arousal, we are unable to learn, even though emotional arousal does not automatically lead to learning" (Värlander, 2008, p. 148). In these ways, emotions have social meanings and occur in relation to social interactions (Värlander, 2008) as typified in learning conversations.

Given the interplay between emotions and learning, studies have set out to further explain the role of emotion in learning (e.g. Johnson, 2016) and have found that emotions generated by feedback comments can motivate adaptive or maladaptive behaviours (Rowe, 2017). However, these studies have typically considered all discrete emotions such as joy, anger, sadness or shame, as either "negative" or "positive" affective states. With a reductionist classification system, we can forget that different emotions have "different antecedents, functions, and outcomes" in learning environments (Gooty, Gavin, Ashkanasy, & Thomas, 2014). As stated by Rowe (2017, p. 161) "emotions are preceded by an event (student receives extensive praise for their work), serve a particular function (feelings of pride lead the student to desire obtaining further praise in the future) and lead to outcomes (increased effort for the next assessment)". A more nuanced understanding of how emotions influence feedback processes and how the processes in turn influence emotions is required. We now turn to focus specifically on the feedback and emotion literature identifying a number of discourses which may inform and challenge our understanding of the role of emotions in feedback. The discourses include: (1) emotion as static in feedback; (2) softening the blow of feedback; (3) emotion being integral to trust and alliance; and (4) emotion as part of sense-making.

Emotion as Static in Feedback

Generally speaking, emotional and relational aspects of feedback are not sufficiently attended to, both for learners and teachers, and both in the classroom and workplace-based setting (Molloy et al., 2013; Ryan & Henderson, 2018; Telio, Ajjawi, & Regehr, 2015). Rather, learners and educators are often exposed to feedback techniques, e.g. feedback sandwich designed to put aside emotions, that is, get rid of the static, or noise, to allow the content or "message" to do its work.

Conceptualising feedback as an information artefact delivered by the educator does not allow space for recognising and grappling with emotions, yet they are ever present in the plethora of research articles asking students and staff about their feedback experiences. Indeed, the feedback techniques designed to reduce learners' emotions bubbling to the surface may well have perpetuated the notion that emotion is a hindering force within the process—something to suppress, get over, push back or get used to.

The consequence of this approach is that by removing control from the learner through backwards-looking feedback, there is no part for them to play other than "take it on the chin" (corrective) potentially amplifying feelings of resentment, incompetence, dissent and/or resistance. Indeed,

6 Attending to Emotion in Feedback 87

the emotional legacy of negative feedback comments, including quite personal comments, has been reported extensively in the literature (Lipnevich & Smith, 2009; Pitt & Norton, 2017; Price, Handley, & Millar, 2011; Rowe, 2017). This emotional legacy can be damaging to learners' self-esteem, and its effects may persist long after the actual encounter (Urquhart et al., 2014). Pitt and Norton (2017) found that emotions interplayed with confidence, effort and achievement which carried forward to future assessments.

The timing of feedback encounters is often seen as a decision-point for educators, with the perceived emotional needs or capacity of the learner, a key influence on when to "deliver feedback". That is, a conscious rescheduling of the feedback encounter may reduce the static that may have prohibited learning. This is particularly prevalent in the literature on feedback in medical education, where learners or trainees are judged to be too emotional (e.g. after a patient procedure went poorly) to engage in a dialogue about their own performance (Ende, 1983). There is literature in the cognitive psychological field promoting "optimal zone of development" (Epstein, Siegel, & Silberman, 2008) where a manageable affective operational state is viewed to optimise an individual's learning and performance, and this would support "holding off" feedback encounters until a point where the learner has the emotional capacity to engage. Whilst this decision to delay a feedback exchange after a highly emotive event may reap benefits for learners on some occasions, ideally this would be a collaborative decision between learner and educator. It may well be, however, that an immediate discussion, incorporating and acknowledging the emotion of both parties, may hold learning potential that could be otherwise lost. In other words, acknowledging and better understanding how to work with emotion, i.e. the *static/noise* in workplace practices may be a focus for the feedback discussion in itself.

Softening the Blow of Feedback

The anticipation of a learner's emotional response (primarily an emotional response through threat to identity) makes educators (or others as "source of feedback") act in strange ways. The most common of these is to engage in acts of "vanishing feedback" (Ende, 1983; Ende et al., 1995) or mealy mouthed feedback (Molloy et al., 2013). The avoidance of honest communication can give learners confusing mixed messages about the quality of their work and also may be seen as patronising in that the teacher is making assumptions about what the learner is capable of taking in. That is, an attempt at softening the blow may be experienced as a blow in itself, in that there are disparate non-verbal and verbal messages, and a shift in tenor of the interaction, compared with when the two players discuss aspects of performance that went according to plan (or met standards).

With a dominant discourse on the potential for feedback information to have a limiting or detrimental impact on learners ("hard to take"), it follows that professional development for feedback providers is about giving equal volume of "positive" and "negative" information so that learners too leave the conversation "balanced". Feedback is often seen by students as comments from teachers that help to explain the mark on an assignment or performance (Boud & Molloy, 2013; Carless, 2006). These early understandings of feedback, including students' perceptions of their responsibilities as recipients within the process, can be further reinforced in classrooms and work-based learning settings where teachers "tell" learners what went wrong in the task (Fernando, Cleland, McKenzie, & Cassar, 2008). With these "conversation" rituals characterised by educator telling, we should probably be less surprised when students report that they see feedback as information they are subject to, rather than a process that they drive and manage for their own learning benefit.

Attending to Feedback Emotions Through Trust and Alliance

Trust, with its embedded emotional facets, as an integral part of feedback, is a surprisingly new subject of focus in feedback research. This may be due to the dominant view of "feedback as information" which has an accompanying assumption that when delivered well is automatically (and neutrally) absorbed by the learner. Moving away from such a conception of feedback has led us to look more closely at what the learner does, but also at what the learner and teacher do together. The educational alliance

6 Attending to Emotion in Feedback   89

is one such theory that repositions feedback from information given to a learner to seeing feedback as co-construction in the context of a safe and mutually respectful relationship for the purpose of supporting growth (Ajjawi & Regehr, 2018). Developing an effective educational alliance relies on establishing shared goals, shared activities and a bond between the learners and educators (Farrell, Bourgeois-Law, Ajjawi, & Regehr, 2017; Telio, Regehr, & Ajjawi, 2016).

Research (Farrell et al. 2017; Telio et al. 2016) highlights that feedback is emotional business, yet the valence of the emotional reaction is related to the strength of the educational alliance rather than the positive or negative direction of the actual feedback content. In other words, how learners react to feedback comments is not merely related to what is said, but also how it is said and the context in which it is said. In one study, participants were more likely to have negative emotional reactions in the setting of weak educational alliances (Telio et al., 2016). Where there were stronger judgements of the educational alliance, this was associated with candid styles of disclosure and highly receptive approaches to feedback, even when the content of the feedback was negative (critical). Where there was a poor bond (based on credibility judgements of competence of the educator and their positive regard and intent, lack of shared goals and activities), learners tended to avoid feedback interactions, be less receptive, and adopted a guarded style of disclosure of their own feelings, thoughts or actions (Telio et al., 2016).

Trust plays an important role in learners and others' co-construction of learning (Ajjawi & Regehr, 2018). Trust is a "primary emotion" that impacts almost all social endeavours, including the formation of empathic relationships. Socio-emotional aspects of trust include openness, benevolence and honesty (Leighton & Bustos Gómez, 2018). Trust itself is highly influenced by emotions and perceptions of another's intentions and credibility, that is, trustworthiness (as person, as clinician, as educator, etc.). Therefore, emotions in learning and feedback are not only raised due to the feedback process but emotions are integral to the actual process where emotions will influence how messages are interpreted, how much information is shared, the nature of knowledge that is co-constructed and how the relationship develops.

Emotion Is Part of Sense-Making

The effects of feedback on learner development are mediated by "the complex interplay of emotional, intellectual and intimate constructions of learning" (Gleaves & Walker, 2013, p. 258). "Arousal" intersects with cognition, and this creates productive and unproductive consequences. Too much arousal interferes with cognitive processing, yet affective mobilisation is required within the learner to generate and use knowledge (Molloy et al., 2013; Ryan & Henderson, 2018). Emotion and how we deal with it influence our perceptions of the situation and related judgements. Inability to manage emotional responses has been found to negatively influence learning and professional identity formation in medical students (Helmich, Bolhuis, Laan, & Koopmans, 2011). Knowledge of the "zone of optimal control", as identified in the above section, may teach learners/practitioners how to recognise and work with emotion in order to promote learning, performance and productive relationships, all of which are mutually informing.

Within our disciplines or professions, our role modelling around emotion communicates important messages to our learners. For example, the sentiment of "dampen your emotions so you can think clearly" may perpetuate the notion that emotion is a form of unhelpful static. For example, in medicine (in particular, in high stakes assessment), there is value placed on "objective" data rather than acknowledging subjectivity of judgement and practitioners who are able to push through emotional affairs and who are not paralysed by emotion (Molloy & Bearman, 2019). For example, nurses are offered debriefing after patient deaths or procedures that go poorly, whereas surgeons or physicians working in the same team, with the very same patient, are often not expected to partake in a debriefing process. This form of emotional labour, where emotions are treated as threats to rational and objective decision-making, is under-recognised in certain professions and may take a toll on individuals' well-being as well as threaten the functioning of a team.

In summary, the literature behoves us to pay more attention to emotions in learning and in particular in relation to feedback, an activity that requires vulnerability and can threaten self, particularly if the learner's work is highly enmeshed with their identity (Molloy & Bearman, 2019). Emotion mediates sense-making, relationship building and influences current and future feedback behaviours and effects. Next, we use an integrative theory of emotion to illustrate key aspects of emotions within a feedback intervention. We then synthesise recommendations for practice and research that takes better account of attending to emotions in feedback.

An Alternative Way of Seeing the Intersection Between Emotion and Feedback: Control-Value Theory

Control-Value Theory (CVT) is a social cognitive theory of emotional regulation that offers an integrative framework for analysing emotional regulation in academic contexts (Pekrun, 2006; Pekrun & Stephens, 2010). Emotional regulation is the ability to manage impulses, feelings and behaviours, is a valuable effect to cultivate and one that is necessary for the feedback process. CVT focusses on achievement emotions, which, as the name suggests, are emotions related to achievement activities and outcomes, such as joy related to learning or frustration and anger that arise when feedback is perceived to be an attack on the self. These also include exam anxiety, shame of failure and hope for success (Pekrun, 2006). There is also a temporal element to achievement emotions that is worth noting, and they can be transient or habitual and recurring. Two key components of CVT relate to: (1) students' individual control over themselves and their circumstances (similar to autonomy) and (2) value beliefs underlying their situational appraisal which influence their emotions. The reciprocal is also true that emotions can influence students' appraisal of the situation and their level of control/value as well as regulate students' interest and motivation to learn. Hence, there are reciprocal linkages between control and value appraisals as antecedents of emotion and emotions reciprocally effecting these appraisals (Pekrun & Stephens, 2010). There's clearly much complexity that belies emotions that make it difficult to disentangle.

Students' beliefs regarding their internal control and value (how invested they are) based on CVT can potentially be influenced through pedagogical design, thus influencing emotional regulation and outcomes. There are activities that have influenced feedback practices that we see now as enabling perceived control and value for the student which might positively influence emotions and achievement. For example, we have used interactive cover sheets that prompt students to self-evaluate their own work and that encourages them to seek feedback on specific aspects of their work (Barton, Schofield, McAleer, & Ajjawi, 2016). Students who took advantage of these opportunities used them in ways that held value to them resulting in bridging of classroom and workplace learning through feedback design and evidence of effects on self-regulation of learning (Ajjawi & Boud, 2018). Therefore, as educators, we can create conditions (or environmental antecedents) that promote perceptions of control and value, thus optimising feedback behaviours. With these pedagogical designs that place the learner in the centre of feedback processes, we no longer need to resort to simple positive-negative balanced approaches such as the well-chewed (and hopefully soon to be spat out) feedback sandwich (Molloy et al., 2019).

Student feedback literacy is gaining momentum in the literature and in practice as a way of optimising learning and action as a result of feedback. Part of learner feedback literacy is indeed learning how to anticipate and manage emotions in relational activities, particularly when there is discrepancy in perspectives on performance (Carless & Boud, 2018). Feedback literacy helps students recognise that they are active agents in feedback processes, therefore raising perceptions of control and value. Improving students' and educators' feedback literacy holds potential.

Although we do not entirely subscribe to the dichotomous (positive-negative) characterisation of emotions and learning offered by CVT, its relevance bears fruit in a number of ways when we turn to feedback. We need to take into account the nature of the task, the social environment, students' appraisals of control and value as well as effects in relation to emotions (activity and outcome emotions) and performance consequences. Students' perceptions of internal control matter for their emotional regulation and outcome emotions. For example, students might deflect seemingly negative feedback to avoid intensity of emotions (a form of regulation) attached to it reducing the need for action. It is important to note that positive emotions do not always result in positive action (and vice versa with negative emotions). For example, a student might receive mainly positive comments on a formative task resulting in relief which then deactivates further action. Another example of seemingly negative feedback content leading to constructive behaviours and emotions within a strong educational alliance can be explained through CVT. A student who perceives that there is a strong educational alliance with their educator may therefore have a strong sense of internal control (through co-construction of goals and activities) and investment (value in maintaining the relationship) which can prompt positive achievement emotions and outcomes despite what could be perceived as quite "negative" feedback.

An Illustrative Case Study: "A Feedback Literacy Program for Students in the Health Workplace: Learning to Recognise and Manage Emotion"

As educators, we have observed the challenges experienced by students when engaging in feedback processes, particularly in workplace settings. When considering how to attend to affect in workplace feedback experiences, CVT offers a useful lens to examine the student experiences of feedback and assists in explaining how a feedback literacy programme contributes to students' ability to manage emotion in feedback. In this section, we present a case study where healthcare students engaged in a feedback literacy programme before commencing their placement in a local hospital. In this case, the *environmental antecedents* of clinical placements are described and present an overview of how a feedback literacy programme influenced students' *perceived value* and *perceived control* whilst engaging in placement feedback activities. We explore how this engagement contributed to *positive achievement emotions.*

Setting the Scene

This study took place in a large and busy teaching hospital where healthcare professional students from a local university engage in work-based clinical placements. Typically, students are sent to a clinical placement (most often in a hospital system) and are expected to learn, under the supervision of a more senior colleague, through engaging in work-based tasks. Students also learn through observing other qualified health practitioners go about their work. In this context, feedback has been seen as a key mechanism to help accelerate learners' performance and professional socialisation, through informal opportunities and through formal, scheduled feedback conversations. A recent survey study found that these students highly valued feedback from placement supervisors and co-workers yet found it challenging to engage in feedback whilst navigating complex workplace settings (Billett, Cain, & Le, 2016). To assist the students' navigation through placement feedback experiences, we designed and delivered a feedback literacy programme which aimed to improve health professional students' ability to understand, engage with and generate feedback (Noble et al., 2019). Healthcare professional students, e.g. social work, nursing and medical students, engaged in the programme before commencing their clinical placement.

The programme intention was to prime students to understand feedback, that is, appreciating feedback (Carless & Boud, 2018) as a process based on learner improvement, e.g. presented conceptual underpinnings of Feedback Mark 2 (Boud & Molloy, 2013). The intervention was delivered in three phases and three times to a total of 105 students and included: (1) e-learning module; (2) workshop; and (3) reflective activities in the workplace. We evaluated the programme and student experiences of feedback processes during their clinical placements using questionnaires and interviews. We identified an unexpected narrative related to students' feedback emotions before the intervention that changed after the intervention. These findings were unexpected, because, whilst nodding to emotions, the focus of the programme was on promoting students' understanding of feedback processes and roles.

Environmental Antecedents of Clinical Placements

As part of their degree programmes, healthcare students are typically required to engage in work-based (clinical) placements. The performance standards are not always apparent in the workplace setting, nor are the learning curriculum or pedagogical practices (Billett, 2006) when compared to classroom settings. Thus, students often experience diminished agency, in terms of feedback engagement (Molloy, 2009). Also, the learning experiences, for students, can be largely dependent on how they engage with the affordances of the workplace including with supervisors. However, because of these *environmental antecedents,* students often complain that they are not getting enough feedback whilst on clinical placements (Urquhart et al., 2014).

Moreover, in this context, the stakes are high for students, in that, they are trying on their future professional identities, e.g. nursing students are experiencing what it is like to be a nurse and the feedback they garner provides a barometer for how they are tracking in their professional identity formation. Because of these high stakes, for some groups of students, the experience of seeking feedback in the workplace is considered to be a *risky business* for fear of receiving poor feedback (Delva et al., 2013). The mechanisms underpinning this perceived risk include weighing up of ego costs against how their image is perceived by others and the perceived benefits of the feedback (Bok et al., 2013). These types of negative emotional responses can contribute to disengagement, or deactivation, in feedback processes.

Perceived Value of Placement Feedback

Students unanimously reported valuing (or anticipating valuing) their placement learning experiences. This was attributed to opportunities to engage with authentic tasks, compared to course work, and working with experienced practitioners and patients. However, the legacy of the students' previous experiences of feedback, e.g. within higher education settings, meant they did not wholly value feedback processes. For example, when interviewed, the students noted that their previous feedback lacked specificity (e.g. "that was good") and lacked plans for improving their performance. In these ways, students' previous experiences of feedback meant that they did not necessarily appreciate the importance, use and value of feedback processes.

After engaging in the feedback literacy programme and then implementing some of these new perspectives as they engaged in placement feedback, individual students participated in an in-depth interview exploring their feedback experiences (Noble et al., under review; 2019). Several students described a shift in how they valued feedback because their understanding of their role in feedback had changed from having feedback done to them to having agency in the process. Furthermore, they positively described feedback experiences where they had adopted a feedback seeker role and established trusted relationships with supervisors. These descriptions resonate strongly with the descriptions of educational alliances (Telio et al., 2015).

Perceived Control of Placement Feedback

Again, students' past experiences of feedback influenced their perception of control over the process. In the main, feedback, prior to the literacy programme, was understood as a process where they were provided information about their performance with limited agency to influence their own learning. Also, in the context of complex clinical environments, students' perceived degree of control was further complicated as they were unsure of the performance standards and how to engage supervisors who had busy service demands in parallel with their teaching/supervision mandate. Further, the fragmented and short nature of clinical placements potentially influences the development of educational relationships.

Following the feedback literacy programme, the feedback experiences reported by the students suggested that their perception of control improved. Because they understood the features and purposes of effective feedback processes, they described experiences of repositioning their ways of engaging with feedback. For example, they were critiquing their workplace feedback experiences, and when they experienced discrepancies between understood models of feedback and enacted feedback, they contributed to the feedback process by "filling in the gaps":

> *Nursing student*: What I mean is someone that says to you, oh God, you did really well, and left it at that. I'm thinking, well, okay, but you've not told me anything more than that. That's the kind of feedback I don't like.
> *Facilitator*: Do you probe a bit, or ask them to provide more details?
> *Nursing student*: I do, because it's—like I've said, it's okay to say that, but I want to know why did you say that. Am I good team player? Did I meet all the standards, the criteria required? (Nursing student 1)

After the intervention, some of the learners provided examples of risk-taking in feedback encounters, e.g. seeking clarification or self-evaluating their performance (what might be viewed as exposing themselves to their supervisors through self-analysis) and suggested that this made them feel less vulnerable due to the switch in agency. Likewise declaring areas of need in terms of their learning goals (or specific goals for an observed task-priming the supervisor's gaze) were examples of learners claiming control.

In their interviews post-placement, students did not use the word control but implied that their new approaches to feedback enabled them to shift from being a "sitting duck" or "on the ropes" waiting for a blow from a knowledgeable other to being more agentic.

> I don't know what makes it different but it just feels like a different rapport compared to just wait for them to give you that feedback. I don't know it just feels like a little bit more equal. (Nursing student 1)

Achievement Emotions

Following their engagement in the feedback literacy programme, the student interviews provided rich insights into how changes in their perception of feedback control and value contributed to achievement emotions, that is, emotions relate directly to achievement activities or achievement outcomes (Pekrun, Frenzel, Goetz, & Perry, 2007). Indeed, the emotions related to both the activity, i.e. engaging in feedback and its outcomes, i.e.

learning from feedback interactions was described positively, e.g. having a sense of enjoyment and pride. For example, students described a sense of enjoyment (activity emotion) when seeking feedback because they recognised its value as an authentic activity and now understood their role in the feedback engagement (enhanced perception of control). These experiences resulted in pride in their learning in the clinical setting as students described being able to identify and engage in subsequent tasks to improve their performance based on the feedback received (outcome emotion). These findings suggest that the literacy programme began to influence students' achievement emotions and their subsequent engagement in feedback by influencing their perception of their *control* workplace feedback practices.

The feedback literacy programme itself encouraged students to explore their own views about feedback, including sharing their experiences of emotion through feedback in different contexts (education settings and beyond). As an activity in their workshop, learners were asked to anticipate the potential emotions in providing self-evaluation that differs from an externally generated opinion and, likewise, were prompted to discuss the emotion involved in asking "busy others" in their environment to comment on their performance. In a role-play activity, students were asked to assume the role of both learner, and educator, to "try on" the expectations, responsibilities, needs and risks of both parties in the dialogue. The debriefing after the role-plays attended to how the parties felt before, during and after the process. In summary, the design of the feedback literacy intervention explicitly catered for attending to and learning about emotion.

Implications for Practice and Research

In terms of practice implications for attending to emotion in feedback, and as noted by others (Dennis, Foy, Monrouxe, & Rees, 2017), we need to acknowledge the integral influence of emotion on feedback processes, rather than sweeping it under the carpet and hoping for the best. In other words, feedback can generate emotional response and at the same time, emotions influence feedback behaviours. The effects of our interventions might be in improving students' feedback literacy, emotional regulation and ultimately learning.

Our case study suggests that supporting feedback literacy development enhances emotional regulation yet does not fully attend to the interplay between feedback and emotion. Feedback literacy could be further developed by engaging both students and educators in discussions about their shared feedback experiences. Educators could consider developing a feedback literacy curriculum, rather than a one-off programme, to support students to progressively engage in feedback processes. Curricular design should offer students choice to enable a sense of control—such as asking them to self-evaluate or to encourage them to identify which aspects of the work they would like feedback information on. Creating a safe environment, where there is trust and shared goal/activities—that is a strong educational alliance—may also offer students a greater sense of control and value which may drive productive achievement emotions.

Educators might be encouraged to share with students the value of engaging in feedback processes rather than assuming this value is understood. A safe environment would be supportive of open discussion of fears and anxieties openly including discussing mistakes and giving students permission and strategies if they do feel deflated after a particular performance. It is important to underline the core role of emotions in learning and to explore meaning-making in the context of emotions and a developing professional identity. The effects of a feedback literacy programme would be to prepare students to be socio-emotionally and cognitively ready to productively participate in assessment and feedback activities. Such open dialogue and acknowledgement of feedback as threats to self are likely to foster a stronger bond and conditions of trust within the educational alliance. Interesting questions that emerge from this discussion are: If we cultivate feedback literacy of learners and educators to notice, and manage emotions, how do we measure this impact? And what effects are we looking for beyond improved performance on the next task? These questions open up a different research agenda for feedback that makes a difference.

Research Implications

We have argued that emotion and feedback are interdependent, yet the relationship is complex. Thus, it would be prudent for future research to explore the nature of the relationship between emotion and feedback, and theoretical perspectives, such as CVT, could be helpful. Visualising the complexities of feedback whilst unpacking the emotional responses using methodologies such as video observation or video reflexive ethnography (VRE) would further assist in understanding the relationship between emotion and feedback. Indeed VRE capitalises on the potential for emotions to tell us things and prompt us to act. Moreover, this approach would capture instances of feedback seeking, feedback sense-making and episodes of vulnerability whilst fostering reflection between both parties to establish "emotionally safe places".

There is limited empirical research exploring the longitudinal effects of emotion on feedback and vice versa. We would encourage researchers to consider longitudinal methodologies such as longitudinal audio diaries (LADs) to capture learner or other stakeholders' perceptions of changes in knowledge or practice or identity. LADs prompt participants to tell stories with the researcher in mind, a more immediate and embodied story that is replete with emotional talk (Monrouxe, 2009). Narrative analysis of stories would explore how the story is told as well as what is told, exploring the use of emotional talk and laughter. Laughter co-produced by participants and the researcher in an interview or LAD might be a coping strategy when recollecting a particularly painful or humiliating feedback experience (Urquhart et al., 2014). The use of narrative analysis techniques would offer insight into the emotional legacy of feedback as well as the ways in which emotions mediate sense-making during feedback encounters and over a long(er) period of time.

Conclusion

In this chapter, we have laid out and tried to untangle the complex factors when it comes to emotion and feedback in higher education. We have claimed that the dominant discourse in this subset of literature is about "reducing emotion" or "putting it to the side" so that the real messages of feedback can land on the listener. We have challenged this notion of "emotion as static" and present an alternative approach where emotions are acknowledged and mobilised so that feedback can make a difference. That is, that learners and teachers (or any other feedback agent) would benefit from understanding that emotion is an inherent part of feedback processes and that developing skills in emotional regulation and capacities in developing educational alliances might have considerable impact on what feedback can achieve. Students and educators would do well from fine-tuning their capacity to recognise and work with emotions within their feedback experiences.

The research is starting to highlight that trust is a key requisite condition for productive feedback processes. Trust itself is highly influenced by emotions and perceptions of another's intentions and trustworthiness. Better understanding of how trust between parties is established may be one of the keys to better understanding productive feedback.

We present CVT as a frame for examining the intersection of emotion and feedback whereby enhancing students' perceptions of control and value may result in positive emotional regulation, positive feedback behaviours and learning. Further, we suggest that students may be rewarded (intrinsic ally and extrinsic ally) for taking risks in conversations about their own work and in demonstrating proactivity in priming others to give feedback on certain aspects of their work.

The case study of feedback literacy in the health professions demonstrated that proactivity may also take the form of seeking opportunities to improve subsequent work. We argue that investing in these activities, and experiencing the benefits first hand, may help in activating productive emotions for learners when engaging in feedback, that is, a learner with a stance of openness to change, and an appetite and skill set to seek information and sets of circumstances to best help them enact change. A better understanding of how emotions influence learning through feedback and how feedback processes influence emotions may help us better prepare all parties for the processes. This heightened understanding may also help us to better set up conditions that support interactions whereby learners feel they have some degree of control over their circumstances, at both the anticipatory and experienced level.

References

Ajjawi, R., & Boud, D. (2018). Examining the nature and effects of feedback dialogue. *Assessment & Evaluation in Higher Education*, 1–14. https://doi.org/10.1080/02602938.2018.1434128.

Ajjawi, R., & Regehr, G. (2018). When I say … feedback. *Medical Education*. https://onlinelibrary.wiley.com/doi/abs/10.1111/medu.13746. doi:https://doi.org/10.1111/medu.13746.

Barton, K. L., Schofield, S. J., McAleer, S., & Ajjawi, R. (2016). Translating evidence-based guidelines to improve feedback practices: The interACT case study. *BMC Medical Education, 16*(1), 1–12. http://dx.doi.org/10.1186/s12909-016-0562-z.

Billett, S. (2006). Constituting the workplace curriculum. *Journal of Curriculum Studies, 38*(1), 31–48. http://www.informaworld.com/10.1080/00220270500153781.

Billett, S., Cain, M., & Le, A. H. (2016). Augmenting higher education students' work experiences: Preferred purposes and processes. *Studies in Higher Education*, 1–16. http://dx.doi.org/10.1080/03075079.2016.1250073.

Bok, H. G. J., Teunissen, P. W., Spruijt, A., Fokkema, J. P. I., van Beukelen, P., Jaarsma, D. A. D. C., & van der Vleuten, C. P. M. (2013). Clarifying students' feedback-seeking behaviour in clinical clerkships. *Medical Education, 47*(3), 282–291. http://dx.doi.org/10.1111/medu.12054.

Boud, D., & Molloy, E. K. (2013). Rethinking models of feedback for learning: The challenge of design. *Assessment & Evaluation in Higher Education, 38*(6), 698–712. http://dx.doi.org/10.1080/02602938.2012.691462.

Carless, D. (2006). Differing perceptions in the feedback process. *Studies in Higher Education, 31*(2), 219–233. http://dx.doi.org/10.1080/03075070600572132.

Carless, D., & Boud, D. (2018). The development of student feedback literacy: Enabling uptake of feedback. *Assessment & Evaluation in Higher Education*, 1315–1325. https://doi.org/10.1080/02602938.2018.1463354.

Delva, D., Sargeant, J., Miller, S., Holland, J., Alexiadis Brown, P., Leblanc, C., … Mann, K. (2013). Encouraging residents to seek feedback. *Medical Teacher, 35*(12), e1625–e1631. http://dx.doi.org/10.3109/0142159X.2013.806791.

6 Attending to Emotion in Feedback 103

Dennis, A. A., Foy, M. J., Monrouxe, L. V., & Rees, C. E. (2017). Exploring trainer and trainee emotional talk in narratives about workplace-based feedback processes. *Advances in Health Sciences Education*. https://doi.org/10.1007/s10459-017-9775-0.

Ende, J. (1983). Feedback in clinical medical education. *JAMA: The Journal of the American Medical Association, 250*(6), 777–781. http://jama.ama-assn.org/content/250/6/777.abstract; https://doi.org/10.1001/jama.1983.03340060055026.

Ende, J., Pomerantz, A., & Erickson, F. (1995). Preceptors' strategies for correcting residents in an ambulatory care medicine setting: A qualitative analysis. *Academic Medicine, 70*, 224–229.

Epstein, R. M., Siegel, D. J., & Silberman, J. (2008). Self-monitoring in clinical practice: A challenge for medical educators. *Journal of Continuing Education in the Health Professions, 28*(1), 5–13.

Farrell, L., Bourgeois-Law, G., Ajjawi, R., & Regehr, G. (2017). An autoethnographic exploration of the use of goal oriented feedback to enhance brief clinical teaching encounters. *Advances in Health Sciences Education, 22*(1), 91–104. http://dx.doi.org/10.1007/s10459-016-9686-5.

Fernando, N., Cleland, J., McKenzie, H., & Cassar, K. (2008). Identifying the factors that determine feedback given to undergraduate medical students following formative mini-CEX assessments. *Medical Education, 42*(1), 89–95. http://dx.doi.org/10.1111/j.1365-2923.2007.02939.x.

Gleaves, A., & Walker, C. (2013). Richness, redundancy or relational salience? A comparison of the effect of textual and aural feedback modes on knowledge elaboration in higher education students' work. *Computers & Education, 62*, 249–261. http://www.sciencedirect.com/science/article/pii/S0360131512002606; https://doi.org/10.1016/j.compedu.2012.11.004.

Gooty, J., Gavin, M. B., Ashkanasy, N. M., & Thomas, J. S. (2014). The wisdom of letting go and performance: The moderating role of emotional intelligence and discrete emotions. *Journal of Occupational and Organizational Psychology, 87*(2), 392–413. Retrieved from https://onlinelibrary.wiley.com/doi/abs/10.1111/joop.12053; https://doi.org/10.1111/joop.12053.

Helmich, E., Bolhuis, S., Laan, R., & Koopmans, R. (2011). Early clinical experience: Do students learn what we expect? *Medical Education, 45*(7), 731–740. http://dx.doi.org/10.1111/j.1365-2923.2011.03932.x.

Johnson, M. (2016). Feedback effectiveness in professional learning contexts. *Review of Education, 4*(2), 195–229. https://doi.org/10.1002/rev3.3061.

Leighton, J. P., & Bustos Gómez, M. C. (2018). A pedagogical alliance for trust, wellbeing and the identification of errors for learning and formative assessment. *Educational Psychology, 38*(3), 381–406. https://doi.org/10.1080/01443410.2017.1390073.

Lipnevich, A. A., & Smith, J. K. (2009). "I really need feedback to learn": Students' perspectives on the effectiveness of the differential feedback messages. *Educational Assessment, Evaluation and Accountability, 21*(4), 347–367. https://link.springer.com/content/pdf/10.1007%2Fs11092-009-9082-2.pdf. http://dx.doi.org/10.1007/s11092-009-9082-2.

McConnell, M., & Eva, K. (2015). Emotions and learning: Cognitive theoretical and methodological approaches to studying the influence of emotions on learning. In *Researching Medical Education* (pp. 181–192). Hoboken: Wiley.

McNaughton, N. (2013). Discourse(s) of emotion within medical education: The ever-present absence. *Medical Education, 47*(1), 71–79. Retrieved from https://onlinelibrary.wiley.com/doi/abs/10.1111/j.1365-2923.2012.04329.x; https://doi.org/10.1111/j.1365-2923.2012.04329.x.

Molloy, E. (2009). Time to pause: Giving and receiving feedback in clinical education. In C. Delaney & E. Molloy (Eds.), *Clinical education in the health professions: An educator's guide.* Chatswood, NSW: Elsevier Australia.

Molloy, E., & Bearman, M. (2019). Embracing the tension between vulnerability and credibility: 'Intellectual candour' in health professions education. *Medical Education, 53*(1), 32–41. Retrieved from https://onlinelibrary.wiley.com/doi/abs/10.1111/medu.13649; https://doi.org/10.1111/medu.13649.

Molloy, E., Borello, F., & Epstein, R. (2013). The impact of emotion in feedback. In D. Boud & E. Molloy (Eds.), *Feedback in higher education* (pp. 50–71). London: Routledge.

Molloy, E., Ajjawi, R., Bearman, M., Noble, C., Rudland, J., & Ryan, A. (2019). Challenging feedback myths: values, learner involvement and promoting effects beyond the immediate task. *Medical Education* (accepted Nov 2018). https://doi.org/10.1111/medu.13802.

Monrouxe, L. V. (2009). Solicited audio diaries in longitudinal narrative research: A view from inside. *Qualitative Research, 9*(1), 81–103. Retrieved from http://qrj.sagepub.com/content/9/1/81.abstract; https://doi.org/10.1177/1468794108098032.

Noble, C., Bilett, S., Armit, L., Collier, L., Hilder, J., Sly, C., & Molloy, E. (under review). "It's yours to take": Generating learner feedback literacy in the workplace.

Noble, C., Sly, C., Collier, L., Armit, L., Hilder, J., & Molloy, E. (2019). Enhancing feedback literacy in the workplace: A learner-centred approach. In S. Bilett, J. M. Newton, G. Rogers, & C. Noble (Eds.), *Augmenting health and social care students' clinical learning experiences: Outcomes and processes.* Dordrecht, The Netherlands: Springer.

Pekrun, R. (2006). The control-value theory of achievement emotions: Assumptions, corollaries, and implications for educational research and practice. *Educational Psychology Review, 18*(4), 315–341. Retrieved from http://dx.doi.org/10.1007/s10648-006-9029-9; https://doi.org/10.1007/s10648-006-9029-9.

Pekrun, R., Frenzel, A. C., Goetz, T., & Perry, R. P. (2007). Chapter 2—The control-value theory of achievement emotions: An integrative approach to emotions in education. In P. A. Schutz & R. Pekrun (Eds.), *Emotion in education* (pp. 13–36). Burlington: Academic Press.

Pekrun, R., & Stephens, E. J. (2010). Achievement emotions: A control-value approach. *Social and Personality Psychology Compass, 4*(4), 238–255. http://dx.doi.org/10.1111/j.1751-9004.2010.00259.x.

Pitt, E., & Norton, L. (2017). 'Now that's the feedback I want!' Students' reactions to feedback on graded work and what they do with it. *Assessment & Evaluation in Higher Education, 42*(4), 499–516. http://dx.doi.org/10.1080/02602938.2016.1142500.

Price, M., Handley, K., & Millar, J. (2011). Feedback: Focusing attention on engagement. *Studies in Higher Education, 36*(8), 879–896.

Rowe, A. D. (2017). Feelings about feedback: The role of emotions in assessment for learning. In D. Carless, S. M. Bridges, C. K. Y. Chan, & R. Glofcheski (Eds.), *Scaling up assessment for learning in higher education* (pp. 159–172). Singapore: Springer.

Ryan, T., & Henderson, M. (2018). Feeling feedback: Students' emotional responses to educator feedback. *Assessment & Evaluation in Higher Education, 43*(6), 880–892. https://doi.org/10.1080/02602938.2017.1416456.

Telio, S., Ajjawi, R., & Regehr, G. (2015). The "educational alliance" as a framework for reconceptualizing feedback in medical education. *Academic Medicine, 90*(5), 609–614.

Telio, S., Regehr, G., & Ajjawi, R. (2016). Feedback and the educational alliance: Examining credibility judgements and their consequences. *Medical Education, 50*(9), 933–942. http://dx.doi.org/10.1111/medu.13063.

Urquhart, L. M., Rees, C. E., & Ker, J. S. (2014). Making sense of feedback experiences: A multi-school study of medical students' narratives. *Medical Education, 48*(2), 189–203. http://dx.doi.org/10.1111/medu.12304.

Värlander, S. (2008). The role of students' emotions in formal feedback situations. *Teaching in Higher Education, 13*(2), 145–156. https://doi.org/10.1080/13562510801923195.

7

Embracing Errors for Learning: Intrapersonal and Interpersonal Factors in Feedback Provision and Processing in Dyadic Interactions

Jochem E. J. Aben, Filitsa Dingyloudi [iD], Anneke C. Timmermans [iD] and Jan-Willem Strijbos [iD]

Feedback is often considered a valuable approach to improve students' learning and performance (e.g. Hattie & Timperley, 2007; Kluger & DeNisi, 1996). Despite the numerous recent attempts to highlight the dialogic, interactive and socially constructed nature of feedback in educational sciences and predominantly in higher education settings (e.g. Ajjawi & Boud, 2018; Narciss, 2017; Steen-Utheim & Wittek, 2017; Van Gennip, Segers, & Tillema, 2009; Yang & Carless, 2013), feedback is still commonly defined and approached as "information provided by an agent (e.g. teacher, peer, book, parent, self, experience) regarding aspects of

---

J. E. J. Aben (✉) · F. Dingyloudi · A. C. Timmermans · J.-W. Strijbos
University of Groningen, Groningen, The Netherlands
e-mail: j.e.j.aben@rug.nl

F. Dingyloudi
e-mail: filitsa.dingyloudi@rug.nl

A. C. Timmermans
e-mail: a.c.timmermans@rug.nl

J.-W. Strijbos
e-mail: j.w.strijbos@rug.nl

© The Author(s) 2019
M. Henderson et al. (eds.), *The Impact of Feedback in Higher Education*,
https://doi.org/10.1007/978-3-030-25112-3_7

one's performance or understanding" (Hattie & Timperley, 2007, p. 81). Previous research, however, indicates that the effectiveness of feedback is likely to differ depending on the educational context in which feedback is provided and processed (e.g. Ajjawi, Molloy, Bearman, & Rees, 2017; Dingyloudi & Strijbos, 2018).

In the case of dyadic interactions, i.e. interactions between two human actors, the educational feedback context (e.g. teacher-student, student-student, student-teacher feedback, etc.) can vary in terms of, among other things, intrapersonal factors (Narciss, 2008; Winstone, Nash, Parker, & Rowntree, 2017) and interpersonal factors (Levy & Williams, 2004; Strijbos & Müller, 2014). Intrapersonal factors are factors that describe one's personal characteristics. For example, a person's motivation and self-perception potentially play a role while providing or processing feedback (Black & Wiliam, 1998; Narciss, 2008; Winstone et al., 2017). Interpersonal factors are factors that describe the relation between human actors. Those factors, such as how a feedback sender (e.g. teacher, student, peer) or recipient (e.g. teacher, student, peer) as well as the relationship between them is represented in the other's mind, can impact the sender's appraisal of the recipients' performance as well as the recipients' appraisal of the senders' feedback (Levy & Williams, 2004).

These intra- and interpersonal factors may be of particular importance as they affect how people deal with errors while providing and processing feedback. Dealing with errors plays a central role in feedback processes, because effectively dealing with errors, also referred to as productive failure, can contribute to an effective learning process (Kapur, 2014; Rach, Ufer, & Heinze, 2013). Since error-making and problem-solving are crucial for knowledge transfer and learning, and feedback is likely to function as a scaffold to reduce the gap between a current and a desired performance (Ramaprasad, 1983), errors viewed as opportunities for learning have a central role in the provision and processing of feedback (Fong et al., 2018).

The aim of this chapter is to propose a feedback model that aims to capture the interplay of intra- and interpersonal factors and the provision and processing of feedback in education with a specific focus on the process of dealing with errors. Such a model contributes to previous literature, as the concurrent influence and interplay of intra- and interpersonal factors, as well as the role of dealing with errors, are largely overlooked areas in

7 Embracing Errors for Learning: Intrapersonal and Interpersonal ...   109

the field of feedback in educational sciences (Strijbos & Müller, 2014; Vandewalle, 2003). By realising the multifaceted and relational nature of feedback influenced by a complex web of intrapersonal and interpersonal factors, practitioners can design more flexible interventions that explicitly consider and address, for example, actors' relationships, perceptions of one another as well as intrapersonal factors that relate to feedback provision and processing and not only consider content- and message-related aspects.

Irrespective of our specific focus on feedback in education, our model also draws upon prominent feedback models in organisational settings, thus incorporating a wider spectrum of views on feedback. Indicatively, feedback literature in organisational psychology devoted more attention to the source (i.e. the feedback sender) and to dyadic interactions (i.e. social exchange) between sender and recipient underscoring the importance of intra- and interpersonal factors than feedback literature in education (Ilgen, Fisher, & Taylor, 1979; Rubin, Bukowski, Parker, & Bowker, 2008). Our model considers specifically dyads as important units of analysis, because feedback in educational settings usually involves two human actors (e.g. a teacher and a student or two peers). Further-on in the chapter, the model will be illustrated by means of an example of a peer feedback situation involving two students that may occur in everyday classes.

Main Orientations of Current Feedback Models

Current feedback models in educational and organisational settings mainly agree upon the idea that feedback aims to inform the feedback recipient about (1) the gap between a desired state and a current state of knowledge or performance and (2) how this gap can be closed (e.g. Black & Wiliam, 1998; Kluger & DeNisi, 1996). In parallel, most models share two important similarities in representing feedback processes. First, current feedback models either focus on the interplay between feedback processes and intrapersonal factors or on the interplay between feedback processes and interpersonal factors. By focusing on only one set of factors, these models overlook that both sets of factors simultaneously impact feedback provision and feedback processing. Second, current models only implicitly assume that the feedback sender and feedback recipient deal with error identification and error-making. Consequently, it is often neglected whether and how dealing with errors is being considered while providing or processing feedback.

The Concurrent Impact of Intra- and Interpersonal Factors

Feedback provision and feedback processing are affected by an interplay of intrapersonal factors. Intrapersonal factors that appear to be related to feedback provision and processing may include intrinsic and extrinsic motivation (Ilgen et al., 1979), effort (Black & Wiliam, 1998), domain knowledge (Butler & Winne, 1995; Timms, DeVelle, & Lay, 2016), self-efficacy (Bandura, 1986; Nadler, 1979; Narciss, 2008), self-perception (Kenny, 1994), communicative skills (Bandura, 1986), reading skills (Timms et al., 2016) and the Big Five personality traits (Guo et al., 2017; Levy & Williams, 2004).

For example, the intrapersonal factor *domain knowledge* could affect the feedback provision and processing in the following way. A feedback sender's prior domain knowledge may influence the ability to identify a domain-specific error in the target recipient's performance as well as the ability to provide a feedback message that is grounded on deep domain-specific knowledge. Similarly, a feedback recipient's prior domain knowledge may influence the ability to comprehend the feedback sender's domain-specific remarks as well as the ability to associate the domain-specific information provided by the feedback sender with other relevant domain-specific information, which could eventually support or hinder the feedback recipient's feedback uptake.

Besides the relevance of intrapersonal factors to feedback processes that involve dyadic interactions, every form of dyadic interaction contains, by definition, not only a flow *within* participating individuals (i.e. intrapersonal factors), but also *between* them (i.e. interpersonal factors). This implies that each actor of an interaction has to cope with his or her own acts and thoughts and has to adapt them to his or her partner at the same time (Barnlund, 1968). This brings us to the second set of factors that are relevant to feedback processes in dyadic interactions, namely interpersonal factors.

The interpersonal factors affecting feedback processes, such as the perception of the other, are shaped over time. For example, in terms of friendship, students may invest more effort in providing peer feedback when they consider the peer a friend (Finkelstein, Fishback, & Tu, 2017). These factors are gradually shaped over time through past experiences of the actor with the same partner and consequently the actor's developing perception of the partner (Gibson, 1969; Upshaw, 1978). The influence of past experiences may be illustrated by means of the concepts *dyadic meta-perception* and *dyadic meta-accuracy*. Dyadic meta-perception describes how one thinks one is viewed by another, and dyadic meta-accuracy refers to one's ability to know how specific others regard one differently (Kenny, 1994). Dyadic meta-perception and dyadic meta-accuracy are relevant, since feedback senders with a high level of dyadic meta-perception and dyadic meta-accuracy are more likely to tailor their feedback message to a specific feedback recipient.

For example, when a student X with an average domain knowledge and a high dyadic meta-accuracy provides peer feedback to a student with a high domain knowledge (Y_1), X may give a more elaborate argumentation for an in-text correction than when X provides peer feedback to a student with a low domain knowledge (Y_2). This is the result of the assumption that, on the one hand, X will know that Y_1 has to be persuaded, since X will assume that Y_1 knows that X has a lower domain knowledge than Y_1. On the other hand, X will know that Y_2 does not have to be persuaded, since X will assume that Y_2 knows X has a higher domain knowledge than Y_2 and that, therefore, Y_2 is more likely to accept in-text corrections than Y_1.

The Role of Errors in Feedback

The second similarity of previous feedback models is the mere implicitness of the assumption that feedback senders and recipients have to deal with errors. Errors are occurrences of a performance or behaviour that, perhaps unintendedly, do not meet an expectation or requirement (Metcalfe,

2017). While errors and their negative consequences, such as faulty products and erroneous performances, typically receive considerable attention and are deemed undesirable and to be prevented, the field of error management considers errors and their positive consequences, such as learning, innovation and resilience, to be fundamental prerequisites for human development (Sitkin, 1996). Accordingly, learning through errors can take the form of (a) knowledge about the errors themselves to avoid them in the future, (b) understanding of a system after experimentation therein, (c) development of a mindset of how to deal with errors and (d) reducing one's negative emotions as a result of errors (Frese & Keith, 2015).

The central role of errors in the provision and processing of feedback is only implicitly visible in the purposes of feedback to support the problem-solving process, to facilitate learning overall and to decrease the gap between a current and a desired performance (Hattie & Timperley, 2007). Consequently, how an individual deals with error-making and error-based feedback may interfere with the provision and processing of feedback that potentially leads to error correction or knowledge transfer. For this reason, dealing with errors is an inherent and crucial part of feedback provision and processing and requires more systematic explication.

Although previous literature states that feedback can be primarily used to correct errors—or in other words: to decrease the gap between current and desired performance—it does not delineate *how* one deals with errors while providing or processing feedback (e.g. Gibbs & Simpson, 2005; Kulhavy, 1977). That is, the process of "correcting errors" is introduced as a phenomenon that is perceived to be similar in every situation, whereas it may differ depending on the situation. For example, how does feedback recipient Y cope with elements of a performance that are in line with the criteria according to Y, whereas they are not in line with the criteria according to sender X? Can a performance be of high quality when it only partially meets the criteria? Such and similar issues that relate to perceived quality, and therefore focus on how someone deals with errors, are not explicitly addressed in nearly all existing feedback models. An exception to this general observation is the model by Timms et al. (2016), in which the process of dealing with errors in a digital learning environment is explicit and central.

The Role of Errors, Intrapersonal Factors and Interpersonal Factors in Feedback Provision and Processing: A Model

In the light of (a) the scarcity of feedback conceptualisations that focus on the interplay between feedback processes and intrapersonal factors, as well as the interplay between feedback processes and interpersonal factors, and (b) the implicit treatment of the role of dealing with errors while providing and processing feedback, a more holistic feedback model is warranted. The proposed model specifically addresses error-oriented feedback influenced by intra- and interpersonal factors (see Fig. 7.1), embracing the inherent complexity in interpersonal communication (Barnlund, 1968).

The model hypothesises that both the feedback sender and the feedback recipient deal with errors while providing or processing feedback, albeit that the feedback sender and the feedback recipient do that in different ways. On the one hand, the feedback sender may identify an error or multiple errors in a particular performance of the target recipient (represented as "error-x" in Fig. 7.1) or at least have the idea that an error or multiple errors occurred. Thereafter, the sender has to decode this error, i.e. assign meaning to it in order to interpret the error (Akin, Goldberg, Myers, & Stewart, 1970) and evaluate it (Cowan, 2010; Tai, Ajjawi, Boud, Dawson, & Panadero, 2018) which could lead to the encoding of a feedback message on the specific error, i.e. the translation of the interpretation and evaluation into the production of verbal and nonverbal signs (Akin et al., 1970). Finally, this message may be sent to the recipient of the feedback in the form of a feedback message. The sender's feedback provision process is depicted by rectangle A in Fig. 7.1.

On the other hand, the feedback recipient has to identify a received feedback message as feedback and acknowledge from that message that he or she made an error. Thereafter, the recipient has to decode the feedback message, evaluate this message and finally (potentially) encode an "output" (e.g. product, performance, response to the feedback). This output may express disagreement with the feedback or may show the intention to act upon the feedback and to correct the error. If the feedback recipient acts upon feedback, this leads to a revised performance, which ideally is an

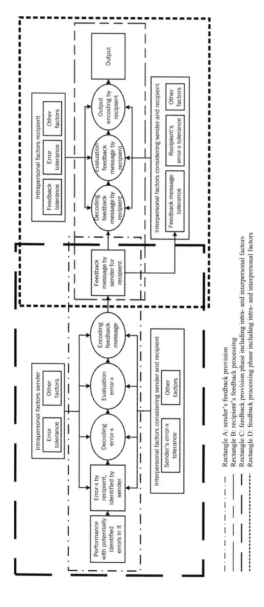

Fig. 7.1 Conceptual model for the processes of providing and processing feedback and the assumed dynamic interplay with intra- and interpersonal factors

improved performance, implying that the initial erroneous performance is (partially) rectified. The feedback processing by the recipient is depicted by rectangle B in Fig. 7.1.

The model also depicts the intra- and interpersonal factors that may affect those feedback provision and feedback processing phases. First, rectangle C represents the feedback provision phase including intrapersonal factors (i.e. the sender's personal characteristics) and interpersonal factors (i.e. the sender's representation of the recipient) that affect the feedback provision phase. Second, rectangle D represents the feedback processing phase including intrapersonal factors (i.e. the recipient's personal characteristics) and interpersonal factors (i.e. the recipient's representation of the sender) that affect the feedback processing phase.

The model assumes that both intrapersonal and interpersonal factors are involved in the process of dealing with errors while providing or processing feedback (Black & Wiliam, 1998; Butler & Winne, 1995; Strijbos & Müller, 2014). Because the model explicitly takes errors as a starting point, two factors are considered especially important: error tolerance and feedback tolerance. In dyadic interactions, both factors are expressed on both the intrapersonal level and the interpersonal level. Error tolerance is one's patience or resilience towards errors occurring in either one's own or another's performance (Rach et al., 2013). One's tolerance towards errors in *general* can be considered as an intrapersonal factor, whereas one's tolerance towards a *specific* error made or identified by a specific other person can be considered as an interpersonal factor since it is likely to be additionally affected by the particular person that made or identified the error. This specificity is represented via "error-x" in Fig. 7.1, as it only appears in the sender's feedback provision process (Rectangle A) and as part of the interpersonal factors (Rectangles C and D), thereby distinguishing error tolerance as an intrapersonal factor from error tolerance as an interpersonal factor. For example, tolerance towards an error might be lower when it is identified by a less liked feedback sender compared to the tolerance towards an error identified by a liked sender (likeableness serving here as an interpersonal factor).

Something similar may hold for feedback tolerance. Feedback tolerance in *general* can be construed as one's patience or resilience towards feedback, and it is therefore an intrapersonal factor. Likewise, a feedback recipient's tolerance towards the feedback of a *specific* other person might be additionally influenced by interpersonal factors. For example, a recipient's feedback tolerance may be low when the feedback was provided by a sender who is not considered a credible source by the recipient. Moreover, the recipient's feedback tolerance towards a specific message from a specific sender is likely to be affected by that specific feedback message.

Illustration of the Model on a Fictional Example

The model conceptualises feedback provision and reception in dyadic settings on a generic level. In this section, we will illustrate the model using a peer feedback example, because interpersonal factors are likely to be even more prevalent and influential in peer feedback compared to a teacher-student setting, due to potentially multiple types of relationships between peers that move beyond the "student-student in-class interactions" (Dingyloudi & Strijbos, 2018). Since a significant portion of peer feedback research has been performed in the area of writing (e.g. Huisman, Saab, van den Broek, & van Driel, 2019; Patchan & Schunn, 2015; Strijbos, Narciss, & Dünnebier, 2010; Wichmann, Funk, & Rummel, 2018), we will present an example of the model in the domain of writing. In this example, we focus on two first-year Bachelor students, named Monica and Chris. Monica has high-level communicative and writing skills (intrapersonal factors), and Chris has low-level communicative and writing skills (intrapersonal factors). Despite Monica and Chris being in the same seminar, they do not really like each other: Chris is one of the popular, talkative students in their class, and Monica is a student that prefers to be a silent listener. Most of the times, Monica tries to avoid any interactions with Chris, but that does not always work out, since they are in the same seminar.

Imagine that Monica and Chris have to write an argumentative text on the impact of social media on elections. As part of the seminar assignment, they are randomly paired to provide feedback to and receive feedback from each other. Monica is not happy to provide feedback to Chris,

7 Embracing Errors for Learning: Intrapersonal and Interpersonal ... 117

since she prefers to avoid any interactions with him. When reading Chris' text, she notices quite some errors. Monica, not wanting to antagonise Chris, decides to point out only a few minor errors and even makes some not earned compliments about Chris' text. Chris, on the other hand, immediately recognises the quality of Monica's text. Not being able to provide high-quality feedback, he quickly writes down some short alternatives for already well-written sentences.

In this feedback provision phase, Monica and Chris formulated comparable feedback messages. The messages focus on lower order concerns and do not reveal any thorough text evaluation. The feedback message composition procedures, however, were different. Whereas Monica's writing skills (i.e. intrapersonal factors, rectangle C) were likely to enable her to provide useful feedback, the interpersonal relationship with Chris (rectangle C) withheld her from doing so. This resulted in Monica identifying errors made by Chris, decoding them, evaluating them and deliberately not encoding a feedback message focusing on all identified errors (rectangle A). In contrast, Chris' writing skills (i.e. intrapersonal factors, rectangle C) were unlikely to enable him to provide useful feedback, and the interpersonal relationship with Monica (rectangle C) did not encourage him to invest effort in trying. The result was Chris poorly identifying errors in Monica's text, not being able to decode and evaluate them, and failing to encode a feedback message focusing on errors regarding higher order concerns (rectangle A).

After the feedback provision stage, Monica and Chris are asked to revise their texts and potentially act upon the provided feedback. Monica, aware of Chris' poor writing skills, does not expect much from Chris' feedback. This low expectation is confirmed when Monica receives the feedback comments by Chris. She immediately recognises that Chris' comments can hardly be called corrections of errors, and therefore, she just scans the remaining comments, ending up ignoring most of them. "Chris is not the one that can correct my text", Monica thinks (rectangle D). In contrast, Chris is willing to correct his text based on Monica's feedback comments. Consequently, Chris corrects most of the errors as suggested by Monica. Chris is quite happy about the final product, further confirmed by Monica's compliments. "Apparently", Chris thinks, "my text is not that bad" (rectangle D).

In this feedback processing phase, Monica and Chris reacted differently upon each other's feedback. Monica started the processing negatively biased and consequently mainly ignored the comments, whereas Chris started the processing positively biased and consequently mainly acted upon the comments (rectangle B). As a result, both students were positive about their final products. Monica saw her own writing skills confirmed, since Chris did not provide useful feedback. Chris was positively surprised about the quality of his text, because even Monica did not provide substantial feedback.

As such, this fictional situation demonstrates that both intra- and interpersonal factors may fundamentally impact the processes and outcomes of feedback provision and feedback processing. Monica did not comment on identified errors, mitigated the perceived quality of Chris' text and processed feedback prejudiced. Chris invested little effort in feedback provision, wrote inappropriate feedback comments and probably overestimated the quality of his text. Maybe even more important, Monica's and Chris' interpersonal relationship did not ameliorate at all and may even have degraded.

Limitations of the Model

The model is not directly applicable to every feedback situation: it cannot be directly applied in the case of confirming feedback, which has a perceived performance that is up to standards as a starting point, and it may be experienced differently in situations of anonymous and automated feedback. First, since the model takes an identified error as the starting point, it inherently does not deal with confirming feedback messages. Confirming feedback, that does not focus on errors, is not included in the model out of a practical consideration: the model stresses improvement-oriented feedback that can potentially be taken up to "close the gap". Nevertheless, the exclusion of confirming feedback does not imply that one should not provide confirming feedback or ignore non-erroneous performances (Hattie & Timperley, 2007; Shute, 2008).

Second, interpersonal factors differently impact the process of dealing with errors in the case of anonymous feedback, compared to non-anonymous feedback. In the case of anonymous feedback, the feedback sender has no knowledge of the feedback recipient and vice versa. Although the interpersonal relationship may initially not seem to impact the feedback process, it may do so as one builds a mental representation of the inferred other when providing anonymous feedback (Strijbos & Müller, 2014) or receiving feedback anonymously (Karabenick, 2011). Elements of this mental representation are, for example, inferred domain knowledge, inferred skills and inferred competence. Since these characteristics of the other are merely inferred from the feedback message, they may or may not correspond to the "real" characteristics of the other or even the characteristics of the other as perceived by that other. Moreover, one may not only infer characteristics of the other, but also a potential other individual; for example, in the case one knows the pool of potential others such as in classroom settings.

Third, in the case of automated feedback, interpersonal factors differently impact the processing of errors. When feedback is automatically provided, the recipient may doubt its quality. For example, one may question the specificity and usability when feedback pops up immediately after submitting a product (e.g. Roscoe, Wilson, Johnson, & Mayra, 2017).

Implications for Feedback Effectiveness in Research and Practice

Our model highlights that when examining disconfirming feedback, in which the role of errors or erroneous performance or behaviour is central, researchers need to bring to the fore and explicitly investigate how oneself deals with error-making (either by oneself or by others), namely one's error tolerance. A closer examination of individuals' error tolerance in disconfirming feedback has the potential to contribute to our understanding of the role of errors in feedback provision and feedback processing, whose role seems to be taken for granted without necessarily being examined. Consequently, the "taken for granted" role of errors in disconfirming feedback leads to feedback models and empirical studies that consider the "feedback message" as the starting point and not the "error" itself from which the feedback cycle emanates and potentially returns to in the form of improvement of performance or learning, by either not repeating the same error in the future or being able to deal with such error-making (either as a sender or recipient).

In addition, our model highlights that when examining disconfirming feedback, which aims to alter or correct an error or one's erroneous performance or behaviour, researchers as well as practitioners need to realise that the individuals involved in a feedback interaction enter the "feedback space" with (a) intrapersonal characteristics (e.g. personality traits, concepts, values, attitudes, expertise, knowledge, skills), indicated as intrapersonal factors, (b) past interpersonal representations of each other, and (c) relationships, which influence the provision and processing of feedback. This implies an "agential" perspective on disconfirming feedback (and feedback in general). In other words, feedback is not merely a feedback message that is simply sent and received, it is rather a set of processes that involve individuals and constellations of individuals (e.g. dyads), who consciously or unconsciously identify themselves and others as well as the relationship between them during all involved processes and as such influencing these processes.

It should be noted that merely evaluating the performance by a specific person, in combination with the interplay of how one' views that specific person and one's intrapersonal factors, can already contribute to one's learning—regardless of whether one subsequently receives feedback from that specific other person or not (cf. evaluative judgement; Boud, Ajjawi, Dawson, & Tai, 2018; Cowan, 2010). However, a deeper discussion is beyond this chapters' perspective on the feedback process as an interpersonal communication exchange and the aim of the model and example presented in this chapter.

Moreover, our model implies that feedback can make a difference even when the product quality and learning capabilities did not change after feedback uptake. In other words, the effect of feedback is not solely reflected by the refined product, knowledge or learning. The interpersonal exchange of feedback may affect the interpersonal relationship and may thereby influence the social interactive learning process. That is, although we conceptualise intra- and interpersonal factors as affecting feedback provision and feedback processing, we do not exclude the possibility of a reciprocal dependence between sender and recipient. As this idea is beyond the scope of this chapter, future research could elaborate on this.

Concerning the effectiveness of feedback in the classroom, the proposed model implies that teachers should at least be aware of the existence of the complex interplay of intra- and interpersonal factors during feedback processes, since a first step towards increasing feedback effectiveness in practice involves feedback actors that are consciously acting. In the case of peer feedback, as arranged in classroom settings, it is important that in particular, teachers are aware of these relationships given their central role in the organisation and management of feedback exchange (Yang & Carless, 2013). A second step regarding implementation of the model in practice is to help actors manage the feedback exchange. Therefore, future research could aim to develop instruments to assist "feedback managers" in the composition of dyads. For instance, when a digital programme would know relevant intrapersonal factors of—and interpersonal relationships between—human actors within a group (e.g. a classroom), such a programme could propose suggestions for the composition of dyads that are likely to exchange feedback effectively.

Not only from a "feedback manager" point of view, but also from the point of view from a feedback recipient, awareness is key. Since processing feedback is likely to evoke negative emotions—especially in response to disconfirming feedback (e.g. Ryan & Henderson, 2018), being mentally prepared for the central role that errors play in feedback may contribute to an effective and congenial feedback processing experience. Consequently, future research could additionally focus on increasing feedback recipients' awareness of the importance of errors for learning.

References

Ajjawi, R., & Boud, D. (2018). Examining the nature and effects of feedback dialogue. *Assessment & Evaluation in Higher Education, 43*(7), 1106–1119. https://doi.org/10.1080/02602938.2018.1434128.

Ajjawi, R., Molloy, E., Bearman, M., & Rees, C. E. (2017). Contextual influences on feedback practices: An ecological perspective. In D. Carless, S. M. Bridges, C. K. Y. Chan, & R. Glofcheski (Eds.), *Scaling up assessment for learning in higher education* (pp. 129–143). Singapore: Springer.

Akin, J., Goldberg, A., Myers, G., & Stewart, J. (1970). *Language behavior: A book of readings in communication.* The Hague, The Netherlands: Mouton & Co.

Bandura, A. (1986). *Social foundations of thought and action.* Englewood Cliffs, NJ: Prentice-Hall.

Barnlund, D. C. (1968). *Interpersonal communication: Survey and studies.* Boston, MA: Houghton Mifflin Company.

Black, P., & Wiliam, D. (1998). Assessment and classroom learning. *Assessment in Education, 5*(1), 7–74. https://doi.org/10.1080/0969595980050102.

Boud, D., Ajjawi, R., Dawson, P., & Tai, J. (Eds.). (2018). *Developing evaluative judgement in higher education: Assessment for knowing and producing quality work.* New York: Routledge.

Butler, D. L., & Winne, P. H. (1995). Feedback and self-regulated learning: A theoretical synthesis. *Review of Educational Research, 65*(3), 245–281. https://doi.org/10.3102/00346543065003245.

Cowan, J. (2010). Developing the ability for making evaluative judgements. *Teaching in Higher Education, 15*(3), 323–334. https://doi.org/10.1080/13562510903560036.

Dingyloudi, F., & Strijbos, J. W. (2018). Just plain peers across social networks: Peer-feedback networks nested in personal and academic networks in higher education. *Learning, Culture and Social Interaction, 18,* 86–112. https://doi.org/10.1016/j.lcsi.2018.02.002.

Finkelstein, S. R., Fishbach, A., & Tu, Y. (2017). When friends exchange negative feedback. *Motivation and Emotion, 41*(1), 69–83. https://doi.org/10.1007/s11031-016-9589-z.

Frese, M., & Keith, N. (2015). Action errors, error management, and learning in organizations. *Annual Review of Psychology, 66,* 661–687. https://doi.org/10.1146/annurev-psych-010814-015205.

Fong, C. J., Schallert, D. L., Williams, K. M., Williamson, Z. H., Warner, J. R., Lin, S., & Kim, Y. W. (2018). When feedback signals failure but offers hope for improvement: A process model of constructive criticism. *Thinking Skills and Creativity, 30,* 42–53. https://doi.org/10.1016/j.tsc.2018.02.014.

Gibbs, G., & Simpson, C. (2005). Conditions under which assessment supports students' learning. *Learning and Teaching in Higher Education, 1,* 3–31.

Gibson, E. J. (1969). *Principles of perceptual learning and development.* East Norwalk, CT: Appleton-Century-Crofts.

Guo, Y., Zhang, Y., Liao, J., Guo, X., Liu, J., Xue, X., et al. (2017). Negative feedback and employee job performance: Moderating role of the big five.

Social Behavior and Personality, 45(10), 1735–1744. https://doi.org/10.2224/sbp.6478.

Hattie, J., & Timperley, H. (2007). The power of feedback. *Review of Educational Research, 77*(1), 81–112. https://doi.org/10.3102/003465430298487.

Huisman, B., Saab, N., van den Broek, P., & van Driel, J. H. (2019). The impact of formative peer feedback on higher education students' academic writing: A meta-analysis. *Assessment & Evaluation in Higher Education, 44*(6), 863–880. https://doi.org/10.1080/02602938.2018.1545896.

Ilgen, D., Fisher, C., & Taylor, S. (1979). Consequences of individual feedback on behavior in organizations. *Journal of Applied Psychology, 64*(4), 349–371. https://doi.org/10.1037/0021-9010.64.4.349.

Kapur, M. (2014). Productive failure in learning math. *Cognitive Science, 38*(5), 1008–1022. https://doi.org/10.1111/cogs.12107.

Karabenick, S. A. (2011). Classroom and technology-supported help seeking: The need for converging research paradigms. *Learning and Instruction, 21*(2), 290–296. https://doi.org/10.1016/j.learninstruc.2010.07.007.

Kenny, D. A. (1994). *Interpersonal perception: A social relations analysis.* New York, NY: Guilford Press.

Kluger, A., & DeNisi, A. (1996). The effects of feedback interventions on performance: A historical review, a meta-analysis, and a preliminary feedback intervention theory. *Psychological Bulletin, 119*(2), 254–284. https://doi.org/10.1037/0033-2909.119.2.254.

Kulhavy, R. (1977). Feedback in written instruction. *Review of Educational Research, 47*(1), 211–232. https://doi.org/10.3102/00346543047002211.

Levy, P., & Williams, J. (2004). The social context of performance appraisal: A review and framework for the future. *Journal of Management, 30*(6), 881–905. https://doi.org/10.1016/j.jm.2004.06.005.

Metcalfe, J. (2017). Learning from errors. *Annual Review of Psychology, 68,* 465–489. https://doi.org/10.1146/annurev-psych-010416-044022.

Nadler, D. A. (1979). The effects of feedback on task group behavior: A review of the experimental research. *Organizational Behavior and Human Performance, 23*(3), 309–338. https://doi.org/10.1016/0030-5073(79)90001-1.

Narciss, S. (2017). Conditions and effects of feedback viewed through the lens of the interactive tutoring feedback model. In D. Carless, S. M. Bridges, C. K. Y. Chan, & R. Glofcheski (Eds.), *Scaling up assessment for learning in higher education* (pp. 173–189). Singapore: Springer.

Narciss, S. (2008). Feedback strategies for interactive learning tasks. In J. Spector, M. Merrill, J. Van Merriënboer, & M. Driscoll (Eds.), *Handbook of research on educational communications and technology* (3rd ed., pp. 125–144). Mahwah, NJ: Lawrence Erlbaum.

Patchan, M., & Schunn, C. (2015). Understanding the benefits of providing peer feedback: How students respond to peers' texts of varying quality. *Instructional Science, 43*(5), 591–614. https://doi.org/10.1007/s11251-015-9353-x.

Rach, S., Ufer, S., & Heinze, A. (2013). Teachers training on students' attitudes towards and their individual use of errors. *PNA, 8*(1), 21–30.

Ramaprasad, A. (1983). On the definition of feedback. *Behavioral Science, 28*(1), 4–13. https://doi.org/10.1002/bs.3830280103.

Roscoe, R. D., Wilson, J., Johnson, A. C., & Mayra, C. R. (2017). Presentation, expectations, and experience: Sources of student perceptions of automated writing evaluation. *Computers in Human Behavior, 70,* 207–221. https://doi.org/10.1016/j.chb.2016.12.076.

Rubin, K. H., Bukowski, W. M., Parker, J. G., & Bowker, J. C. (2008). Peer interactions, relationships, and groups. In W. Damon, M. R. Lerner, D. Kuhn, R. S. Siegler, & N. Eisenberg (Eds.), *Child and adolescent development: An advanced course* (pp. 141–180). Hoboken, NJ: Wiley.

Ryan, R., & Henderson, M. (2018). Feeling feedback: Students' emotional responses to educator feedback. *Assessment & Evaluation in Higher Education, 43*(6), 880–892. https://doi.org/10.1080/02602938.2017.1416456.

Shute, V. J. (2008). Focus on formative feedback. *Review of Educational Research, 78*(1), 153–189. https://doi.org/10.3102/0034654307313795.

Sitkin, S. B. (1996). Learning from failure: The strategy of small losses. In M. D. Cohen & L. S. Sproull (Eds.), *Organizational learning* (pp. 541–577). Thousand Oaks, CA: Sage.

Steen-Utheim, A., & Wittek, A. L. (2017). Dialogic feedback and potentialities for student learning. *Learning, Culture and Social Interaction, 15,* 18–30. https://doi.org/10.1016/j.lcsi.2017.06.002.

Strijbos, J. W., & Müller, A. (2014). Personale faktoren im feedbackprozess. In H. Ditton, & A. Müller (Eds.), *Feedback and evaluation: Theoretical foundations, empirical findings, practical implementation* [Feedback und Rückmeldungen: Theoretische Grundlagen, empirische Befunde, praktische Anwendungsfelder] (pp. 87–134). Münster, Germany: Waxmann.

Strijbos, J. W., Narciss, S., & Dünnebier, K. (2010). Peer feedback content and sender's competence level in academic writing revision tasks: Are they critical for feedback perceptions and efficiency? *Learning and Instruction, 20*(4), 291–303. https://doi.org/10.1016/j.learninstruc.2009.08.008.

Tai, J., Ajjawi, R., Boud, D., Dawson, P., & Panadero, E. (2018). Developing evaluative judgement: Enabling students to make decisions about the quality of work. *Higher Education, 76*(3), 467–481. https://doi.org/10.1007/s10734-017-0220-3.

Timms, M., DeVelle, S., & Lay, D. (2016). Towards a model of how learners process feedback: A deeper look at learning. *Australian Journal of Education, 60*(2), 128–145. https://doi.org/10.1177/0004944116652912.

Upshaw, H. S. (1978). Personality and social effects in judgment. In E. C. Carterette & M. P. Friedman (Eds.), *Handbook of perception: Psychophysical judgment and measurement* (Vol. 2, pp. 143–172). London, UK: Academic Press.

VandeWalle, D. (2003). A goal orientation model of feedback-seeking behavior. *Human Resource Management Review, 13*(4), 581–604. https://doi.org/10.1016/j.hrmr.2003.11.004.

Van Gennip, N., Segers, M., & Tillema, H. H. (2009). Peer assessment for learning from a social perspective: The influence of interpersonal variables and structural features. *Educational Research Review, 4*(1), 41–54. https://doi.org/10.1016/j.edurev.2008.11.002.

Wichmann, A., Funk, A., & Rummel, N. (2018). Leveraging the potential of peer feedback in an academic writing activity through sense-making support. *European Journal of Psychology of Education, 33*(1), 165–184. https://doi.org/10.1007/s10212-017-0348-7.

Winstone, N. E., Nash, R. A., Parker, M., & Rowntree, J. (2017). Supporting learners' agentic engagement with feedback: A systematic review and a taxonomy of recipience processes. *Educational Psychologist, 52*(1), 17–37. https://doi.org/10.1080/00461520.2016.1207538.

Yang, M., & Carless, D. (2013). The feedback triangle and the enhancement of dialogic feedback processes. *Teaching in Higher Education, 18*(3), 285–297. https://doi.org/10.1080/13562517.2012.719154.

Part III

Pedagogies of Feedback Impact

8

Operationalising Dialogic Feedback to Develop Students' Evaluative Judgement and Enactment of Feedback

Edd Pitt ⓘ

Introduction

Previous research (Pitt & Norton, 2017; Pitt, 2017) has suggested that one-way monologic forms of feedback only help certain types of students, namely those who are able to successfully self-regulate: a process of taking control of and evaluating one's own learning and behaviour (Boekaerts, 2006). For the vast majority of students how they process and make use of feedback is a troublesome issue, especially if it is passively received or told to them (Pitt & Winstone, 2019). To address issues surrounding students not proactively receiving feedback many have argued that more dialogic forms of feedback, such as ongoing dialogue with lecturers and dialogic peer feedback, can help students to understand, process and enact feedback in subsequent assessment opportunities (Ajjawi & Boud, 2017; Nicol, 2010).

E. Pitt (✉)
Centre for the Study of Higher Education, University of Kent,
Canterbury, UK
e-mail: E.pitt@kent.ac.uk

© The Author(s) 2019
M. Henderson et al. (eds.), *The Impact of Feedback in Higher Education*,
https://doi.org/10.1007/978-3-030-25112-3_8

More recently, Carless and Boud (2018) have suggested the term student feedback literacy, which involves the understandings, capacities and dispositions needed to use feedback productively. This includes appreciating feedback, making judgements, managing affect and taking action. Feedback literacy also incorporates notions of students appreciating their own and others' roles in the feedback process (e.g. teachers, peers, etc.) (Carless & Boud, 2018). Such a claim is, however, presently rather conceptual and the impact this has upon students' enactment of feedback has not been empirically investigated across differing disciplines. Before we can empirically investigate students' feedback literacy development, we need to understand how differing educational practices that pursue the development of evaluative judgement and enactment of feedback are operationalised in the classroom. In this chapter, I explore how film, comedy, drama and music performance lecturers in the humanities at a UK university operationalise dialogic feedback through differing educational practices. In particular, I seek to further our understanding of the ways lecturers pedagogically design their teaching and assessment to facilitate dialogic feedback interactions between students and lecturers and students and their peers. Alongside describing these innovative pedagogical practices, I examine how each pedagogy might mobilise the intended impact and discuss the challenges with researching impact.

Context of the Research

Eleven lecturers were identified as implementing dialogic feedback practices in their teaching. I interviewed them about their curricula, teaching sessions and assessment and feedback practices. The discussions to follow in this chapter describe how dialogic feedback was implemented by the lecturers and their perceptions of how it affected student learning behaviour and enactment of feedback. The analysis of the interview transcripts followed a constructivist latent theoretical thematic analysis, in which I sought to examine the underlying ideas, assumptions and conceptualisations of the lecturers. Due to my prior theoretical understanding within this area, the data were interpreted in an analyst-driven manner (Braun & Clarke, 2006). In the remainder of this chapter, through examples of lecturers' practices and thoughts, I highlight the salient sociocultural contexts, structural conditions and contextual issues that underpinned their operationalisation of dialogic feedback.

Culture of the Classroom

The lecturers I interviewed all talked at length about how the culture of the classroom was important to enabling dialogic feedback in their teaching practice. This was something which they addressed in week one, session one of the students' university experience, to emphasise the classroom being seen as a safe space for students to try riskier things:

> *RP* I try to create an environment where you could really mess up but that's the point, it's giving them a safe space to experience adversity so they can learn from this.

Students' experiences of feedback prior to their arrival at university often influence their expectations of what feedback will look like in their new setting (Nicol, 2009). Students may, for example on entry to university, lack the necessary self-regulatory skills to successfully utilise feedback information afforded to them. Similarly, as Orsmond, Merry, and Handley (2013) have argued, students often struggle with self-assessment skills, which are crucial to engaging with dialogic feedback. This presents quite a challenge for the lecturer to create the climate whereby students can become more comfortable about engaging with dialogic feedback with the lecturer and their peers. This was particularly the case when the students had not done as well as they expected to do in their performance.

To help students come to understand that failure was not necessarily a disastrous outcome, the lecturers used weekly in-class formative tasks. They wanted students to see them as an opportunity to refine and improve their performance and hopefully enact the feedback prior to the highly weighted summative assessment at the end of the module:

> *RP* the idea is that in 12 weeks' time you get it and you perform and you don't fail. If you're going to fall flat, you're going to do it now, and there's time to make adjustments before the big assessment.

The supportive culture of the classroom manifested within the tasks and scaffolded opportunities for not only repeated exposure to skills that were relevant to the final assessment but more importantly the rich dialogue surrounding these. The lecturers felt that exposure over time seemed to positively affect the students' performance outcomes. However, it is difficult to quantify how successful the students were at enacting their feedback on a week-by-week basis. The lecturers themselves were not always convinced that their students understood or knew how to use the weekly feedback they were getting:

> KM I mean they are getting so much feedback all of the time, it's hard to tell if they are using all of each in the next performance. Sometimes I wonder if they actually can see how to use it, maybe they choose not to, I don't know.

The disciplinary norms in these subjects were that making mistakes was a necessary part of the learning process, central to the development of resilience, self-assessment and self-regulation. Much of this was facilitated by well-organised formative tasks, which provided frequent opportunities for experimentation, failure and development of students' ability to understand their emotional reactions to feedback. The lecturers sought to create an environment whereby students were afforded opportunities to develop their understandings, capacities and dispositions towards learning and feedback. Of course, this is well intentioned but the impact that this has upon students' learning behaviours and enactment of feedback is rather difficult to measure in isolation. The lecturers reflected that positively influencing the culture of the classroom takes time. Most academics understand that failure or disappointment is part of academic life but this is not necessarily as well understood by students. The culture of the classroom the lecturers created facilitated moments where students could engage in dialogue surrounding their own and others' adversity, failure or disappointment alongside opportunities to engage in, generate and receive feedback through ongoing dialogue with their peers and lecturer. The lecturers' perceptions of the relative success of pedagogical approaches that promote dialogue, including how these effects might be influenced, underpin the remainder of the focus in this chapter.

The Use of Exemplars and Dialogic Feedback

It is a real challenge for students to understand and be able to distinguish what quality looks like in their discipline (Carless & Chan, 2017; Sadler, 2010; Tai, Ajjawi, Boud, Dawson, & Panadero, 2017). Exemplars have been suggested as a way to enable students to see and appreciate different levels of quality within their discipline. More importantly, such exposure is designed to facilitate students' understanding of how the quality of work can be distinguished (Tai et al., 2017). The lecturers used exemplars at the beginning of the students' undergraduate degree, a time when they were naturally inexperienced and often had different understandings of what constitutes quality within their discipline to their lecturers. Multiple exemplars from the professional world were used in each subject: Drama (West End Theatre Performances), Comedy (Comedy Club Comedians), Film (Oscar-winning short films), and Music (UK Album Chart Artists). Students were given assessment criteria the lecturers had created and asked them to assess the professional exemplars and discuss with peers why they had assessed them at the varying levels. This was quite a challenge for the students as within these performative subjects, students are often unaware of how their own judgements compare to others within the more established professional field and how they could learn from such exemplars:

> OD like I'll say, "You should look at this comedian because you're a bit like them, and you could see how they do it, which will give you an idea of how you want to do it."

OD argued that students could learn a lot from seeing different examples of quality within professional comedic performances. Furthermore, in film LJ used short films, which were in a sense published works to demonstrate the level of quality available within the film studies field:

> LJ I do model as many things as possible. So, I show them a short film every week and usually what happens is it telescopes narrative. So, it might be nonlinear, it might be linear, but it's a snapshot of something usually. So, they have that as a sort of standard.

Through these lecturer-initiated exemplars, students were afforded opportunities to calibrate standards and their understanding of quality based upon professional-level (disciplinary standards) outputs through dialogic discussion between peers and with the lecturer.

Others have used exemplars to promote students' evaluative judgement. For example, Sadler (2010) used exemplars with students by asking them to identify strengths and weaknesses in a written piece of work. Further, students were tasked with writing feedback related to how the work might be improved, developing their judgement of quality and how feedback can be constructed to improve the work. The use of exemplars in Sadler's research arguably represented the early stages towards the development of feedback literacy, but one opportunity to engage with and to enact evaluative judgements would not be sufficient. Ongoing dialogue surrounding the features of quality or indeed lack of quality within exemplars is essential for students to be able to productively comprehend how lecturers make academic decisions about student work (Tai, Canny, Haines, & Molloy, 2016). The implication here is that exemplar-based teaching sessions are lecturer led; however, as To and Carless (2015) have argued, student ownership of the process is very important in order for them to fully appreciate what constitutes quality in their discipline.

If we apply this framework to the current situations the lecturers have described, then it appears to have the potential to increase the impact of such an experience as the students are afforded agency to make and defend their judgements, which could promote the development of evaluative judgement over time. This was operationalised by the lecturers through initially scaffolding the dialogic element of the exemplars pedagogy, and as the modules progressed, the dialogue between peers became more student driven as they developed their expertise and evaluative judgement.

The humanities lecturers designed their teaching sessions to allow participants the opportunity to see their peers' ongoing in-class performances and initially facilitated a dialogue surrounding said performances to help them to develop their evaluative judgement. In a sense, these exemplars were live and in the moment. The lecturers were not in control of the quality of the students' performance outputs nor the ensuing dialogue as the students were providing feedback and discussing this as they saw the performances. This is a very interesting pedagogical development as it affords students more agency and removes the more teacher-led exemplars that I have discussed so far in this chapter. The humanities lecturers had previously given students exposure to professional-level quality work;

8 Operationalising Dialogic Feedback to Develop Students' ...   135

students had the opportunity to see their peers face adversity, failure or indeed success in the moment:

> SQ After we have done the exemplars from professionals, they get a series of practical workshops, and most of those workshops, the majority of time in those workshops is taken up with students presenting a small piece of stand-up they've been working on, to the class, just like a gig. This is like a live exemplar really. We talk about gags that don't work. The reason that we talk about things that don't work, is not to say that we think it isn't good, but how could it work better. They are able to apply what they have learnt from the exemplars and the quality of other students' work they have seen here.

As SQ indicates, the students performed their work in progress, peers watched and then a whole group discussion relating to the level of the performance referential to previous professional exemplars took place. The lecturers then asked students to give their peers specific feedback following the performance and the performer was asked to consider how they might enact this feedback in subsequent performances. Interestingly, the lecturers seemed to prefer the use of students' actual work in progress in their teaching as they felt that relying upon exemplars from the professional world could sometimes present issues surrounding how achievable the standards were for the students:

> RH you're using the students' performance in the class as a teaching object. if you're using someone like Brian May, it's so removed from their world, and of course the guy's a mega star so of course he sounds amazing, he's Brian May. There's no point in that being the only exemplar you use. For the students it's sometimes better to see what their peers are doing.

The pedagogic operationalisation of exemplars within these formative in-class performance opportunities was underpinned by dialogue that allowed different student perspectives to come to the fore in order to help them construct a collective understanding of what constituted quality in their discipline (Carless & Chan, 2017). As Handley and Williams (2011) have suggested, the student-led dialogue surrounding the exemplars helped the students to see first-hand different levels of quality and allowed them insight into their lecturers' tacit ways of interpreting criteria. The impact of this pedagogical operationalisation of exemplars is difficult to quantify in the short term. The development of evaluative judgement takes time and students will not always progress in a linear way. The lecturers attempted to qualitatively judge impact by encouraging students to incorporate the feedback into their subsequent performance:

> *KP* It's really a challenge to get them to always use the feedback they have received from either myself or their peers. What I have started to do is ask them to discuss with their peers how they plan to or have used the feedback in their performances. This I think has helped them to see over time how the feedback is helping them to improve.

I was struck by some of the lecturers' candour in their reflections relating to impact of feedback. We are increasingly asked as practitioners to demonstrate or quantify the impact of our various pedagogical approaches, but this may not always be appropriate or easy to do. The lecturers I interviewed wanted to encourage the students to enact the feedback information and facilitated this through iterative in-class task design, which gave them opportunities to track the effects at least in part. They conceived impact to be about students understanding the purpose of feedback and over time realising how it could be enacted to improve performance. In many cases, the impact of the feedback may not have been immediate or manifest in the next opportunity; rather, it may have been much later in their studies.

Developing Students' Evaluative Judgement Using Exemplars

Tai et al., (2017) have suggested the term evaluative judgement, which they argue, is the "capability to make decisions about the quality of work of self and others" (p. 5). Students need opportunities to develop their evaluative judgement over time. As I have previously outlined in this chapter, the exemplars and live exemplars that the lecturers operationalised played a very important part in trying to enable this. They created an environment where students were afforded the agency to appreciate the various subtleties of their performative disciplines. Further, these opportunities happened largely within class contact hours, and as Tai et al. (2017) suggest, students

8 Operationalising Dialogic Feedback to Develop Students' ...   137

are making judgements independently without the need for teacher-driven direction and thus is not as labour intensive for the lecturer. The learner was placed within a dialogic culture, where constant dialogic appraisal of peers' work, and referenced to this, their own work became over time normalised. As such, the environment, tasks and culture replicated the disciplinary norms students could expect to encounter in the professional world following graduation (Tomlinson, 2012).

This framework of consistent exposure to opportunities for developing evaluative judgement over time reflected the need for the lecturers to appreciate that students needed multiple opportunities if they were to improve. The lecturers indicated that some students demonstrated an ability to recognise different levels of quality and provided useful feedback comments to their peers. PF described how some students also enacted the feedback they received in subsequent performances towards the end of their module suggesting it had an impact upon them:

> *PF* I think the students, having gone through the period and the continuous assessment stuff, they're able to see different levels of quality and apply it to their own performance. You see that in the quality of the comments and how each student responds to them in the later weeks of the module.

Earlier in this chapter, I reflected upon some of the lecturer's candour in their understanding of the impact of their feedback. PF's thoughts are an example whereby he indicates that impact is conceived as being enactment in later weeks of the module (indicating enactment in the highly weighted performance assessment at the end). However, the students' journeys towards developing evaluative judgement are not always linear and progressive. Despite some students appearing to develop an understanding of what constitutes quality in their discipline and being able to construct helpful and useful feedback for others related to their performance, WW explained that they were not always able to apply this judgemental feedback to their own work:

> *WW* What I'll often say to them is, "Don't forget when you're giving advice, you're also learning for yourself." So, for example there's a student who gives lots of good suggestions to other students, and actually her own writing is a bit underdeveloped. So, I said, "Look you need to give yourself the advice you're giving to other ..." Which I know is hard, because it's

> your own stuff, you've got very close to it. But just come up with the
> ideas and then say to yourself what you would say to others.

In this example, the impact of feedback appears to be very different. In one respect, the student's ability to generate feedback in relation to criteria appears to have been positively impacted upon by her experience. However, the impact this has had upon her ability to apply this knowledge to her own work is less developed. This is an interesting situation and highlights the complexities of understanding impact and indeed measuring it across an entire cohort of students. It would have been very easy for the lecturer to interject and almost tutor the student to apply the feedback she had given to her peers. However, WW's role in the process of students developing evaluative judgement is to know when not to say anything and trust the underpinning process. The student is less likely to develop evaluative judgement and know how to take action into the future if they are told; rather, it is up to them to make connections between what they have identified in others' work and how this then applies to their own work (Tai et al., 2017). The challenge here is that any possible impact this has may come much further down the line in the student's studies. The culture of the classroom that the lecturers created (including the pedagogical approaches adopted) can theoretically influence the development of students' evaluative judgement. In all the examples I have discussed in this chapter, formative ongoing opportunities to practice, refine and enact feedback received were apparent, alongside dialogue surrounding how students did or indeed did not do this. This continual refinement in a safe and supportive environment affords students agency but also gives them the freedom and opportunity to make judgements and take action, therefore, increasing the potential for feedback processes to be impactful on feedback literacy and learning.

The Use of Peer Dialogic Feedback

Several of the examples offered above have utilised peer dialogue. By definition, a peer is an equal in one or more of the following aspects: age, educational level or level of expertise (Panadero, Jonsson & Alqassab,

8 Operationalising Dialogic Feedback to Develop Students' ...

2018). In this chapter, I conceive peer feedback as referring to any information about a student's performance that they generated for or received from a peer within their studies. Peer feedback is not a new concept, and many researchers have suggested how it can be used formatively in practice, harnessed for feedback generation and reception and development of students' evaluative judgement (Tai et al., 2017). In peer feedback, students are placed in a director role where they are active givers and receivers of feedback. The benefits of exposure to peer feedback for students have clear links to increasing the impact of feedback if we are to interpret such situations as fostering opportunities where students can use the feedback information they receive to enhance future work. The opportunities for peer feedback in different forms were underpinned by the students' previous experiences of exemplars and evaluative judgement development.

It was evident that despite students previously experiencing opportunities to develop a sense of what constituted quality within their discipline and an ability to make evaluative judgements, peer feedback was still a difficult area for students to participate in:

> KQ There can be sessions where it's like getting blood from a stone. But I'm not sure that's lack of engagement as such, I think it's not knowing exactly how to spot what they should be getting or giving feedback on maybe. So, in the first couple of weeks, it's quite hard to get beyond students just kind of looking at each other's work and going, "Oh that's nice, I enjoyed that." Or, "Yeah that was good." And you have to push them quite hard to elaborate on what they mean by good. Then the next barrier is getting them to give each other what we'd phrase as suggestions for improvement, but identifying negatives about work.
>
> RP Initially everyone's like "Oh it was really good, brilliant." And then as the weeks go by they become more critical and constructive about what the performer can do to improve next time. I think it happens after they have seen lots of different acts in the session and they can distinguish the quality between them all.

Both KQ and RP's examples pose an interesting question in relation to when it may be best to introduce peer feedback in teaching sessions and the potential impact this feedback might have. The areas I have outlined in earlier sections of this chapter appear to

140   E. Pitt

underpin the process of introducing peer feedback. Students' giving and receiving meaningful feedback, with the intention of helping their peers to improve without the necessary pre-development of evaluative judgement and disciplinary understanding of quality, may for example reduce the potential impact that peer feedback has.

Opportunities for students to generate for and receive feedback from their peers were frequently available in the courses studied. As I have previously outlined, students were afforded many opportunities to develop their evaluative judgements through critique of exemplars, dialogue about quality and a safe space to hone performative elements and to take action within their discipline. Central to the development of these academic skills were opportunities the lecturers created, in the face-to-face teaching time, for peer feedback to be generated and dialogue surrounding this to be fostered. Here I explain a few strategies in more detail, unpicking the challenge of tracking impact for each.

Comedy Buddies

Comedy buddies were used within the comedy performance course. The lecturer was particularly keen to set the peer feedback framework up so as to expose students to conflicting thought processes from their own. This framework often resulted in students generating and receiving more critical feedback from their peers. Matching students for example from different comedy performance skills sets (i.e. slapstick vs. observational) seemed to allow students to receive peer feedback that originated from a different disciplinary interpretation:

> *OD* I often set up a thing called comedy buddies. Ideally you want to get somebody who's more cerebral and material based matched with somebody who's more instinctive and performance based. Because they learn more from each other. If you have people with the same strengths and weaknesses working together, they can just reinforce their weaknesses.

Dialogic feedback between peers was the key pedagogical strategy underpinning the comedy buddies approach. The lecturers indicated that the peer feedback dialogue offered students conflicting ideas relating to their

8 Operationalising Dialogic Feedback to Develop Students' ... 141

comedic performance. The challenge for the student was to be able to generate feedback for a peer that had a fundamentally different approach to their own and then to articulate this within a meaningful dialogic exchange with their peer. The lecturers intended for feedback to be impactful for students enacting this feedback in their subsequent performances. This is a rather nuanced situation, and as I have previously argued in this chapter, enactment is difficult to measure in the immediate term. This appears to be especially the case here as the feedback was being generated by someone with a very different thought process to the student and suggests isolated situations like this might not always produce feedback information that can be enacted.

The Script Writers Forum

The script writer's forum was an initiative within the film studies course. This practice was reliant upon students producing weekly film script ideas that were pitched to their lecturer and peers during the teaching time. Film students had previously been exposed to exemplars of professional quality and had engaged with dialogue with their peers about these:

> *EM* In the script writer forum you are going to get 10 comments from your screenplay or on your film. None of them might be terrible, but one of them will be gold dust. So that's oral feedback from me, but also from people sitting round the table each week on the work they produce. The peer feedback is usually very good quality, critical and tactfully given. As the weeks go by, they are making more developed judgements and learn from each other on that and really help each other to improve.

As EM indicated, the design of the forum gave students an opportunity to generate peer feedback information for others on their script ideas, but also to receive it. In this situation, the impact of feedback could potentially be measured by the lecturer through observing and participating in the dialogic feedback interactions. Students could enact the feedback in the subsequent refinement of the film script for the following week's session. In particular, students could share their ongoing work in progress with their peers and participate in a dialogue surrounding its strengths and

142 E. Pitt

weaknesses, reflecting upon how they had enacted feedback. Students could also make ongoing judgements of what constituted quality in their discipline through exposure to other students' work in progress and this could potentially have an impact upon their own work.

Speed Dating Peer Feedback

In drama, after 10 weeks of observing the students' ongoing performances peers were asked to give each other detailed feedback in 1-2-1 meetings in order to engage them in a dialogue surrounding their progress and how they had incorporated previous feedback. The approach in particular allowed students to generate feedback for their peers but also to articulate how they had subsequently incorporated feedback into their act:

> LN In week 10, I do what I call speed dating feedback. So, as the weeks have gone by they have all taken notes on everybody's act, and then they move round so that each performance group or soloist talks to every other performance group or soloist. Each person spends three minutes with each act, so they get really detailed feedback and actually the quality of feedback they produce is really good, which suggests to me that there are people with brilliant feedback for each other who aren't always piping up with it in the group based discussions that happen earlier in the term.

LN interpreted the dialogue between peers as being underpinned by what had gone before in the module. The speed dating feedback happened from week 10 onwards, which meant that students had already had opportunities to develop their evaluative judgement within the comedy performance discipline, through exemplars of professional comedy performance and live exemplars of differing quality in their peers' comedy performances. These experiences were afforded by the lecturers in order to calibrate students' understanding of what constitutes quality in the discipline so they could potentially generate critical evaluative feedback for one another in relation to their own and others' performances. The lecturer perceived that the intimate and more specific 1-2-1 peer dialogic feedback opportunities afforded seemed to assist some students who were perhaps less inclined to offer feedback to others in the whole class discussions which happened ear-

8 Operationalising Dialogic Feedback to Develop Students' ... 143

lier in the module. Impact therefore took a different form in this example as it related more to being able to generate feedback and share with peers, than it being about enactment of feedback in subsequent work.

The Potential for Impactful Feedback

The educational potential of peer feedback relied heavily upon students having a developed sense of quality within their discipline and an ability to make evaluative judgements. The lecturers created opportunities for students to develop both of these areas in the early stages of their experience. The lecturers all alluded to the potential impact of peer feedback suggesting that it could be as useful as lecturer feedback as peers often have the same understanding of language used within the discipline and provide more non-directive comments to their peers. As the students experienced more instances of generating and receiving feedback from their peers, they appeared to become more capable of distinguishing the quality of the peer feedback they received. For many lecturers, this indicated that feedback had an impact as the students became better at understanding its purpose and potential for enactment. This is an interesting way of considering impact, which moves our understanding of impact from a position of it being about enactment in a subsequent assessment towards one of making sense of information and incorporating into a performance schema (in-the-moment interpretations of information and what/how to integrate) and a deeper engagement with the information being received. Although I have highlighted what the lecturers did and their perceptions of its success, I am not making claims relating to its effects on student learning per se. However, the lecturers' practices and interpretations of impact appear to suggest a different consideration of how feedback can be conceived not only by practitioners but also by students themselves. It is clear that more longitudinal empirical research would need to be carried out in order to support the lecturers' perceptions of impact. The approach one might take to researching this might explore the thought processes of students when deciding to enact or not enact feedback they receive from peers or their lecturer. Similarly, the role that emotions play in the processing and enactment of feedback and how this interacts with the generation of feedback for peers within the dialogic classrooms. This contrasts starkly with research seeking to see a change in grade on a subsequent piece of work.

Engaging students in feedback dialogue both gives students more *and* demands more of them as learners. Furthermore, the demands placed upon the lecturer in the early developmental stages are larger than normal, but this potentially reduces as students become more familiar and capable of leading the dialogue. I have suggested that all lecturers could amend their current pedagogical practice to integrate activities such as exemplars of professional or high quality work, live exemplars of varying levels of quality of students' work in progress and multiple dialogic peer feedback opportunities to allow time for students to develop their evaluative judgement and therefore to increase the potential impact of feedback processes. The impact of these educational practices could be empirically explored through for instance student audio/visual diaries, whereby students document their "in the moment" thoughts, feelings and understandings. Such a research design could help us to understand the impact that feedback has in the short, medium and long term, not only between in-class tasks, or within one module but across an entire programme of study.

The pedagogical approaches operationalised by the lecturers I have discussed in this chapter were underpinned by scaffolding such opportunities strategically in order to positively enhance students understanding of the purpose and potential for enactment of feedback within their performative assessments. In other words, the practices explored in this chapter hold great potential for developing students' evaluative judgements and feedback literacy in the longer terms through careful scaffolding of pedagogical opportunities. One of the limitations of this chapter is that it is focused upon the lecturer's perceptions of the relative success of their educational practices in promoting impactful feedback. Understanding the long term impact such approaches have upon students, requires further empirical research which seeks to explore the student role in the dialogic process, and how the approaches affect their enactment over time and across multiple disciplines.

References

Ajjawi, R., & Boud, D. (2017). Researching feedback dialogue: An interactional analysis approach. *Assessment & Evaluation in Higher Education, 42*(2), 252–265. https://doi.org/10.1080/02602938.2015.1102863.

Boekaerts, M. (2006). Self-regulation and effort investment. In W. Damon, R. A. Lerner, K. A. Renninger, & I. E. Sigel (Eds.), *Handbook of child psychology volume 4: Child psychology in practice* (pp. 345–377). New York, NY: Wiley. https://doi.org/10.1002/9780470147658.

Braun, V., & Clarke, V. (2006). Using thematic analysis in psychology. *Qualitative research in Psychology, 3*(2), 77–101.

Carless, D., & Boud, D. (2018). The development of student feedback literacy: Enabling uptake of feedback. *Assessment & Evaluation in Higher Education, 43*(8), 1315–1325. https://doi.org/10.1080/02602938.2018.1463354.

Carless, D., & Chan, K. K. H. (2017). Managing dialogic use of exemplars. *Assessment & Evaluation in Higher Education, 42*(6), 930–941. https://doi.org/10.1080/02602938.2016.1211246.

Handley, K., & Williams, L. (2011). From copying to learning: Using exemplars to engage students with assessment criteria and feedback. *Assessment & Evaluation in Higher Education, 36*(1), 95–108. https://doi.org/10.1080/02602930903201669.

Nicol, D. (2009). Assessment for learner self-regulation: Enhancing achievement in the first year using learning technologies. *Assessment & Evaluation in Higher Education, 34*(3), 335–352.

Nicol, D. (2010). From monologue to dialogue: Improving written feedback processes in mass higher education. *Assessment & Evaluation in Higher Education, 35*(5), 501–517. https://doi.org/10.1080/02602931003786559.

Orsmond, P., Merry, S., & Handley, K. (2013). Students' social learning practice as a way of learning from tutor feedback. In S. Merry, M. Price, D. Carless, & M. Taras (Eds.), *Reconceptualising Feedback in Higher Education.* Routledge.

Panadero, E., Jonsson, A., & Alqassab, M. (2018). Peer feedback used for formative purposes: Review of findings. In A. Lipnevich & J. K. Smith (Eds.), *The Cambridge handbook of instructional feedback* (pp. 409–431). Cambridge: Cambridge University Press. https://doi.org/10.1017/9781316832134.

Pitt, E. (2017). Students' utilisation of feedback: A cyclical model. In D. Carless, S. Bridges, C. Chan, & R. Glofcheski (Eds.), *Scaling up assessment for learning in higher education* (pp. 145–158). Singapore: Springer, https://doi.org/10.1007/978-981-10-3045-1.

Pitt, E., & Norton, L. (2017). Now that's the feedback I want!' students' reactions to feedback on graded work and what they do with it. *Assessment & Evaluation in Higher Education, 42*(4), 499–516. https://doi.org/10.1080/02602938.2016.1142500.

Pitt, E., & Winstone, N. (2019). Dialogic feedback in a digital world. In M. Bearman, P. Dawson, J. Tai, R. Ajjawi, & D. Boud (Eds.), *Re-imagining university assessment in a digital world*. New York: Springer.

Sadler, D. R. (2010). Beyond feedback: Developing student capability in complex appraisal. *Assessment & Evaluation in Higher Education, 35*(5), 535–550. https://doi.org/10.1080/02602930903541015.

Tai, J., Ajjawi, R., Boud, D., Dawson, P., & Panadero, E. (2017). Developing evaluative judgement: Enabling students to make decisions about the quality of work. *Higher Education, 76*(3), 467–481. https://doi.org/10.1007/s10734-017-0220-3.

Tai, J., Canny, B. J., Haines, T. P., & Molloy, E. K. (2016). The role of peer-assisted learning in building evaluative judgement: Opportunities in clinical medical education. *Advances in Health Sciences Education, 21*(3), 659–676. https://doi.org/10.1007/s10459-015-9659-0.

To, J., & Carless, D. (2015). Making productive use of exemplars: Peer discussion and teacher guidance for positive transfer of strategies. *Journal of Further and Higher Education, 40*(6), 746–764. https://doi.org/10.1080/0309877X.2015.1014317.

Tomlinson, M. (2012). Graduate employability: A review of conceptual and empirical themes. *Higher Education Policy, 25*(4), 407–431. https://doi.org/10.1057/hep.2011.26.

9

Turning Self-Assessment into Self-Feedback

Ernesto Panadero ⓘ, Anastasiya Lipnevich and Jaclyn Broadbent ⓘ

Over the past few decades, the field of education has accumulated extensive literature on self-assessment and its effects on educational outcomes (Boud & Falchikov, 1989; Brown, & Harris, 2013; Panadero, Brown & Strijbos, 2016a; Panadero, Jonsson, & Botella, 2017; Sitzmann, Ely, Brown, & Bauer, 2010). In general, existing definitions of self-assessment have a common underlying idea, and it's that of learners' engagement

---

E. Panadero (✉)
Departamento de Psicología Evolutiva y de La Educación, Universidad Autónoma de Madrid, Madrid, Spain

Centre for Research in Assessment and Digital Learning (CRADLE), Deakin University, Geelong, VIC, Australia

A. Lipnevich
Queens College and the Graduate Center, City University of New York, New York, NY, USA

J. Broadbent
Centre for Research in Assessment and Digital Learning (CRADLE), Deakin University, Geelong, VIC, Australia
e-mail: jaclyn.broadbent@deakin.edu.au

© The Author(s) 2019
M. Henderson et al. (eds.), *The Impact of Feedback in Higher Education*,
https://doi.org/10.1007/978-3-030-25112-3_9

with a process or product of their own learning to describe their perceived progress or result. However, the outcome of self-assessment can be purely summative (e.g., self-grading) to mostly formative (e.g., creating qualitative information that can be applied for a resubmission of the work). Andrade (2018), in her overview of self-assessment research, encouraged to define self-assessment through its purpose. She stated that "the purpose of self-assessment is to generate feedback that promotes learning and improvements in performance" (p. 377). In turn, the purpose of feedback is in modifying processes and products that enhance learning. Thus, we will define self-feedback as the implementation of self-assessment in ways that generate feedback information and processes for students' own purposes (e.g., achieving educational gains).

This definition emphasizes the importance of using self-assessment for formative purposes, creating space and opportunities for students to reflect on their work and improve upon it, while offering information for the teachers on how to modify their instruction. Instead of using self-assessment for purely grading purposes, as was the tendency not so long ago (e.g., Panadero et al., 2016a), it encourages students to generate feedback that could close the gap between their current performance and the expected goal. This can be interpreted as a change in paradigm, turning self-assessment from grade assignment into something more powerful—self-feedback.

This conceptualization could have a strong impact on education if we consider previous research findings. For example, previous meta-analyses have revealed that self-assessment has an impact on student achievement (Brown & Harris, 2013), self-regulated learning and self-efficacy (Panadero et al., 2017), and motivation (Sitzmann et al., 2010). Interestingly, these reviews included studies from earlier years, in which the formative purposes of assessment were not as clearly defined as they are today. In other words, the majority of studies included in the aforementioned reviews discussed summative versions of self-assessment, which might have had a weaker influence on learning. Therefore, it is to be expected that in the future research will take into account multiple operationalizations of self-assessment, in particular, equating self-assessment with self-feedback and encouraging the use of it formatively (Andrade, 2018; Panadero et al., 2016a). We want to extend this argument further, incorporating new

Shifting from Summative Implementations of Self-Assessment to Self-Feedback

In the early days of self-assessment, the primary purpose thereof was in students' guessing or predicting their grade in an attempt to explore its correlation to teachers' grades (Falchikov & Boud, 1989). Although this trend is currently shifting with more researchers trying to uncover intricacies of learning-oriented purposes of self-assessment, a large portion of current studies on self-assessment is still focused on student-predicted grades and their correlation with scores assigned by teachers. For example, Andrade (2018) found that out of the fifty-two articles published on self-assessment from 2013 to 2016 thirty explored students' accuracy (note: she used the term consistency). These studies are informative and further our understanding of students' ability to effectively evaluate their work, and the conditions under which this process is particularly effective. Yet, we would argue that students get the most benefit through the deep reflection that can accompany self-assessment (see, for example, Panadero et al., 2016a). An increasing volume of research has focused on how to use self-assessment in ways that would promote direct reflection on the qualities of the performed work, not just the grade (e.g., Brown & Harris, 2013; Sitzmann et al., 2010), but the field can clearly improve.

Unfortunately, the summative tradition in self-assessment research has had a negative impact on the number and depth of formative self-assessment studies. As a consequence, there is barely any educational research focusing on the type of feedback students give to themselves. To our knowledge, one notable exception is a study by Yan and Brown (2017) who employed retrospective interviews to examine processes that students used when meaningfully engaging in self-assessment for the purposes of improving learning. They found that students usually went through three phases (1) determining the performance criteria, (2) self-directed feedback seeking that can come via inquiry from external sources or self-monitoring, and (3) self-reflection based on the feedback sought. This study is interesting because it shows the behavioral, cognitive, and affective processes students actively employ when processing self-feedback, but we need to keep in mind that the data are limited as it comes from self-report. Acknowledging that this type of research is very scarce, we will focus next on six aspects that will be key to achieving implementations that truly help to develop students' effective self-feedback.

Making the Implicit Explicit to Correct for Self-Bias

A very distinct aspect of self-feedback is that it refers to the self, wherein a student serves both as a provider and a receiver of feedback. Butler and Winne's (1995) review pointed out that learners had their own internal path to feedback that occurred regardless of the reception of explicit and direct external feedback from teachers or peers. Therefore, even if teachers did not actively encourage formal self-assessment, students tended to create their own internal feedback. In fact, studies show that we continuously engage in this type of self-referenced activities in all domains of our lives and tend to dismiss information from outside sources that are inconsistent with our stable perceptions of performance and ability (Dunning, Heath, & Suls, 2004). The dismissal of inconsistent information is particularly important for us because probably the strongest factor influencing self-feedback is individual bias.

There is an extensive body of research that has consistently demonstrated that human beings are imperfect at assessing themselves, especially when it comes to low academic achievers (Dunning et al., 2004). The more we help students to be mindful of their own performance and self-evaluation, the more likely they are to reflect upon those processes that are usually "internal objects of reflection." Boud (1999) pointed out that self-assessment is more powerful as an instructional and learning activity if it involves external sources of feedback such as teachers or peers, an aspect also pointed out by feedback models proposed by Butler and Winne (1995) and Narciss (2008). This external feedback will help students to correct biases because in educational settings they have a negative impact on academic achievement. Probably the most promising way to achieve this goal is through direct instruction and demonstration of activities lead-

9 Turning Self-Assessment into Self-Feedback 151

ing to self-feedback because students need to be shown external reference values to achieve higher accuracy and learn to create self-feedback (Narciss, 2008).

To enhance student self-feedback occurrence in the classroom educators should use this as an instructional goal deeply embedded into the curriculum, which implies that educators need to turn an inherent internal process into an explicit external one that the educators can model (Eva & Regehr, 2008). Boud (1999) noted that self-assessment should not be viewed as an isolating, individualized activity. Rather, it can and it should involve the available social circle of teachers, peers, and parents. The nature of self-assessment suggests students' seek feedback from their social environments and then adjust their own feedback and evaluation to improve processes and products of learning. Having students engage in an effective cycle of self-feedback may be possible through the implementation of scaffolds such as modeling, formulating explicit criteria, using exemplars, and other instructional tools (Panadero, Jonsson, & Strijbos, 2016b). As a result of these instructional interventions, students will be able to create their own feedback based on external reflection induced by scaffolding tools. Panadero et al. (2016b) combined recommendations from Andrade and Valtcheva (2009) and Ross (2006) and came up with a list of guidelines for implementation that would increase the likelihood of self-feedback to occur (p. 318):

1. Define the criteria by which students assess their work.
2. Teach students how to apply the criteria.
3. Give students feedback information on their self-assessments.
4. Give students help in using self-assessment data to improve performance.
5. Provide sufficient time for revision after self-assessment.
6. Do not turn self-assessment (*exclusively*) into self-evaluation by counting it toward a grade.

As it can be seen, these guidelines emphasize the intentional shift from internal self-feedback processes into explicit moments of instruction. Receiving external feedback from teachers and peers will allow for

Shifting from Scoring Accuracy to Content Accuracy

There is a vast number of studies on scoring accuracy in self-assessment (Brown, Andrade, & Chen, 2015), and there is empirical evidence suggesting that having students calculate their own grades on a task results in significant performance gains. Sanchez, Atkinson, Koenka, Moshontz, and Cooper (2017) synthesized the findings of 33 reports on peer and self-grading. They found that students who engaged in self-grading performed better than students who did not (g = 0.34). Importantly, this meta-analysis mixed pure summative interventions with formative ones, making it hard to discern the sole impact of summative self-assessment. It is clear, however, that the act of reflecting on one's performance with the goal to generate a grade is likely to have positive effects on students' subsequent performance because self-grading makes the student reflect upon his/her performance and situate it in a scoring schema. The benefits of self-grading can also be explained from the information processing perspective. The sheer act of reflecting upon one's performance strengthens memory traces and may facilitate subsequent information retrieval (Bjork, Storm, & de Winstanley, 2010). Further, if this reflection goes beyond the grade and students focus on the task itself, they will generate more productive self-feedback (e.g., Andrade, 2018; Panadero et al., 2016a).

In order to get closer to effective self-feedback, we could move self-assessment accuracy from scoring to content accuracy. This is because "...*it may be much more educationally powerful if students are accurate when describing the qualities of their work (i.e., its strengths or weaknesses that need to be improved) in terms of subject, discipline, or course 'content-matter' accuracy*" (Panadero et al., 2016a, p. 812), as compared to the perfect calibration in terms of self-grading. This type of accuracy is closer to self-feedback because with that type of information the learner is more capable of answering the three critical questions (Where am I? Where am I going next? How do I get there?) as they relate to the content of the task itself, and not just the grade. Therefore, we need to start researching how to get our self-assessment interventions closer to content accuracy.

Developmental Approach: The Power of Practice/Expertise

Another important aspect to consider when moving toward self-feedback is practice and expertise. Panadero et al. (2016a) proposed a developmental approach that required self-assessors to have some practice with the particular task they were supposed to assess. Without adequate familiarity with a task, it is unlikely that self-assessors can make accurate and realistic evaluations of one's performance due to lacking criteria, standards, and performance models. This idea was first outlined in regards to self-grading accuracy by the meta-analysis from Falchikov and Boud (1989): "Self-assessment may be regarded as a skill and, as such, needs to be developed. It has been suggested that good assessment practice, whether ratings be made by students or by teachers, should include training of assessors" (p. 426). Panadero et al. (2016a) extended this idea past summative self-assessment and grading alone and included formative self-assessment, which, in its effective form, culminates in self-feedback. The authors argued that skill development should be embraced throughout the self-feedback process: "Just as we cannot ask students to perform a novel task with the ease and fluency of an expert, so we should not expect students to conduct self-assessment with ease and accuracy, until they have mastered the relevant skills" (p. 819).

Panadero et al. (2016a) also argued that there were two reasons why prior knowledge and expertise in the task domain mattered. First, consistently with the cognitive load theory, when students are performing a task for the first time, the actual performance consumes most of the cognitive resources (Kirschner, 2002) leaving too little room for self-monitoring or strategic self-evaluation. The lacking cognitive schemata increase cognitive load, as practice is required to build up such schemas and automatize some of the processes that require significant cognitive investments. The second reason refers to motivational aspects. That is, if students lack experience and are not sure what to do with a novel task, it will be highly unlikely that they will find the exercise to be enjoyable and helpful. This could result in a "threat to the self and/or even encourage learned helplessness and decreased self-efficacy" (Panadero et al., 2016a, p. 819). This practice, particularly in high stakes assessment contexts (e.g., grades), may have a negative effect on self-assessors' willingness and motivation to perform self-assessment in the future via negative effects on self-efficacy, emotions, and other psychosocial variables.

To circumvent these issues, Panadero and colleagues proposed four key considerations. First, practice is key for a successful self-assessment implementation culminating in self-feedback. Hence, giving students multiple opportunities to engage with the task and subsequent self-monitoring and self-assessment is required. Second, an incremental structured implementation should be exercised in order to achieve optimal results. For example, assessors should be first introduced to simpler forms of self-feedback, and tasks should gradually increase in complexity as students gain practice and expertise. Third, differential interventions might be more beneficial for different stages of expertise, which means that we need to be aware of the current stage students are in before implementing self-feedback in an appropriate manner. Fourth, the focus should be on skill development, rather than exclusively on student content knowledge. In other words, teachers should be aware that the final goal is to develop the ability to create self-feedback, not just to be accurate at the particular task the student is performing at that specific moment (e.g., mathematical equations). In conclusion, this developmental approach should help to develop self-feedback expertise for the students so they can more accurately answer the three key feedback questions: "where am I going, where am I, where to next?".

Connecting Self-Feedback and Self-Regulated Learning

In order to increase students' opportunities to generate more productive self-feedback, our interventions need to be embedded into models of how learning strategies are enacted. The theory of self-regulated learning presents such models and "*refers to self-generated thoughts, feelings, and*

9 Turning Self-Assessment into Self-Feedback 155

actions that are planned and cyclically adapted to the attainment of personal goals" (Zimmerman, 2000, p. 14). The most prominent self-regulated learning models include the idea of self-feedback under the umbrella term of self-evaluation (Panadero et al., 2017). Beyond theoretical models, a fruitful line of empirical research has consistently shown that self-assessment interventions had a positive effect on student self-regulation and self-efficacy (Panadero et al., 2017).

Nevertheless, there seems to be tension. Within the assessment literature, especially within its formative niche, self-assessment is seen as an "instructional process used by the teacher as an educational resource" (Panadero & Alonso-Tapia, 2013, p. 554). In contrast, self-regulated learning scholars see it as a "process that pupils carry out to self-regulate" (p. 554). These differential paradigms have been translated into practice by formative assessment scholars focusing more on pedagogical and instructional aspects of self-assessment (e.g., Tan, 2012), whereas self-regulated learning scholars have focused on trying to understand the impact of self-assessment on cognitive, motivational, and emotional processes (e.g., Sitzmann et al., 2010). It seems it would be more beneficial to fuse both approaches to conceptualize how, from an instructional and learning perspectives, self-feedback can be effectively generated by learners. Butler and Winne (1995) presented initial attempts to bring together the two approaches as they anchored their work in self-regulated learning theory while reviewing the links between external and internal feedback. However, not much empirical research was published back in the day on this topic.

Luckily, we are reaching the point where self-assessment and self-regulated learning cross-disciplinary empirical research is gaining momentum. One example of such a trend would be a recent meta-analysis that showed the positive effects of self-assessment interventions on self-regulated learning (Panadero et al., 2017). Another example from be Nicol and McFarlane-Dick (2006) who presented a theoretical exploration of how seven principles of good feedback practice—that reflect on the self-feedback concept presented here—influenced students' self-regulation. Nicol and McFarlane-dick's approach is advantageous because, by being anchored within pedagogical foundations, it is easier to bring the concept of self-feedback into real classrooms. Finally, Panadero, Broadbent,

Boud, and Lodge (2019) have recently presented how formative assessment practices—including self-assessment—impact three self-regulated models. Through the use of graphical representations these authors clarify how assessment influence the students strategic learning behavior.

All in all, self-regulated learning conceptualizes students as both agentic, that is, responsible for their own learning and strategic, i.e., capable of using different strategies to reach their goals. This type of conceptualization is needed for self-feedback where students need to be active seekers of their own feedback while resorting to self-regulated learning to obtain such information.

Individual Characteristics and Interpersonal Variables

Lipnevich, Berg, and Smith (2016) proposed that student's individual characteristics (e.g., personality facets, prior achievement) affect student receptivity to feedback and their actions in response to teacher-provided feedback. It is safe to presume that individual characteristics would matter even more for self-assessment. After all, it is the person delivering feedback and evaluative judgments to him or herself, and whether or not a person views him or herself as a competent, self-efficacious, or conscientious person would affect the quality of self-feedback as well as subsequent actions. Hence, we need to understand how different students might variably benefit from self-assessment. Understanding these differences will be critical for our attempts to make self-assessment more productive.

For example, there is initial research examining differences between low and high achieving students' self-assessment accuracy (e.g., Boud, Lawson, & Thompson, 2013). Existing literature suggests that the average student has the most to gain from the process (e.g., Boud et al., 2013) with low achievers gaining the least (Sitzmann et al., 2010). If we were to understand better how students process self-feedback, we could be more effective in helping low achievers—a category of students that are in the greatest need of most support.

Further, there has been some interest in exploring gender differences in self-assessment. A recent meta-analysis on the effects of self-assessment interventions revealed that female students' self-efficacy increased more than males,' whereas self-regulatory strategies were the same for both genders (Panadero et al., 2017). Interestingly, gender differences in the perceived value of self-assessment are observed at the teacher level and can explain, at least to a degree, the aforementioned impacts of self-assessment on self-efficacy. Lipnevich and Gjikali (2019) reported initial evidence for such differences, with female teachers viewing self-assessment as more useful and beneficial than their male counterparts. Teacher reports on instructional practices matched the above finding, with female teachers reporting a more frequent implementation of self-assessment (medium effect sizes). This finding calls for further investigations, as well as clear communication of benefits of self-assessment to both male students and teachers. Articulating benefits and providing supports for effective generation of self-feedback should be advised to all instructors.

Also, it is not surprising there has been a number of studies showing that motivated students use more often self-assessment as a learning strategy (Ibabe & Jauregizar, 2010). Tapping into student motivation by activating their attainment, intrinsic, and utility values (e.g., Eccles & Wigfield, 2002) of self-feedback could be a boon to student achievement.

To our knowledge, self-assessment literature has not focused on individual characteristics for reasons that might seem obvious (i.e., it is one's self-evaluation). However, this gap needs to be corrected as a variety of individual factors may influence the quality of self-feedback that students generate. So, for example, future studies may explore whether students with different personality profiles would vary in their willingness to engage in self-feedback, and thus, explore opportunities for helping them to develop this important skill. Further, studies may examine student characteristics (e.g., personality, prior knowledge, gender), alone and in combination, to investigate potential differences in self-feedback delivery. After all, studies report differential responses to teacher-provided feedback depending on student characteristics (e.g., Lipnevich & Smith, 2009) and it is self to speculate that they will be pronounced in the context of self-feedback as well.

Evaluative Judgment: Changing the View from Task-Specific to Long-Term Learning

Lastly, it is important to situate self-feedback in a larger assessment paradigm to potentiate its implementation along with other assessment practices (e.g., peer assessment). Recently, there has been a push for evaluative judgment, which is defined as *"the capability to make decisions about the quality of work of self and others"* (Tai, Ajjawi, Boud, Dawson, & Panadero, 2018). The pedagogical idea behind is that in higher education we need to help students to develop the capacity to evaluate their own work and that of others. Importantly, students' development of evaluative judgment can only be achieved through a shift in how assessment and feedback are conceptualized and implemented in our universities. Our courses will need to offer opportunities to develop evaluative judgment which should be enhanced through activities such as peer assessment, formative teacher's feedback and, of course, self-feedback. These allow the students to develop their capacity to evaluate work via explicit instruction of the evaluative judgment's components (e.g., assessment criteria, standards) and a dialogic approach to feedback so that students are motivated to engage in recursive loops that will enhance students' self-feedback ability (Jonsson & Panadero, 2018; Winstone, Nash, Parker, & Rowntree, 2016). This way, helping students to become effective self-feedback agents should represent an instructional goal, as opposed to being a side activity, which is how self-assessment is implemented in many instances (Brown & Harris, 2013).

This idea of having self-feedback embedded in the curriculum has implications for our interventions. We are no longer asking students to self-assess for a particular task in our course; it is for a broader skill that implies developing self-feedback capabilities independently of the content task. That is, students need to know that when they approach a new task/course they need to look for assessment criteria, standards, exemplars, etc., to gain knowledge about the task. At the same time, they need to practice it before they can accurately estimate their learning and performance.

The Impact of Self-Feedback in the Leverage of Feedback Processes

In previous sections, we have presented different ideas on how to move from self-assessment to self-feedback. This shift will have a triple impact on students' learning. First, if they turn into advanced self-feedback agents, they will be adopting an active role in the feedback process, not only with themselves but also with the teachers. This means that, for example, that students will be more likely to ask for more precise and helpful feedback from teachers because by creating their own feedback, they would be capable of identifying where they are in comparison with where they are supposed to be and would be more inclined to ask for advice in regards to how to get there. Second, the more advanced self-assessment strategies students employ, the higher the chances that these will turn into long-term learning for the students, transcending contexts and academic domains. And, thirdly, it is our belief that teaching students to be effective generators of self-feedback is the ultimate goal of any instructional activity. We, as educators, provide feedback to help students succeed. However, we cannot always be there, so our goal is to teach students to generate great quality self-feedback and thus, not depend on us. Hence, self-feedback may represent one of the most important outcomes of any educational setting.

Conclusions

In this chapter, we focused on the concept of self-feedback proposing different areas for research and implementation and discussing its effects on student learning and performance. Self-feedback should be seen as the most formative use of self-assessment, in which the learners create their own feedback, one that is anchored in content accuracy, in the development of practice and expertise, and framed within self-regulated learning theories. We hope this chapter will encourage the field to redefine our approach to self-assessment and employ different pedagogical practices to help students to generate good quality self-feedback and thus achieve greater academic success.

References

Andrade, H. (2018). Feedback in the context of self-assessment. In A. A. Lipnevich & J. K. Smith (Eds.), *The Cambridge handbook of instructional feedback* (pp. 376–408). Cambridge: Cambridge University Press.

Andrade, H., & Valtcheva, A. (2009). Promoting learning and achievement through self-assessment. *Theory into Practice, 48*(1), 12–19. https://doi.org/10.1080/00405840802577544.

Bjork, E. L., Storm, B. C., & de Winstanley, P. A. (2010). *Learning from the consequences of retrieval: Another test effect.* In A. S. Benjamin (Ed.), *Successful remembering and successful forgetting: A festschrift in honor of Robert A. Bjork* (1st ed.). New York: Psychology Press.

Boud, D. (1999). Avoiding the traps: Seeking good practice in the use of self-assessment and reflection in professional courses. *Social Work Education, 18*(2), 121–132. https://doi.org/10.1080/02615479911220131.

Boud, D., & Falchikov, N. (1989). Quantitative studies of student self-assessment in higher-education: A critical analysis of findings. *Higher Education, 18*(5), 529–549. https://doi.org/10.1007/BF00138746.

Boud, D., Lawson, R., & Thompson, D. G. (2013). Does student engagement in self-assessment calibrate their judgement over time? *Assessment & Evaluation in Higher Education, 38*(8), 941–956. https://doi.org/10.1080/02602938.2013.769198.

Brown, G. T. L., Andrade, H., & Chen, F. (2015). Accuracy in student self-assessment: Directions and cautions for research. *Assessment in Education: Principles, Policy & Practice,* 1–14. https://doi.org/10.1080/0969594x.2014.996523.

Brown, G. T. L., & Harris, L. R. (2013). Student self-assessment. In J. McMillan (Ed.), *The Sage handbook of research on classroom assessment* (pp. 367–393). Thousand Oaks, CA: Sage.

Butler, D. L., & Winne, P. H. (1995). Feedback and self-regulated learning: A theoretical synthesis. *Review of Educational Research, 65*(3), 245–281. https://doi.org/10.3102/00346543065003245.

Dunning, D., Heath, C., & Suls, J. M. (2004). Flawed self-assessment: Implications for health, education, and the workplace. *Psychological Science in the Public Interest, 5*(3), 69–106. https://doi.org/10.1111/j.1529-1006.2004.00018.x.

Eccles, J. S., & Wigfield, A. (2002). Motivational beliefs, values, and goals. *Annual Review of Psychology, 53,* 109–132.

Eva, K. W., & Regehr, G. (2008). "I'll never play professional football" and other fallacies of self-assessment. *Journal of Continuing Education in the Health Professions, 28*(1), 14–19. https://doi.org/10.1002/chp.150.

Falchikov, N., & Boud, D. (1989). Student self-assessment in higher education: A meta-analysis. *Review of Educational Research, 59*(4), 395–430. https://doi.org/10.3102/00346543059004395.

Ibabe, I., & Jauregizar, J. (2010). Online self-assessment with feedback and metacognitive knowledge. *Higher Education, 59*(2), 243–258. https://doi.org/10.1007/s10734-009-9245-6.

Jonsson, A., & Panadero, E. (2018). Facilitating students' active engagement with feedback. In A. A. Lipnevich & J. K. Smith (Eds.), *The Cambridge handbook of instructional feedback.* Cambridge: Cambridge University Press.

Kirschner, P. A. (2002). Cognitive load theory: Implications of cognitive load theory on the design of learning. *Learning and Instruction, 12*(1), 1–10. https://doi.org/10.1016/S0959-4752(01)00014-7.

Lipnevich, A. A., Berg, D. A. G., & Smith, J. K. (2016). Toward a model of student response to feedback. In G. T. L. Brown & L. R. Harris (Eds.), *Handbook of human and social conditions in assessment* (pp. 169–185). New York: Routledge.

Lipnevich, A. A., & Gjikali, K. (2019, January). *What we know about feedback: Teacher beliefs and practices in a nutshell.* Paper presented at CUNY Graduate Student Summit, New York, NY.

Lipnevich, A. A., & Smith, J. K. (2009). Effects of differential feedback on students' examination performance. *Journal of Experimental Psychology: Applied, 15*(4), 319–333. https://doi.org/10.1037/a0017841.

Narciss, S. (2008). Feedback strategies for interactive learning tasks. In J. M. Spector, M. D. Merrill, J. J. G. van Merriënboer, & M. P. Driscoll (Eds.), *Handbook of research on educational communications and technology* (pp. 125–144). Mahwah, NJ: Lawrence Erlbaum.

Nicol, D., & McFarlane-Dick, D. (2006). Formative assessment and self-regulated learning: A model and seven principles of good feedback practice. *Studies in Higher Education, 31*(2), 199–218. https://doi.org/10.1080/03075070600572090.

Panadero, E., & Alonso-Tapia, J. (2013). Self-assessment: Theoretical and practical connotations. When it happens, how is it acquired and what to do to develop it in our students. *Electronic Journal of Research in Educational Psychology, 11*(2), 551–576. http://dx.doi.org/10.14204/ejrep.30.12200.

Panadero, E., Brown, G. T. L., & Strijbos, J. W. (2016a). The future of student self-assessment: A review of known unknowns and potential directions.

Educational Psychology Review, 28(4), 803–830. https://doi.org/10.1007/s10648-015-9350-2.

Panadero, E., Jonsson, A., & Botella, J. (2017). Effects of self-assessment on self-regulated learning and self-efficacy: Four meta-analyses. *Educational Research Review, 22,* 74–98. https://doi.org/10.1016/j.edurev.2017.08.004.

Panadero, E., Jonsson, A., & Strijbos, J. W. (2016b). Scaffolding self-regulated learning through self-assessment and peer assessment: Guidelines for classroom implementation. In D. Laveault & L. Allal (Eds.), *Assessment for learning: Meeting the challenge of implementation* (pp. 311–326). New York: Springer.

Panadero, E., Broadbent, J., Boud, D., & Lodge, J. M. (2019). Using formative assessment to influence self- and co-regulated learning: The role of evaluative judgement. *European Journal of Psychology of Education, 34*(3), 535–557. https://doi.org/10.1007/s10212-018-0407-8.

Ross, J. A. (2006). The reliability, validity, and utility of self-assessment. *Practical Assessment Research & Evaluation, 11.* Retrieved from http://pareonline.net/getvn.asp?v=11&n=10.

Sanchez, C. E., Atkinson, K. M., Koenka, A. C., Moshontz, H., & Cooper, H. (2017). Self-grading and peer-grading for formative and summative assessments in 3rd through 12th grade classrooms: A meta-analysis. *Journal of Educational Psychology,* No Pagination Specified. https://doi.org/10.1037/edu0000190.

Sitzmann, T., Ely, K., Brown, K. G., & Bauer, K. N. (2010). Self-assessment of knowledge: A cognitive learning or affective measure? *Academy of Management Learning & Education, 9*(2), 169–191.

Tai, J., Ajjawi, R., Boud, D., Dawson, P., & Panadero, E. (2018). Developing evaluative judgement: Enabling students to make decisions about the quality of work. *Higher Education, 76*(3), 467–481. https://doi.org/10.1007/s10734-017-0220-3.

Tan, K. H. K. (2012). *Student self-assessment: Assessment, learning and empowerment.* Singapore: Research Publishing.

Winstone, N. E., Nash, R. A., Parker, M., & Rowntree, J. (2016). Supporting learners' agentic engagement with feedback: A systematic review and a taxonomy of recipience processes. *Educational Psychologist,* 1–21. https://doi.org/10.1080/00461520.2016.1207538.

Yan, Z., & Brown, G. T. L. (2017). A cyclical self-assessment process: Towards a model of how students engage in self-assessment. *Assessment & Evaluation in Higher Education, 42*(8), 1247–1262. https://doi.org/10.1080/02602938.2016.1260091.

Zimmerman, B. J. (2000). Attaining self-regulation: A social cognitive perspective. In M. Boekaerts, P. R. Pintrich, & M. Zeidner (Eds.), *Handbook of self-regulation* (pp. 13–40). San Diego, CA: Academic Press.

10

How Debriefing Can Inform Feedback: Practices That Make a Difference

Margaret Bearman®, Walter Eppich® and Debra Nestel®

Introduction

Feedback has a bad reputation in higher education. Student satisfaction surveys often point to higher dissatisfaction levels with feedback than with other aspects of university education. This may relate to how educators and students conceive feedback, namely as explicit information regarding performance. However, while students may receive information—generally written or verbal comments on their work—they frequently ignore

---

M. Bearman (✉)
Centre for Research in Assessment and Digital Learning (CRADLE),
Deakin University, Geelong, VIC, Australia
e-mail: margaret.bearman@deakin.edu.au

W. Eppich
Northwestern University, Evanston, IL, USA
e-mail: w-eppich@northwestern.edu

D. Nestel
Monash University and University of Melbourne, Melbourne, VIC, Australia
e-mail: debra.nestel@monash.edu

© The Author(s) 2019
M. Henderson et al. (eds.), *The Impact of Feedback in Higher Education*,
https://doi.org/10.1007/978-3-030-25112-3_10

this "feedback" or simply may not understand what they might do differently. This problem of making no difference at all to student work has led to calls for "feedback that has an effect" on students (Jackel, Pearce, Radloff, & Edwards, 2017; Molloy et al., 2019, in press; Price, Handley, Millar, & O'Donovan, 2010).

Unfortunately, it may be difficult to work out what type of "effect" feedback is supposed to have on higher education students. Generally, feedback effects can be nebulous, tacit and, worryingly, harmful (Kluger & DeNisi, 1996). There are relatively few studies to provide educators with guidance. Some papers outline the ways in which feedback can boost the "know what" (declarative knowledge) and the "know how" (procedural knowledge) (Esterhazy & Damşa, 2017; Vardi, 2009). This is made more difficult because "feedback" is a contested term (Price et al., 2010), laden with assumptions (van der Leeuw, Teunissen, & van der Vleuten, 2018). In recent times, researchers highlight feedback as a process optimally integrated with educational design (Boud & Molloy, 2013). Current definitions of feedback, including the one proposed in Chapter 2 ("processes where the learner makes sense of the performance-relevant information to promote their learrning") emphasizes the role of the learner, the presence of "performance information" and the "effect" on the quality of work.

Outside higher education literature, an overlooked but related area of research and practice has a strong empirical base and a less contested definition. "Debriefing" refers to developmental conversations that take place after simulated or real work performances. These conversations most frequently occur as a group process. For example, a healthcare team comes together to debrief after a simulated or real resuscitation. Similarly, a trainee teacher can debrief with their mentor after teaching students. Drawing from Tannenbaum and Cerasoli (2013, p. 233), we define debriefing as: a "reflection on specific events or performance" episodes, with "developmental intent" "through iterative process of reflection and planning" drawing from at least one external source of information. Note that a facilitator is not necessarily required (Boet et al., 2011; Dine et al., 2008), nor do debriefings need to take a particular form or structure (Tannenbaum & Cerasoli, 2013). A particular variation in simulation is the "microdebrief" or "pause and discuss", which provide targeted conversations within short pauses during the learning activity (Eppich, Hunt, Duval-Arnould, Siddall, & Cheng, 2015; Flanagan, 2008).

These overviews of feedback and debriefing suggest that both are developmental sense-making activities drawing on information about a task or performance. In short, debriefing is a particular form of feedback. An extensive and long-standing body of debriefing literature shows its positive effects on what the learner does next (Tannenbaum & Cerasoli, 2013). Therefore, exploring productive pedagogical features associated with debriefing may provide guidance on how feedback can have "an effect". This chapter aims to identify debriefing practices that might inform how feedback processes may be conceptualized and enacted within higher education in new ways. Although evidence exists for debriefing in general, this chapter primarily focuses on debriefing in healthcare simulation as it represents the largest body of evidence (Tannenbaum & Cerasoli, 2013) and has a strongly articulated set of accepted practices (Krogh, Bearman, & Nestel, 2016). Moreover, simulation is a familiar modality within higher education (Lean, Moizer, Towler, & Abbey, 2006).

Debriefing in healthcare simulation is always associated with a real or simulated enactment, usually where students or trainees enact an authentic scenario taken from healthcare practice. To give a concrete example, consider a simulation-based learning activity, designed for medical students' development of effective patient-centred communication skills. The activity takes place in a mock consultation room, with one-way glass to an observation room. Four students attend a 3-hour session taking turns to either interview the simulated patient (actor) or observe four different scenarios. The facilitator briefs the students about the overall session and uses simulation as an educational method. Before each encounter, the facilitator also discusses the particular scenario with the individual assuming the role of a medical student on a general practice rotation. The simulation then unfolds: the student interacts with a simulated patient to discuss reasons why the patient's cold does not require a prescription for antibiotics. The other students and the facilitator observe the student through the one-way glass. Finally, the facilitator, four students and simulated patient all participate in a debriefing. This often commences with the role-playing student talking about how they felt during the encounter and their thoughts on what happened. The facilitator leads a complex and

168   M. Bearman et al.

comprehensive conversation about the performance, including a balance between strengths and potential areas of improvement. Finally, the facilitator closes the entire activity by leading a short summary and reflection session across all four scenarios. See Appendix 1 for a more comprehensive outline of the debriefing pedagogies.

This example of communication skills education illustrates a particular example of the complexity of debriefing practices in healthcare simulation. There are, however, many different kinds of simulation activities. For example, psychomotor skills, such as inserting a breathing tube into a mannequin, require a different educational approach to learning communication skills with a simulated patient. Complex team-based scenarios provide yet another type of experience. These scenarios involve the integration of clinical and teamwork skills in high-pressure situations, such as treating patients whose clinical status rapidly deteriorates and demands immediate life-saving intervention. While we treat simulation as a whole body of work for the purposes of this discussion, debriefing varies across different simulation modalities and educational purposes.

Evidence About the Impacts of Debriefing

Simulations and their associated debriefings have long-lasting and transformative effects on participants, often many years after the original experience (Bearman, Greenhill, & Nestel, 2019, in press). A range of quantitative studies supports debriefing as a means to improve performance (Cheng et al., 2014; Tannenbaum & Cerasoli, 2013) with a 2013 meta-analysis of debriefing indicating that debriefs improve performances by 25% (Tannenbaum & Cerasoli, 2013). The literature offers multiple examples of measurable gains associated with the presence of debriefing in healthcare simulation, including improved cardiopulmonary resuscitation quality (Dine et al., 2008) and improved retention of surgical knot-tying techniques (Xeroulis et al., 2007). The type of debriefing also makes a difference, although under what circumstances are less clear (Cheng et al., 2013; 2014; Van Heukelom, Begaz, & Treat, 2010). Tannenbaum and Cerasoli (2013) outlined three useful findings from their meta-analysis. Firstly, multimedia aids such as video did not affect the efficacy of the debriefing. Secondly, debriefings for teams and for individuals should occur differently. For example, a debriefing conducted to improve team function should occur with the team and take team-level performance into account; a debriefing focused on an individual should include judgements about the performance of the individual. Finally, the authors found that debriefing has similar impacts in simulated and real settings. This supports the contention that is not *simulation* per se that leads to learning but is the cumulative effect of the activity and the feedback that accompanies it.

The rest of this chapter explores how debriefing practices might inform feedback in higher education. We outline two major facets of debriefing, which we think have particular value for the feedback literature. The first of these explores how debriefing is embedded in experiential learning processes. The second considers the culture of debriefing in healthcare simulation. By "culture", we examine the habits of heads, hands and hearts (Shulman, 2005) that underpin debriefing practices.

The Embedded Nature of Debriefing

Within simulation, debriefing frequently comprises an integral part of the simulation design, likely significantly contributing to its effectiveness. We reflect on some of the specific conventions surrounding debriefing, which may lead to positive impacts upon learning.

Setting Up Expectations

Briefings (often called prebriefings) prepare learners for the entire simulation activity. They represent a key part of debriefing practice (Der Sahakian et al., 2015; Kneebone & Nestel, 2005; Rudolph, Raemer, & Simon, 2014) and a recent systematic review affirms that briefings improve learning (Tyerman, Luctkar-Flude, Graham, Coffey, & Olsen-Lynch, 2019). Experts agree on what the briefing phase entails (Der Sahakian et al., 2015; Rudolph et al., 2014; Tyerman et al., 2019). Briefings provide an opportunity to stress the developmental aspect of simulation and describe how the learning experience will unfold. They serve as an essential precursor to debriefing in several important ways as they: (a) declare expectations and standards; (b) clarify learners' needs; and (c) situate the activity in the broader educational experience.

Through briefings, simulation facilitators raise the goals of the task and the expected standards of performance (what Hattie & Timperley [2007] refer to as "feed up") (Cheng et al., 2018). This process allows joint agreement on criteria for success prior to the learning activity. Briefings also offer the opportunity to clarify the learners' needs. This can be a simple request for learners to raise their hands if they have completed a similar task, to more complex requests. For example, Kneebone and Nestel (2005, p. 88) describe asking simulation participants questions such as: "What are you hoping to learn during this exercise? Is there anything in particular that you would like us to observe?"

Briefings also outline expectations for any form of *debriefing*, both during or after the simulation. Ideally, this primes participants in three ways. Firstly, facilitators describe the debriefing process (including who participates and how the conversation will be facilitated) and the general topics for discussion within the debrief. In this way, learners commence the simulation aware of how they will interact with the fellow participants, debriefers and observers in the future. Secondly, the timing of the debriefing interactions is clarified. Facilitators indicate whether debriefing takes place "on the fly" within the simulation activity or after the activity ends. If the timing of debriefing is dynamic, facilitators must clearly communicate the logistics of how this happens in order to avoid misunderstandings. For example, learners or facilitators may use a hand signal to pause the simulation activity and initiate a short focused debriefing to help clarify confusion (McMullen et al., 2016). Finally, an effective briefing orients the learners to how the debriefing might inform future performances. See the table in Appendix 1, particularly rows 1, 2 and 3 for concrete examples of briefing within a healthcare simulation.

These briefing practices have parallels in higher education. Clearly stated expectations and standards often represent a key part of feedback and assessment within higher education, through activities such as co-constructing rubrics or use of exemplars (Ajjawi & Bearman, 2018). Boud and Molloy (2013) propose a model of feedback, Feedback Mark 2, in which learners must nominate what part of their work they would like

10 How Debriefing Can Inform Feedback ...   171

scrutinized. The positive experience of briefing practices attests to the value of this approach. However, the higher education literature inadequately addresses student control of feedback processes, particularly with respect to learners initiating the timing and tenor of conversations about their work. For example, students could signal their desire for comments on an assignment from faculty or peers. This is more than submitting a copy of the essay for feedback information, but rather a deeper consideration of how students request, record and react to insights from faculty or peers. The lessons from simulation suggest that the potential benefit for students outweighs any logistical challenges.

Activities That Generate Rich Performance Relevant Information

Both in simulation and workplace learning, useful information about a performance derives only partly from the educators' judgements. In information-rich environments, the context itself provides useful data for the learner, what van der Leeuw et al. (2018) call "performance relevant information" (PRI). PRI "focuses on how learners interpret their performance…in terms of what is relevant information for their learning" and "includes all potential sources of information for learning arising from the interpretation of one's performance and interaction" (van der Leeuw et al., 2018, p. 557). A fundamentally important aspect here is that learners determine what is relevant. While the authors frame PRI as a workplace phenomenon, this notion applies equally in all experiential learning settings. Thus, PRI also represents valuable learning cues in simulated learning environments, such as: the physical characteristics of the simulated patient; authentic responses of other team members; observation of those watching the simulation; and a video record of the performance. During structured debriefings, educators can explicitly highlight potential PRI in a learner-centred fashion (Cheng et al., 2016). Such conversations enable sense-making of simulated encounters so that learners can derive learning that is relevant for them (Rudolph, Simon, Raemer, & Eppich, 2008). In addition, emerging work highlights the potential of using simulations to sensitize medical learners to potential sources of PRI dur-

172   M. Bearman et al.

ing team interactions, as this will assist future workplace learning (Eppich, Rethans, Dornan, & Teunissen, 2018; Kneebone & Nestel, 2005).

This work on PRI highlights the benefit of situating learning activities in generative environments. Esterhazy points to the productive feedback opportunities located within authentic disciplinary tasks with many tutors. Rich, generative environments allow learners to orient themselves to useful cues, not only in order to complete the task at hand, but for their future career. Having said this, the simulation experience suggests additional key lessons: (a) environments must be suited to the learner and (b) novices and experts perceive cues differently (Kneebone, 2009). In other words, replicating workplaces in order to produce "authentic" cues does not always benefit learning.

Iteration and the Role of Microdebriefing

Simulation offers key advantages, namely allowing learners to repeat tasks multiple times, taking the information from successive debriefings on board. This principle is often formalized through the use of concurrent facilitation strategies, which steers performances as they unfold (Eppich et al., 2015; Hunt et al., 2014). Promoting successful performance serves as a guiding principle for such approaches. For example, when medical trainees prepare to care for patients in cardiac arrest, rapid cycles of practice-microdebrief-practice allow trainees to apply feedback information immediately under the watchful guidance of an educator coach (Eppich et al., 2015). The microdebriefings, embedded within brief pauses in the performance, maximize learners' opportunity to refine their performance and *experience* success rather than merely *discussing* how they might achieve it. This strategy seems to have particular benefit when learners strive to master algorithmic approaches to particular clinical situations.

This microdebriefing example demonstrates the importance of opportunities to enact changes immediately. Terminal (post-simulation) debriefing has benefit when learners have a chance to put the information into action (Auerbach, Kessler, & Foltin, 2011). Evidence is also mounting that concurrent debriefings also have a real impact on practice (Hunt et al., 2014). However, Cheng et al.'s (2014) systematic literature review suggests that this matter is not straightforward. The authors reported three studies examining the value of terminal versus concurrent briefing. One study comparing surgical knot-tying concluded that there was no difference in learning; one study on learning endoscopy skills concluded that concurrent briefing was more effective; and finally, one study looking at medical resuscitation concluded that terminal briefing was more effective.

Recent work is exploring the benefit of focused microdebriefings for *whole team* performance. Studies have explored bouts of concurrent team reflection *during* performance events characterized by high time pressure and uncertainty. These brief moments of team reflection focused on team goals, processes and strategies to improve current and future performance (Schmutz & Eppich, 2017). Larger medical teams perform better during emergency simulations when they engage in periodic bursts of shared reflection (Schmutz, Lei, Eppich, & Manser, 2018).

These examples of effective mid-performance feedback for both individuals and teams hold potential value for higher education. In particular, they offer strategies for in-class or online tasks that often mostly contain informal feedback opportunities. (A concrete illustration of such a task is given by Esterhazy and Damsa, who describe the rich informal group and tutor interactions supporting undergraduate biology students' graphing activity.) This type of small-scale social activity, whether online or in-class, could benefit from structured iterations of microfeedback. For example, if students undertake a series of low stakes but challenging tasks around a particular concept, then they can microdebrief one task before tackling the next one. Similarly, if they are working in teams on authentic projects or problems, then moments of pausing and focusing on team performance may also help keep the group on track and calibrate team function.

The Culture of Debriefing

The previous section explores the advantages of integrating the learning activity and the feedback approach. This next section considers the cultural traditions of debriefing in healthcare simulation. Interestingly, debriefing has a different origin to feedback, which is fundamentally about performance information. Debriefing commenced in the military, whereby those who had completed dangerous missions "talked through" their experience (Samter et al., 1993). This almost therapeutic practice shifted over time to include a developmental focus. This history leads to a somewhat different set of assumptions, values and norms to those underlying feedback in education, which we refer to as the "culture" of debriefing in healthcare simulation. This culture includes both the tacit habits of hands, head and heart associated with a certain practice as well as strategies to deliberately cultivate it. We outline some key points regarding the culture of debriefing below.

Values-Based Debriefing

A common myth in health professional education is that if you know the right words, then you will be able to "deliver" feedback (Molloy et al., 2019). However, feedback is more than learning a series of stock phrases. As Telio et al.'s (2015) work on the educational alliance suggests, feedback not only represents information, but also incorporates the dynamics of a relationship in which learners perceive an interpersonal bond as well as shared goals and tasks. A relational focus may be a particular feature of feedback within the healthcare environment (Armson, Lockyer, Zetkulic, Könings, & Sargeant, 2019).

An interview study of expert debriefers with immersive healthcare simulations (Krogh et al., 2016) indicated that experts hold defined philosophies of debriefing. These revolved around values such as dedication, honesty, curiosity, learner-centredness and a desire to help learners improve clinical practice. These values were seen as the core of debriefing practice, not the micro-skills of debriefing such as frameworks and asking questions.

Rudolph et al. (2014) draw from the literature and their own expert practice to describe how values are essential to briefings, and by extension, debriefing. In this work, the authors propose that with adequate briefings, the simulation environment can offer a "psychologically safe" place, where learners can take risks. Part of this is values-based: the teachers must respect the learners' internal sense-making and underpin the learning with two assumptions. Educators assume that learners (a) work "towards a goal as best he or she could in the moment" and (b) are "capable of competent action and self-transformation" (Rudolph et al., 2014, p. 343). In other words, educators must acknowledge the part learners play in their own learning and assume that learners intend to learn and believe in their capacity for successful completion. These assumptions may help educators provide useful comments to learners they more readily accept. They reorient the role of the information provider from "telling" to respecting, accepting and believing learners.

Keeping these values in mind may support better feedback practices in higher education. If educators can draw on the values espoused by the debriefing literature, then they may reframe their feedback comments towards how to achieve and what has been achieved rather than what has not been achieved. Current faculty development generally focuses on the mechanics of feedback, for example such as what to say or write or design. Educators may profit by focusing on both the developmental value of feedback and the role of the learner in their own learning, rather than on "how to do feedback". Interestingly, the debriefing experiences shows that values propagate "rhizomatically" (Deleuze & Guattari, 1987), that is to say, they propagate as social practices as much as through a centralized approach to training.

Embracing Emotions: The Learning Potential in Productive Tensions

Debriefing involves "meaning-making" in all senses of the word—not just in terms of the cognitive development—but the affective and interpersonal dimensions as well. This is a key part of simulation as emotions are expected and therefore accounted for in the debrief approach. Debriefing allows for the "venting" phase, whereby learners release their emotions. Debriefers are asked to consciously track and engage participants, to ensure that they are not overwhelmed by emotion. Helping participants make connections between their emotions and their performance is a signature of many simulations in health care and working with emotions comprises part of the debriefer's role (Janzen et al., 2016). Actively probing for emotional states and linking them with performance contrasts with many pedagogical approaches to feedback. See Row 4 in the table within Appendix 1 for an example of working with emotions when debriefing a simulation.

We should highlight here that unpleasant emotions have the potential to influence learning positively. Eppich, Dornan, Rethans, and Teunissan (2019) interviewed 17 doctors-in-training about their experiences engaging in patient care related telephone talk with other health professionals. The authors found that learning through work-related telephone talk was partly driven by productive conversational tensions. These productive conversational tensions arose from experiencing and dealing with tensions related to: hierarchy, pushback and uncertainty. As a specific example, pushback occurs when a conversation partner rejects a suggestion or contribution without due consideration, something doctors-in-training reported as unpleasant. These moments of productive conversational tensions, however, provided doctors-in-training with moments of valuable feedback about their ability to deal with these tensions in the spirit of performance relevant information discussed previously. Of course, there is a fine line between productive tensions and disruptive behaviour and frank conflict, the latter of which is highly unproductive. Nonetheless, these productive tensions seemed to motivate junior doctors to modify their telephone talk in future encounters. Further, during these telephone interactions with other health professionals, astute doctors-in-training noted implicit or "disguised feedback" in the form of conversational interruptions and questions that complemented productive conversational tensions as important learning cues (Eppich et al., 2018). We surmise that this notion of productive conversation tension has relevance for feedback and debriefing conversations in general. While we do not advocate for creating tension intentionally, in our view educators may not need to smooth over all tensions during feedback and debriefing since there may some positive influence on learning.

The role of emotions in feedback is well recognized but is often seen as something to reduce and manage (see Chapter 6). Given debriefing's history as an almost therapeutic process, it is unsurprising that key practices acknowledge and embrace emotions. This suggests that in some higher education contexts, when a student is asked to comment or reflect on their performance or on others views of their performance, the first question from the educator might be "how do you feel?", while the last question might be: "how do you feel now?" In this way, students can come to recognize the key role that emotions play in learning, without "managing" them or "reducing" them.

Improvement Through Debriefing the Debriefers

Simulation facilitators must invest time and effort to develop their debriefing skills. A focus on continual professional development is an essential part of expert debriefing practice (Krogh et al., 2016). Since participation in multi-day faculty development events may be prohibitive for some, peer coaching embedded within authentic teaching experiences represents an often untapped development opportunity. In both settings, a range of tools outline standards of debriefing behaviours and these can structure peer observation and feedback. These tools allow peers to observe a debriefing in both simulated and real educational scenarios and afterwards discuss the performance with the debriefer, often with a video recording.

Two prominent consensus standards address debriefer behaviours.

* The *Objective Structured Assessment of Debriefing* (OSAD) (Arora et al., 2012) comprises eight categories. An example of both the OSAD as a tool and of debriefing overall is provided in Appendix 1, where we outline associated exemplar practices.
* The *Debriefing Assessment for Simulation in Health care* (DASH) (Brett-Fleegler et al., 2012; Simon, Rudolph, & Raemer, 2009) comprises six elements related to: (1) establishing a foundation for a supportive learning environment; (2) maintaining an engaging learning context; (3) structuring the conversation; (4) promoting engaging discussion; (5) identifying and exploring performance gaps; and (6) helping trainees achieve or sustain good performance.

Use of such debriefing assessment instruments helps create shared understandings and expectations within simulation programs (Cheng et al., 2017).

Peer assessment within faculty development is not unknown in higher education; for example, peer review of teaching is an accepted practice,

178   M. Bearman et al.

although not necessarily frequently employed. More commonly, teacher moderation of assessments by building joint consensus around grades is an example of how peers can work together in higher education. However, peer assessment of *feedback* could radically change what teachers do by: identifying valuable approaches in certain contexts; improving individual performance; and building a culture of feedback based on shared values.

Implications for Feedback in Higher Education

This brief analysis outlines the reasonable evidence that debriefings positively influence performance. It also suggests that the impact of debriefing may stem from: (1) its embedded nature with the entire learning activity and (2) the development of a culture which encourages learner-centred values, productive tensions and lifelong development. These have sizeable implications for feedback practice.

Debriefing practice involves more than focusing only on what happens after a learning activity ends, but also includes critical educator behaviours before the activity as well. Simulation practitioners routinely prepare learners for the task at hand, ensuring learners know the feedback processes and their own contribution to learning. Although this type of briefing is not yet "essential" in higher education, we suggest this discussion is critical for both learners and educators. Moreover, while simulation naturally generates valuable PRI for learners and educators to assimilate, this does not apply to all activities in higher education. In order to improve feedback processes, educators may have to give some thought to how the tasks generate rich PRI. Finally, evidence that explores the different timing of debriefing also has potential application in higher education. It may be valuable for educators to consider the question: when is "terminal" feedback more or less useful?

A "values-based" approach to feedback already occurs by default as practitioners adopt certain models and approaches to feedback. However, the debriefing literature suggests these underlying values are more important than generally articulated. The current "culture" of debriefing encourages educators consider the following: (a) hold learners in "positive regard"

(Rudolph et al., 2014); (b) acknowledge the role of emotions and productive tensions (Eppich et al., 2019); and (c) constantly improve their debriefing in line with consensus standards (OSAD, DASH). If educators can similarly seek to interrogate the fundamental values underpinning feedback practices and focus on integrating them into their work, then we believe this will help build feedback that "makes a difference".

Appendix 1: Debriefing Pedagogies and the Objective Structured Assessment of Debriefing (OSAD)

This form illustrates both exemplar debriefing behaviours and the OSAD (London Handbook for Debriefing, n.d.). It does so through recording facilitator's practices from the example of a communication skills training simulation. For ease, we have named the facilitator as Dr Chan and the simulated patient as Mr Lee. Scores have not been presented here since our purpose is to illustrate what a simulation facilitator might do in this type of debriefing. The observations are applied to the whole session including the briefing. While we don't provide any improvement oriented observations, it is possible to see how the OSAD could be used for this purpose (Table 10.1).

Table 10.1 Debriefing pedagogies and OSAD (London Handbook for Debriefing, n.d., pg 13)

Category	Description	Observations
1. Approach	"Manner in which the facilitator conducts the debriefing session, their level of enthusiasm and positivity when appropriate, showing interest in the learners by establishing and maintaining rapport and finishing the session on an upbeat note"	Dr Chan warmly welcomed the students to the session—smiling, with a handshake and indicating where the students might sit. She seemed very student-centred, giving them her complete attention. She asked the student about the curriculum activities they had been doing immediately before the session At the end of the session, Dr Chan thanked the simulated patient and the students for their full participation and that she looked forward to meeting the students again after they had had the opportunity to practice their skills on clinical placements. Again, she shook hands and smiled as they left
2. Establishes learning environment	"Introduction of the simulation/learning session to the learner(s) by clarifying what is expected of them during the debriefing, emphasizing ground rules of confidentiality and respect for others and encouraging the learners to identify their own learning objectives"	Establishing the learning environment mainly took place at the beginning of the session. Dr Chan took time to orient the students to the structure of the session, the physical environment—showing them the consultation and observation rooms. She arranged the chairs in the observation room in a circle so that they could all easily make eye contact with each other during the briefing and debriefing. She asked the students about their prior experiences of learning with simulated patients—what they liked, what they did not, what was valuable and what was not. She outlined the learning objectives and invited the students to respond to them relative to their experiences—what they have found easy, what they have found hard and what they would like to be observed. She also asked the students to share their specific learning objectives and if they had any concerns about either the simulation or the proposed scenarios. She also asked students to treat the simulation as if it was an encounter with a real patient and as such professional behaviour was expected within the simulation and in the surrounding discussions. Dr Chan checked in with each of them for their personal commitment

(continued)

Table 10.1 (continued)

Category	Description	Observations
3. Engagement of learners	"Active involvement of all learners in the debriefing discussions, by asking open questions to explore their thinking and using silence to encourage their input, without the facilitator talking for most of the debriefing, to ensure that deep rather than surface learning occurs"	Dr Chan engaged the students by letting them know the logistics for the whole session and her expectations of them. She sought their agreement. Dr Chan nominated a student to use a patient-centred communication skills rating form in each encounter and to be prepared to share their ratings with the interviewing student. The other two observing students were also given observation tasks that varied depending on the scenario (e.g. building on a learning point from the previous scenario). Dr Chan gave the students an opportunity to pause and reflect immediately before the debriefing began. She made sure that each student had an opportunity to contribute to discussions across the session
4. Reaction	"Establishing how the simulation/learning session impacted emotionally on the learners"	Dr Chan explored and/or acknowledged the students' feelings before and after each scenario and at the end of the session. She helped the students to make links between their feelings and their behaviour building awareness of this state. She also invited Mr Lee to share if he had identified the students' emotions within the scenario. The observers' emotions were also sought at particular times across the session since learning can occur for all participants irrespective of whether they are observer or interviewer

(continued)

Table 10.1 (continued)

Category	Description	Observations
5. Reflection	"Self-reflection of events that occurred in the simulation/learning session in a step-by-step factual manner, clarifying any technical clinical issues at the start, to allow ongoing reflection from all learners throughout the analysis and application phases, linking to previous experiences"	Dr Chan supported reflection in three ways. Firstly, as soon as the simulation had finished and the interviewing student and Mr Lee had entered the observation room where the debriefing took place, she asked the students to pause for a minute. She requested students to think about what had just happened in the simulation, how it related to their prior experiences, their expectations, to the learning objectives and anything else they noticed. Secondly, towards the end of each debriefing, she summarized what had been discussed and asked the students to identify something that was especially meaningful for their own practice that they might take forward to the next scenario. Thirdly, at the end of the session, students were invited to draw together their learning from each scenario and think about how and when they would maintain and extend their patient-centred communication skills in real patient encounters
6. Analysis	"Eliciting the thought processes that drove a learner's actions, using specific examples of observable behaviours, to allow the learner to make sense of the simulation/learning session events"	After students had shared their judgements of their own performance, Dr Chan asked them to explain why they had asked questions in a particular sequence, noticed (or not) verbal and emotional cues from the simulated patient or made little use of transition statements as they changed topics, etc. Mr Lee was also invited to ask the students about why they had used specific communication skills during the encounter. He was encouraged to offer his preferences in skills to help the students appreciate his patient perspective from within the encounter. The communication skills rating form was used as a benchmark for expected behaviours although not every skill was explored in every scenario

(continued)

Table 10.1 (continued)

Category	Description	Observations
7. Diagnosis	"Enabling the learner to identify their performance gaps and strategies for improvement, targeting only behaviours that can be changed, and thus providing structured and objective feedback on the simulation/learning session"	Dr Chan invited the interviewing student to be the first participant to verbalize how they thought they had performed in each scenario. She varied this approach, sometimes encouraging a focus on what had been done well before moving to areas for development, while at other times enabling the student to simply share their judgements as they wished. One student was visibly upset by their performance, and so Dr Chan shifted the order of sharing information enabling the student to gain composure and offer their experience. All the students and Mr Lee participated in building a profile of the performance highlighting strengths and areas for development, exploring why they had occurred and what could be done to maintain or improve the performance. Dr Chan also returned to the student specific learning objectives (if there were any) and made some judgements and strategies for development as required
8. Application	"Summary of the learning points and strategies for improvement that have been identified by the learner(s) during the debrief and how these could be applied to change their future clinical practice"	Dr Chan had allocated individual students the task of summarizing learning points from each scenario and that she expected this to be shared. At the end of the session, these learning points were jointly distilling to three key learning points that the students considered relative to their clinical placements. The students agreed that they would undertake occasional peer observation of interviewing while on clinical placements with these three points in mind

References

Ajjawi, R., & Bearman, M. (2018). Problematising standards: Representation or performance? In *Developing evaluative judgement in higher education* (pp. 57–66): Abingdon: Routledge.

Armson, H., Lockyer, J. M., Zetkulic, M., Könings, K. D., & Sargeant, J. (2019). Identifying coaching skills to improve feedback use in postgraduate medical education. *Medical Education, 53*(5). https://doi.org/10.1111/medu.13818.

Arora, S., Ahmed, M., Paige, J., Nestel, D., Runnacles, J., Hull, L., ... Sevdalis, N. (2012). Objective structured assessment of debriefing: Bringing science to the art of debriefing in surgery. *Annals of surgery, 256*(6), 982–988. https://doi.org/10.1097/sla.0b013e3182610c91.

Auerbach, M., Kessler, D., & Foltin, J. C. (2011). Repetitive pediatric simulation resuscitation training. *Pediatric Emergency Care, 27*(1), 29–31. https://doi.org/10.1097/pec.0b013e3182043f3b.

Bearman, M., Greenhill, J., & Nestel, D. (2019, in press). The power of simulation: A large-scale narrative analysis of learners' experiences. *Medical Education, 53*(4). https://doi.org/10.1111/medu.13747.

Boet, S., Bould, M. D., Bruppacher, H. R., Desjardins, F., Chandra, D. B., & Naik, V. N. (2011). Looking in the mirror: Self-debriefing versus instructor debriefing for simulated crises. *Critical Care Medicine, 39*(6), 1377–1381. https://doi.org/10.1097/CCM.0b013e31820eb8be.

Boud, D., & Molloy, E. (2013). Rethinking models of feedback for learning: The challenge of design. *Assessment & Evaluation in Higher Education, 38*(6), 698–712. https://doi.org/10.1080/02602938.2012.691462.

Brett-Fleegler, M., Rudolph, J., Eppich, W., Monuteaux, M., Fleegler, E., Cheng, A., & Simon, R. (2012). Debriefing assessment for simulation in healthcare: Development and psychometric properties. *Simulation in Healthcare, 7*(5), 288–294. https://doi.org/10.1097/sih.0b013e3182620228.

Cheng, A., Eppich, W., Grant, V., Sherbino, J., Zendejas, B., & Cook, D. A. (2014). Debriefing for technology-enhanced simulation: A systematic review and meta-analysis. *Medical Education, 48*(7), 657–666. https://doi.org/10.1111/medu.12432.

Cheng, A., Grant, V., Huffman, J., Burgess, G., Szyld, D., Robinson, T., & Eppich, W. (2017). Coaching the debriefer: Peer coaching to improve debriefing quality in simulation programs. *Simulation in Healthcare, 12*(5), 319–325. https://doi.org/10.1097/SIH.0000000000000232.

Cheng, A., Hunt, E. A., Donoghue, A., Nelson-McMillan, K., Nishisaki, A., LeFlore, J., ... EXPRESS Investigators. (2013). Examining pediatric resuscitation education using simulation and scripted debriefing: A multicenter randomized trial. *JAMA Pediatrics, 167*(6), 528–536. https://doi.org/10.1001/jamapediatrics.2013.1389.

Cheng, A., Morse, K. J., Rudolph, J., Arab, A. A., Runnacles, J., & Eppich, W. (2016). Learner-centered debriefing for health care simulation education: Lessons for faculty development. *Simulation in Healthcare, 11*(1), 32–40. https://doi.org/10.1097/sih.0000000000000136.

Cheng, A., Nadkarni, V. M., Mancini, M. B., Hunt, E. A., Sinz, E. H., Merchant, R. M., ... Auerbach, M. (2018). Resuscitation education science: Educational strategies to improve outcomes from cardiac arrest: A scientific statement from the American Heart Association. *Circulation,* e82–e122. https://doi.org/10.1161/cir.0000000000000583.

Deleuze, G., & Guattari, F. (1987). *A thousand plateaus: Capitalism and schizophrenia.* Minneapolis: University of Minnesota Press.

Der Sahakian, G., Alinier, G., Savoldelli, G., Oriot, D., Jaffrelot, M., & Lecomte, F. (2015). Setting conditions for productive debriefing. *Simulation & Gaming, 46*(2), 197–208. https://doi.org/10.1177/1046878115576105.

Dine, C. J., Gersh, R. E., Leary, M., Riegel, B. J., Bellini, L. M., & Abella, B. S. (2008). Improving cardiopulmonary resuscitation quality and resuscitation training by combining audiovisual feedback and debriefing. *Critical Care Medicine, 36*(10), 2817–2822. https://doi.org/10.1097/CCM.0b013e318186fe37.

Eppich, W., Dornan, T., Rethans, J.-J., & Teunissen, P. W. (2019). "Learning the lingo": A grounded theory study of telephone talk in clinical education. *Academic Medicine,* Publish Ahead of Print. https://doi.org/10.1097/acm.0000000000002713.

Eppich, W., Hunt, E. A., Duval-Arnould, J. M., Siddall, V. J., & Cheng, A. (2015). Structuring feedback and debriefing to achieve mastery learning goals. *Academic Medicine, 90*(11), 1501–1508. https://doi.org/10.1097/ACM.0000000000000934.

Eppich, W., Rethans, J.-J., Dornan, T., & Teunissen, P. W. (2018). Learning how to learn using simulation: Unpacking disguised feedback using a qualitative analysis of doctors' telephone talk. *Medical Teacher, 40*(7), 661–667. https://doi.org/10.1080/0142159X.2018.1465183.

Esterhazy, R., & Damşa, C. (2017). Unpacking the feedback process: An analysis of undergraduate students' interactional meaning-making of feedback comments. *Studies in Higher Education*, 1–15. https://doi.org/10.1080/03075079. 2017.1359249.

Flanagan, B. (2008). Debriefing: Theory and technique. In R. Riley (Ed.), *Manual of simulation in healthcare* (pp. 155–170). Oxford: Oxford University Press.

Hattie, J., & Timperley, H. (2007). The power of feedback. *Review of Educational Research, 77*(1), 81–112. https://doi.org/10.3102/003465430298487.

Hunt, E. A., Duval-Arnould, J. M., Nelson-McMillan, K. L., Bradshaw, J. H., Diener-West, M., Perretta, J. S., & Shilkofski, N. A. (2014). Pediatric resident resuscitation skills improve after "Rapid Cycle Deliberate Practice" training. *Resuscitation, 85*(7), 945–951. https://doi.org/10.1016/j.resuscitation.2014. 02.025.

Jackel, B., Pearce, J., Radloff, A., & Edwards, D. (2017). *Assessment and feedback in higher education: A review of literature for the higher education academy*. Retrieved from https://www.heacademy.ac.uk/system/files/hub/download/acer_assessment.pdf.

Janzen, K. J., Jeske, S., MacLean, H., Harvey, G., Nickle, P., Norenna, L., ... McLellan, H. (2016). Handling strong emotions before, during, and after simulated clinical experiences. *Clinical Simulation in Nursing, 12*(2), 37–43. https://doi.org/10.1016/j.ecns.2015.12.004.

Kluger, A. N., & DeNisi, A. (1996). The effects of feedback interventions on performance: A historical review, a meta-analysis, and a preliminary feedback intervention theory. *Psychological Bulletin, 119*(2), 254–284.

Kneebone, R. (2009). Perspective: Simulation and transformational change: The paradox of expertise. *Academic Medicine, 84*(7), 954–957.

Kneebone, R., & Nestel, D. (2005). Learning clinical skills—The place of simulation and feedback. *The Clinical Teacher, 2*(2), 86–90. https://doi.org/10. 1111/j.1743-498X.2005.00042.x.

Krogh, K., Bearman, M., & Nestel, D. (2016). "Thinking on your feet"—A qualitative study of debriefing practice. *Advances in Simulation, 1*(1), 12. https://doi.org/10.1186/s41077-016-0011-4.

Lean, J., Moizer, J., Towler, M., & Abbey, C. (2006). Simulations and games: Use and barriers in higher education. *Active Learning in Higher Education, 7*(3), 227–242. https://doi.org/10.1177/1469787406069056.

McMullen, M., Wilson, R., Fleming, M., Mark, D., Sydor, D., Wang, L., ... Burjorjee, J. E. (2016). "Debriefing-on-Demand": A pilot assessment of using a "Pause button" in medical simulation. *Simulation in Healthcare, 11*(3), 157–163. https://doi.org/10.1097/sih.0000000000000140.

Molloy, E., Bearman, M., Ajjawi, R., Ryan, A., Noble, C., & Rudland, J. (2019). Challenging feedback myths: Values, learner involvement and promoting effects beyond the immediate task. *Medical Education.* https://doi.org/10.1111/medu.13802.

Price, M., Handley, K., Millar, J., & O'Donovan, B. (2010). Feedback: All that effort, but what is the effect? *Assessment & Evaluation in Higher Education, 35*(3), 277–289. https://doi.org/10.1080/02602930903541007.

Rudolph, J. W., Raemer, D. B., & Simon, R. (2014). Establishing a safe container for learning in simulation: The role of the presimulation briefing. *Simulation in Healthcare, 9*(6), 339–349. https://doi.org/10.1097/sih.0000000000000047.

Rudolph, J. W., Simon, R., Raemer, D. B., & Eppich, W. J. (2008). Debriefing as formative assessment: Closing performance gaps in medical education. *Academic Emergency Medicine, 15*(11), 1010–1016. https://doi.org/10.1111/j.1553-2712.2008.00248.x.

Samter, J., Fitzgerald, M. L., Braudaway, C. A., Leeks, D., Padgett, M. B., Swatz, A. L., ... Dellinger, N. F. (1993). From military origin to therapeutic application. *Journal of Psychosocial Nursing and Mental Health Services, 31*(2), 23–27.

Schmutz, J. B., & Eppich, W. J. (2017). Promoting learning and patient care through shared reflection: A conceptual framework for team reflexivity in health care. *Academic Medicine, 92*(11), 1555–1563. https://doi.org/10.1097/ACM.0000000000001688.

Schmutz, J. B., Lei, Z., Eppich, W. J., & Manser, T. (2018). Reflection in the heat of the moment: The role of in-action team reflexivity in health care emergency teams. *Journal of Organizational Behavior, 39*(6), 749–765. https://doi.org/10.1002/job.2299.

Shulman, L. S. (2005). Signature pedagogies in the professions. *Daedalus, 134*(3), 52–59.

Simon, R., Rudolph, J., & Raemer, D. B. (2009). Debriefing assessment for simulation in healthcare. Retrieved from https://harvardmedsim.org/debriefing-assessment-for-simulation-in-healthcare-dash/.

Tannenbaum, S. I., & Cerasoli, C. P. (2013). Do team and individual debriefs enhance performance? A meta-analysis. *Human Factors, 55*(1), 231–245. https://doi.org/10.1177/0018720812448394.

Telio, S., Ajjawi, R., & Regehr, G. (2015). The "educational alliance" as a framework for reconceptualizing feedback in medical education. *Academic Medicine, 90*(5), 609–614. https://doi.org/10.1097/acm.0000000000000560.

The London handbook for debriefing: Enhancing performance debriefing in clinical and simulated settings. (n.d.). London: Imperial College.

Tyerman, J., Luctkar-Flude, M., Graham, L., Coffey, S., & Olsen-Lynch, E. (2019). A systematic review of health care presimulation preparation and briefing effectiveness. *Clinical Simulation in Nursing, 27,* 12–25. https://doi.org/10.1016/j.ecns.2018.11.002.

van der Leeuw, R. M., Teunissen, P. W., & van der Vleuten, C. P. M. (2018). Broadening the scope of feedback to promote its relevance to workplace learning. *Academic Medicine, 93*(4), 556–559. https://doi.org/10.1097/ACM.0000000000001962.

Van Heukelom, J. N., Begaz, T., & Treat, R. (2010). Comparison of post-simulation debriefing versus in-simulation debriefing in medical simulation. *Simulation in Healthcare, 5*(2), 91–97. https://doi.org/10.1097/SIH.0b013e3181be0d17.

Vardi, I. (2009). The relationship between feedback and change in tertiary student writing in the disciplines. *International Journal of Teaching and Learning in Higher Education, 20*(3), 350–361.

Xeroulis, G. J., Park, J., Moulton, C.-A., Reznick, R. K., LeBlanc, V., & Dubrowski, A. (2007). Teaching suturing and knot-tying skills to medical students: A randomized controlled study comparing computer-based video instruction and (concurrent and summary) expert feedback. *Surgery, 141*(4), 442–449. https://doi.org/10.1016/j.surg.2006.09.012.

11

Impact of Personalized Feedback: The Case of Coaching and Learning Change Plans

Jocelyn M. Lockyer, Heather A. Armson,
Karen D. Könings, Marygrace Zetkulic
and Joan Sargeant

Introduction

Acceptance and use of feedback, in the health care setting, is a complex interplay involving the recipient, the educator, the delivery mechanism(s), the context, and the intended outcomes (Colquhoun et al., 2017; Lau et al., 2016; Michie, van Stralen, & West, 2011; Ramani, Könings, Mann, Pisarski, & van der Vleuten, 2018; Winstone, Nash, Parker, & Rowntree, 2017). As noted by a postgraduate (resident) trainee in the context of feedback in the hospital setting:

J. M. Lockyer (✉) · H. A. Armson
University of Calgary, Calgary, AB, Canada
e-mail: lockyer@ucalgary.ca

H. A. Armson
e-mail: armson@ucalgary.ca

K. D. Könings
School of Health Professions Education,
Maastricht University, Maastricht, The Netherlands
e-mail: kd.konings@maastrichtuniversity.nl

© The Author(s) 2019
M. Henderson et al. (eds.), *The Impact of Feedback in Higher Education*,
https://doi.org/10.1007/978-3-030-25112-3_11

... you're interacting with multiple groups of people—with people that know less than you, know more than you, your peers. And synthesizing that information, doing different things and watching what happens to the patient. You are kind of gathering, well—"The attending [supervisor] feels this way, the fellow [senior peer] feels this way, the intern [peer] thinks this, and I think this." And you see how the patient goes through that. And based on that you kind of see what the outcome of your actions was. Was the attending right? Was I right? Was there not a right answer and the patient was sick either way? (Sargeant et al., 2010)

Learners find it difficult to self-assess (Sargeant et al., 2010) and to understand and use feedback to improve knowledge, skills, and attitudes. Feedback comes from many sources—internal (e.g., perceptions about one's work, beliefs about what worked) and external (e.g., tests, verbal comments, formal reviews) (Sargeant et al., 2010; Winstone et al., 2017). Faced with multiple feedback sources, learners interpret the data through reflection, comparison, calibration, and filtering. In the end, they may accept and use the feedback, seek further clarifying information, ignore or reject it (Sargeant et al., 2010). Feedback can be compromised by perceptions that it lacks utility, detail, clarity, individualization, can't be implemented or recalled (Bing You et al., 2018; Jonsson 2013; Nash, Winstone, Gregory, & Papps, 2018).

Educators can find providing feedback challenging. In some situations, it can be difficult to define "competence." Skills, resources, and time to deliver feedback can be lacking. Some other impediments to engaging students include personal attitudes toward specific students, normative beliefs about feedback, concern about appeals, and cultures of kindness or excellence (Cleland, Knight, Rees, Tracey, & Bond, 2008; Dudek, Marks,

---

M. Zetkulic
Hackensack Meridian School of Medicine at Seton Hall,
Nutley, NJ, USA
e-mail: Marygrace.Zetkulic@hackensackmeridian.org

J. Sargeant
Dalhousie University, Halifax, NS, Canada
e-mail: Joan.sargeant@dal.ca

& Regehr, 2005; Kogan, Conforti, Bernabeo, Iobst, & Holmboe, 2015; Nichols, Kulaga, & Ross, 2013; Ramani et al., 2017).

The context in which feedback takes place also affects the type and nature of the assessments as well as the approaches taken to providing feedback (Colquhoun et al., 2017; Lau et al., 2016; Winstone et al., 2017). Feedback may consist largely of quantitative or numerical assessment data with insufficient elaboration for learners. And, it may be provided too late in the experience for learners to reasonably apply. Alternately, it may involve longer sit-down sessions in which a careful review of performance is undertaken with planning for the next educational experience(s). Policy and legislation through accreditation standards and national examination systems influence the types of assessment and feedback systems adopted (Lau et al., 2016).

Given the complex systems in which feedback occurs and the challenges learners experience using feedback, ensuring impactful feedback is challenging. This chapter offers a recently developed, research-based feedback approach, the R2C2 model (Armson, Lockyer, Zetkulic, Könings, & Sargeant, 2019; Graham & Beuthin, 2018; Sargeant et al., 2015, 2017, 2018). The R2C2 model is based on research and theories related to informed self-assessment, person-centered psychological and motivational theories, and coaching (Sargeant et al., 2010). While developed and tested within the health professions education context, the theory and research on which it is based may translate well to other workplace learning contexts and higher education fields in which feedback is oral and supported by observation and/or written documentation. The R2C2 model stresses building a **relationship (R)** between the educator and the learner, exploring **reactions (R)** to performance data and feedback, clarifying the **content (C)** of the feedback and **coaching** for **change (C)** through collaborating in the co-development of a learning change plan to optimize the impact of the feedback. This chapter describes the R2C2 model, followed by the evidence and theory supporting the two primary mechanisms operating within the model, coaching and learning change plans. The chapter concludes with suggestions for application and future research across disciplines and contexts.

The R2C2 Model

The R2C2 model has four phases (Sargeant et al., 2015, 2018). In the first phase, the educator builds the **relationship** in order to engage the learner. The educator describes the purpose of the feedback provides the learner with an opportunity to describe their experiences and their goals for the discussion. In the second phase, the educator explores the learner's **reactions** to ensure the learner feels understood and the learner's perspectives heard and respected. The educator queries initial reactions, surprises, and asks how this feedback compared with previous performance feedback. In the next phase, the educator explores and helps the learner determine the **content** of the feedback to ensure the learner is clear about the feedback and the opportunities it suggests for improvement. The educator clarifies the learner's perceptions about the content by going through it in a systematic way but also by asking enough questions to understand what the learner believes about their own performance. In the final stage, the educator **coaches for change** by helping the learner identify areas for change in order to co-develop an achievable learning change plan. The educator will ensure the learner can describe and commit to specific observable changes, along with the actions that will be required, when they will begin, the resources needed, anticipated barriers and how they will overcome the barriers and how they will know they have achieved their goal. It is iterative and encourages returning to previous stages as the plan develops or clarification is needed.

Material, including a tip sheet, videos, scripts, and a presentation, developed to support the use of the R2C2 model can be found on the Association of American Medical Colleges' *MedEdPORTAL: The Journal of Teaching and Learning Resources* (https://www.mededportal.org/) (Sargeant et al., 2016). Two exemplars of the model featuring an interaction between an educator and a learner are available on YouTube: https://youtu.be/_cSDQYjUEok and https://youtu.be/-ljhCWYujks.

The R2C2 model and its applicability to health care have been examined with practicing physicians who discussed standardized performance reports with a regulator (Sargeant et al., 2015) and nurse practitioners who participated in a multisource feedback process (Graham & Beuthin, 2018). More in-depth work was undertaken with postgraduate (PG) medical trainees (i.e., residents) who adopted the format for their 4–6 month progress meetings with educators (Armson et al., 2019; Sargeant et al., 2017, 2018). The R2C2 model enabled feedback discussions to occur in a collaborative, non-threatening environment using a series of open-ended questions to promote a respectful educator-learner relationship focused on continual improvement.

Practicing physicians found the feedback process was helpful and they appreciated the reflection stimulated by the discussion. (Sargeant et al., 2015). Similarly, nurse practitioners found that coaching was valuable, enjoyable, and supportive enabling them to pursue professional development and make changes in practice (Graham & Beuthin, 2018).

In the research with PG trainees (Armson et al., 2019; Sargeant et al., 2017, 2018), both learners and educators found the model facilitated engagement in a reflective feedback conversation about their assessment data and helped them use it to plan improvement. Learners noted the use of open-ended questions encouraged critical reflection and self-assessment. They recognized that the coaching portion was the most unique aspect of the feedback session while the co-creation of the learning change plan enabled them to create a concrete plan for improvement and changed the orientation of the discussion from "assessment and judgement" to "development and progress." Those who returned to the goals and learning change plans on subsequent feedback sessions spoke about the benefits including an evaluation of the activity and a longitudinal view of progress. While the model worked for both learners who struggled as well as those who were doing well (Sargeant et al., 2017, 2018), there was variability in the effectiveness of the R2C2 model. For example, where the educator's natural style was learner-centered, the R2C2 model seemed easier to implement. When educators and learners wrote out the plan, filed it for reference, and accessed it on a subsequent feedback session, the plan was more likely to be recalled and implemented (Sargeant et al., 2018).

A secondary study (Armson et al., 2019) examined the coaching component of the model. The researchers found that process (e.g., coach and learner preparation, relationship development, reflection, and encouragement) and content (e.g., specific feedback about performance and learner engagement in its discussion, collaboration on goal setting, development of the learning change plan, learner commitment, and follow-up), were intertwined and interdependent. Attention to both was needed to ensure learner's honest self-assessment and the co-development of a viable plan. Effective educators were able to balance a coaching dialogue and a teaching monologue and recognize there were times when they needed to be more directive so the learner could identify goals and come up with a plan. Recent unpublished work suggests that educators, experienced in using the model, have begun to adapt it for use at the end of clinical experiences as well as for progress meetings. The educators found that while phrases needed to be adapted, they could use the strategy to build the **relationship**, query the experience and obtain **reactions**, determine the **content** (goal) the learner would like to pursue and **coach for change** as they co-developed a plan that would achieve the goal.

Two components of the R2C2 model, coaching and the learning change plan with follow-up, appear to be the mechanisms enabling the learner to use the feedback. The follow-up phase aligns with a key tenet of this book, that is, that feedback impact is a necessary part of the process. The follow-up makes both parties accountable for tracking the effect of the co-generated strategies.

Coaching

Coaching Described

There is no universal definition of coaching. There is broad agreement that coaching is a managed conversation that takes place between two people, aims to support sustainable change to behaviors or ways of thinking, and focuses on learning and development (Van Nieuwerburgh, 2017). It must meet three criteria: explicit commitment by learner to improve performance; formal identification of individualized goals; and feedback about an individual's performance in relation to identified goals (Stober & Grant, 2010). Across disciplines, there are variations in why coaching is done, how it is done, when it is done, where it takes place, and what outcomes are sought. For this chapter, coaching is conceptualized as adopting techniques used in coaching without the requirement that it be done by a professional coach.

Theory Supporting Coaching

Several theories support the concept of coaching as enabling learners to move forward with feedback. These include humanistic/person-centered approaches, informed self-assessment approaches, the science of behavior change, and commitment to change (to be described in the section on learning change plans).

Humanistic and person-centered approaches draw on the cognitive and behavioral sciences (Sargeant et al., 2015) and ensure that the recipient sees the messages as individualized and meaningful to them, and that they are a partner in co-developing the plan. Through coaching and encouraging reflection, the recipient's self-awareness and self-direction are enhanced (Rogers, 1969; Rudland et al., 2013).

Informed self-assessment recognizes that individuals will use both internal and external data to understand how well they are doing (Sargeant et al., 2010). Encouraging recipients to draw on external feedback and calibrate it through discussion with someone with more expertise moves the learner beyond their own perceptions to integrate external feedback into the development of a tangible plan for progression.

The science of behavior change from implementation science identifies the importance of having facilitators (or coaches) provide guidance. The facilitator's role is to consider the individual and their motivation, values and beliefs, time and resources, nature of the change required and its complexity, degree of fit, perceived need for change, relative advantage, and environment in which the change will occur. The facilitator then considers these factors in helping the learner make changes recognizing both barriers and enablers (Kitson & Harvey 2016; Semrau et al., 2017).

Evidence for Coaching

Research evidence supporting coaching with feedback in medical education is captured in two reviews of coaching that can be best described as emerging. Surgical coaching has been associated with high learner satisfaction and improvements of skills and knowledge (Gagnon & Abbasi, 2018). In a broader review of the literature, coaching was found to reduce surgical error, improve technical skill acquisition, improve examination scores, and identify learners who were struggling academically (Lovell, 2018).

Nonetheless, the limited research demonstrates coaching success, although the metrics used to assess coaching are variable and fall short of demonstrating improved patient outcomes (Gagnon & Abbasi, 2018; Semrau et al., 2017). Examinations of outcomes as perceived by learners and educators also differ when compared to actual observations of coaching (Alken, Tan, Luursema, Fluit, & van Goor, 2015; Mazer et al., 2018). In part, these differences may be related to the factors that affect all feedback—the learner's engagement, the educator's ability, the message and its delivery, and the context in which coaching is done.

Learning Change Plans

Learning change plans restructure whereby learners can use feedback for planning improvement and future learning by articulating changes they will make, their timeline, resources they will require, challenges and how they will be overcome along with identifiable results (Sargeant et al., 2018). Such plans have variously been termed: learning contracts (Caffarella & Caffarella, 1986); learning plans (Barrington & Street, 2009); learning agreements and learning commitments (Barrington & Street, 2009); study plans (Barrington & Street, 2009); commitment to change statements (Armson, Elmslie, Roder, & Wakefield, 2015; Mazmanian & Mazmanian, 1999; Overton & MacVicar, 2008); and implementation intentions (Saddawi-Konefka, Schumacher, Baker, Charnin, & Gollwitzer, 2016). Clearly, there are differences between statements of intent typically used for short educational activities and learning contracts which apply for a term or a year of study. For the purposes of this chapter, recognizing differences in terminology and meaning, the term "learning change plan" will be used. Plans may be written down, signed or verbal (Mazmanian & Mazmanian, 1999) or part of a learning learner's portfolio. To be effective, they should be followed up to ensure that the person has been able to effect the changes (Pereles, Lockyer, Hogan, Gondocz, & Parboosingh, 1996) as they work best when they are written, made public and are voluntary (Frank & Scharff, 2013).

Theory Supporting Learning Change Plans

Several theories support the use of learning change plans in feedback conversations. At their root, they are behavioral commitments whereby the person's words (oral or written) obligate the individual to behavioral acts (Overton & MacVicar, 2008). Some of the underlying theories include theories of self-directedness and learner-centeredness (Frank & Scharff, 2013; Mazmanian & Mazmanian, 1999; Sargeant et al., 2015); cognitive load theory (Saddawi-Konefka et al., 2016; van Merriënboer & Sweller, 2010); and reflection (Armson et al., 2015).

Learning change plans shift the onus of learning from the teacher to the learner (Barrington & Street, 2009), enabling the teacher to become facilitative not authoritarian (O'Halloran & Delaney, 2011). Learner-centered and self-directed approaches recognize that individuals are more likely to change when they take the initiative, diagnose their own learning needs often with guidance given issues with inaccurate self-assessment (Eva & Regehr, 2008; Sargeant et al., 2010), formulate goals, identify the resources (human and material) needed, choose and implement appropriate approaches and evaluate the outcomes (Mazmanian & Mazmanian, 1999). By enabling people to take responsibility for their own learning, the likelihood of follow-through is increased as plans often require both behavioral and attitudinal changes (O'Halloran & Delaney, 2011; Overton & MacVicar, 2008). Behavioral changes not followed or accompanied by attitudinal changes are less likely to be sustained (Overton & MacVicar, 2008). Learning change plans stimulate the development of motivation, self-efficacy, and self-directedness (Frank & Scharff, 2013).

Learning changes carry a cognitive load which is the mental activity spent using and managing working memory (Saddawi-Konefka et al., 2016). There are three components to the cognitive load, intrinsic load (difficulty inherent in learning the material), germane load (work associated with processing, construction, and automation of schemas) and extraneous load (difficulty generated by non-educational aspects of how the material is presented to learner). Recognizing that individuals have a limited capacity for cognitive load, learning change plans help people reduce extraneous content, focus on their goals, and automate their behaviors, thereby decreasing cognitive load (Saddawi-Konefka et al., 2016). In feedback settings, plans are useful in helping people move forward, particularly if the plan is clearly articulated and identifies timelines, resources, and enables learners to determine how they will know they have achieved their goals (Sargeant et al., 2015, 2018).

Reflection is seen to be a key mechanism, particularly as it enhances deep rather than surface learning. Deep learning requires that the learner critically analyze new information, link it with previous knowledge, interpret the information, and apply it. Learning change plans work by encouraging deep learning as the learner considers their current performance and develops a plan for change. Co-development of the plan, as occurs in coaching settings, appears to increase the likelihood the plan will be implemented (Armson et al., 2019; Sargeant et al., 2018).

Evidence for Learning Change Plans

While there are individual studies demonstrating the efficacy of learning change plans, there has not been a consolidated literature review. Nonetheless, individual studies show they promote reflection on practice and encourage participants to identify and commit to and follow-up specific planned actions (Armson et al., 2015; Könings et al., 2016). Learners report that reflection gives them a sense of future direction and engages them in their own learning (Barrington & Street, 2009). Learning change plans in the form of learning contracts have been successfully used to develop competencies for self-directed learning, increase student ability to translate learning needs into learning objectives in a form that makes it possible to accomplish the objectives, identify human and material resources appropriate to the objectives and select strategies for using learning objectives (Caffarella & Caffarella 1986). Learners who signed their plans were more likely to attend more office hours, prioritize homework and reading and demonstrate a trend toward improvement on exam performance. This led the researchers to note that these plans appear to instill self-discipline to get work done in a timely way and introduce structure into the learning process while still being flexible enough to apply to a wide variety of students (Frank & Scharff, 2013). The more the plan is developed in a focused way (vs. having a global objective) also increases the time that people spend working toward their goals (Saddawi-Konefka et al., 2017). The learning change plan from the commitment to change statement literature has identified the benefits of these statements in changing practice and show that 47–87% of intended changes are implemented (Armson et al., 2015), although they need to be followed up for accountability and sustainability (Overton & MacVicar, 2008; Pereles et al., 1996).

Implications for Application and Future Research

The R2C2 model is relatively simple and adheres to contemporary human resources management approaches which encourage looking for outcomes, discussing reactions, and examining the past, present, and future (Buckingham & Goodall, 2019). The evidence emerging for the R2C2 model, coaching and learning change plans is promising. Nonetheless, many unsolved questions arise about using the model and its components for feedback discussions, both in the health context and the wider higher education context. The R2C2 model needs to be tested with other healthcare professionals and in different higher education settings (Graham & Beuthin, 2018). The model has been largely tested in medical education environments with fairly concrete and often longitudinal data (e.g., progress report meetings, multisource feedback). It may have applicability for educators working with students who are developing research proposals, writing a thesis or dissertation or doing a portfolio review.

Work has begun to adapt the R2C2 model for "in the moment" feedback that might occur during, or at the end of a patient encounter but testing in the workplace needs to be undertaken. This approach may offer an approach to discussions during practical experiences with teachers in training, pharmacy, and nursing students.

The value of ensuring that both learner and educator are knowledgeable about the process has been recognized (Sargeant et al., 2018). Consequently, learners who have participated in an R2C2 discussion may be able to develop strategies to support peer feedback as that has been shown to help learners make peer comparisons and more accurate assessments about their own work and that of others (Tai, Canny, Haines, & Molloy, 2016). Learners would need training and the impact of this assessed.

The research needs to move beyond the question of whether the model can be taught/implemented and end-user satisfaction into studies that examine the impact of coaching on learner performance and the achievement of learning goals.

Conclusions

Providing and receiving feedback are complex with uncertain outcomes. In the context of health professions education, the setting for the research-informed R2C2 model for feedback presented in this chapter, many approaches have been attempted inside the classroom, in simulation centers, and in direct patient care settings. This chapter has identified the factors that appear to impact on learning and improvement and described the R2C2 model which by combining coaching and the co-development of learning change plans appears to be a promising strategy for fostering feedback use. More work is required to examine how a model such as the R2C2 works optimally within various contexts and cultures to help learners progress to meet the competencies expected at different levels of training.

References

Alken, A., Tan, E., Luursema, J. M., Fluit, C., & van Goor, H. (2015). Coaching during a trauma surgery team training: Perceptions versus structured observations. *American Journal of Surgery, 209*(1), 163–169. https://doi.org/10.1016/j.amjsurg.2014.02.009.

Armson, H., Elmslie, T., Roder, S., & Wakefield, J. (2015). Is the cognitive complexity of commitment-to-change statements associated with change in clinical practice? An application of bloom's taxonomy. *Journal of Continuing Education in the Health Professions, 35*(3), 166–175. https://doi.org/10.1002/chp.21303.

Armson, H., Lockyer, J. M., Zetkulic, M. G., Könings, K. D., & Sargeant, J. (2019). Identifying coaching skills to improve feedback use in postgraduate medical education. *Medical Education* (in press). https://doi.org/10.1111/medu.13818.

Barrington, K., & Street, K. (2009). Learner contracts in nurse education: Interaction within the practice context. *Nurse Education in Practice, 9*(2), 109–118. https://doi.org/10.1016/j.nepr.2008.10.004.

Bing-You, R., Varaklis, K., Hayes, V., Trowbridge, R., Kemp, H., & McKelvy, D. (2018). The feedback tango: An integrative review and analysis of the content of the teacher-learner feedback exchange. *Academic Medicine, 93*(4), 657–663. https://doi.org/10.1097/ACM.0000000000001927.

Buckingham, M., & Goodall, A. (2019). The feedback fallacy. *Harvard Business Review, 97*(2), 92–101. ISSN: 0017-8012.

Caffarella, R. S., & Caffarella, E. P. (1986). Self-directedness and learning contracts in adult education. *Adult Education Quarterly, 36*(4), 226–234. https://doi.org/10.1177/0001848186036004004.

Cleland, J. A., Knight, L. V., Rees, C. E., Tracey, S., & Bond, C. M. (2008). Is it me or is it them? Factors that influence the passing of underperforming students. *Medical Education, 42*(8), 800–809. https://doi.org/10.1111/j.1365-2923.2008.03113.x.

Colquhoun, H. L., Carroll, K., Eva, K. W., Grimshaw, J. M., Ivers, N., Michie, S., ... Brehaut, J. C. (2017). Advancing the literature on designing audit and feedback interventions: Identifying theory-informed hypotheses. *Implementation Science, 12*(1), 117. https://doi.org/10.1186/s13012-017-0646-0.

Dudek, N. L., Marks, M. B., & Regehr, G. (2005). Failure to fail: The perspectives of clinical supervisors. *Academic Medicine, 80*(Suppl), 84–87. PubMed PMID: 16199466.

Eva, K. W., & Regehr, G. (2008). "I'll never play professional football" and other fallacies of self-assessment. *Journal of Continuing Education in the Health Professions, 28*(1), 14–19. https://doi.org/10.1002/chp.150.

Frank, T., & Scharff, L. F. V. (2013). Learning contracts in undergraduate courses: Impacts on student behaviors and academic performance. *Journal of the Scholarship of Teaching and Learning, 13*(4), 36–53. ISSN: 1527-9316.

Gagnon, L. H., & Abbasi, N. (2018). Systematic review of randomized controlled trials on the role of coaching in surgery to improve learner outcomes. *American Journal of Surgery, 216*(1), 140–146. https://doi.org/10.1016/j.amjsurg.2017.05.003.

Graham, R., & Beuthin, R. (2018). Exploring the effectiveness of multisource feedback and coaching with nurse practitioners. *Nursing Leadership (Toronto, Ont.), 31*(1), 50–59. https://doi.org/10.12927/cjnl.2018.25472.

Jonsson, A. (2013). Facilitating productive use of feedback in higher education. *Active Learning in Higher Education, 14,* 63–76. https://doi.org/10.1177/1469787412467125.

Kitson, A. L., & Harvey, G. (2016). Methods to succeed in effective knowledge translation in clinical practice. *Journal of Nursing Scholarship, 48*(3), 294–302. https://doi.org/10.1111/jnu.12206.

Kogan, J. R., Conforti, L. N., Bernabeo, E., Iobst, W., & Holmboe, E. (2015). How faculty members experience workplace-based assessment rater training: A qualitative study. *Medical Education, 49*(7), 692–708. https://doi.org/10.1111/medu.12733.

Könings, K. D., van Berlo, J., Koopmans, R., Hoogland, H., Spanjers, I. A. E., Ten Haaf, J., … Van Merriënboer, J. J. G. (2016). Promoting residents' reflection at work: Combining a smartphone app with coaching groups. *Academic Medicine, 91*(3), 365–370.

Lau, R., Stevenson, F., Ong, B. N., Dziedzic, K., Treweek, S., Eldridge, S., … Murray, E. (2016). Achieving change in primary care–causes of the evidence to practice gap: Systematic reviews of reviews. *Implementation Science, 11*(1), 40. https://doi.org/10.1186/s13012-016-0396-4.

Lovell, B. (2018). What do we know about coaching in medical education? A literature review. *Medical Education, 52*(4), 376–390. https://doi.org/10.1111/medu.13482.

Mazer, L. M., Hu, Y. Y., Arriaga, A. F., Greenberg, C.C., Lipsitz, S. R., Gawande, A. A., … Yule, S. J. (2018). Evaluating surgical coaching: A mixed methods approach reveals more than surveys alone. *Journal of Surgical Education, 75*(6), 1520–1525. https://doi.org/10.1016/j.jsurg.2018.03.009.

Mazmanian, P. E., & Mazmanian, P. M. (1999). Commitment to change: Theoretical foundations, methods and outcomes. *Journal of Continuing Education in the Health Professions, 19,* 200–207.

Michie, S., van Stralen, M. M., & West, R. (2011). The behaviour change wheel: A new method for characterising and designing behaviour change interventions. *Implementation Science, 6,* 42. https://doi.org/10.1186/1748-5908-6-42.

Nash, R. A., Winstone, N. E., Gregory, S. E. A., & Papps, E. (2018). A memory advantage for past-oriented over future-oriented performance feedback. *Journal of Experimental Psychology: Learning, Memory, and Cognition, 44*(12), 1864–1879. https://doi.org/10.1037/xlm0000549.

Nichols, D., Kulaga, A., & Ross, S. (2013). Coaching the coaches: Targeted faculty development for teaching. *Medical Education, 47*(5), 534–535. https://doi.org/10.1111/medu.12187.

O'Halloran, K. C., & Delaney, M. E. (2011). Using learning contracts in the counselor education classroom. *Journal of Counselor Preparation and Supervision, 3*(2), 69–81. https://repository.wcsu.edu/jcps/vol3/iss2/1.

Overton, G. K., & MacVicar, R. (2008). Requesting a commitment to change: Conditions that produce behavioral or attitudinal commitment. *Journal of Continuing Education in the Health Professions, 28*(2), 60–66. https://doi.org/10.1002/chp.158.

Pereles, L., Lockyer, J., Hogan, D., Gondocz, T., & Parboosingh, J. (1996). Effectiveness of commitment contracts in continuing medical education. *Academic Medicine, 71*(4), 394. PMID: 8645410.

Ramani, S., Könings, K. D., Mann, K. V., Pisarski, E. E., & van der Vleuten, C. P. M. (2018). About politeness, face, and feedback: Exploring resident and faculty perceptions of how institutional feedback culture influences feedback practices. *Academic Medicine, 93*(9), 1348–1358. https://doi.org/10.1097/ACM.0000000000002193.

Ramani, S., Post, S. E., Könings, K., Mann, K., Katz, J. T., & van der Vleuten, C. (2017). "It's just not the culture": A qualitative study exploring residents' perceptions of the impact of institutional culture on feedback. *Teaching and Learning in Medicine, 29*(2), 153–161. https://doi.org/10.1080/10401334.2016.1244014.

Rogers, C. R. (1969). *Freedom to learn: A view of what education might become.* Columbus, OH: C. E. Merrill Publishing Company.

Rudland, J., Wilkinson, T., Wearn, A., Nicol, P., Tunny, T., Owen, C., & O'Keefe, M. (2013). A student-centred feedback model for educators. *Clinical Teacher, 10*(2), 99–102. https://doi.org/10.1111/j.1743-498x.2012.00634.x.

Saddawi-Konefka, D., Baker, K., Guarino, A., Burns, S. M., Oettingen, G., Gollwitzer, P. M., & Charnin, J. E. (2017). Changing resident physician studying behaviors: A randomized, comparative effectiveness trial of goal setting versus use of WOOP. *Journal of Graduate Medical Education, 9*(4), 451–457. https://doi.org/10.4300/jgme-d-16-00703.1.

Saddawi-Konefka, D., Schumacher, D. J., Baker, K. H., Charnin, J. E., & Gollwitzer, P. M. (2016). Changing physician behavior with implementation intentions: Closing the gap between intentions and actions. *Academic Medicine, 91*(9), 1211–1216. https://doi.org/10.1097/ACM.0000000000001172.

Sargeant, J., Armson, H., Chesluk, B., Dornan, T., Eva, K., Holmboe, E., ... van der Vleuten, C. (2010). The processes and dimensions of informed self-assessment: A conceptual model. *Academic Medicine, 85*(7), 1212–1220. https://doi.org/10.1097/acm.0b013e3181d85a4e.

Sargeant, J., Armson, H., Driessen, E., Holmboe, E., Könings, K., Lockyer, J., … Shearer, C. (2016). Evidence-informed facilitated feedback: The R2C2 feedback model. *MedEdPORTAL, 12*, 10387. https://doi.org/10.15766/mep_2374-8265.10387.

Sargeant, J., Lockyer, J. M., Mann, K., Armson, H., Warren, A., Zetkulic, M., … Boudreau, M. (2018). The R2C2 model in residency education: How does it Foster coaching and promote feedback use? *Academic Medicine, 93*(7), 1055–1063. https://doi.org/10.1097/acm.0000000000002131.

Sargeant, J., Lockyer, J., Mann, K., Holmboe, E., Silver, I., Armson, H., … Power, M. (2015). Facilitated reflective performance feedback: Developing an evidence- and theory-based model that builds relationship, explores reactions and content, and coaches for performance change (R2C2). *Academic Medicine, 90*(12), 1698–1706. https://doi.org/10.1097/acm.0000000000000809.

Sargeant, J., Mann, K., Manos, S., Epstein, I., Warren, A., Shearer, C., & Boudreau M. (2017). R2C2 in action: Testing an evidence-based model to facilitate feedback and coaching in residency. *Journal of Graduate Medical Education, 9*(2), 165–170. https://doi.org/10.4300/jgme-d-16-00398.1.

Semrau, K. E. A., Hirschhorn, L. R., Marx Delaney, M., Singh, V. P., Saurastri, R., Sharma, N., … Gawande, A. A. (2017). Better birth trial group. Outcomes of a coaching-based WHO safe childbirth checklist program in India. *New England Journal of Medicine, 377*(24), 2313–2324. https://doi.org/10.1056/nejmoa1701075.

Stober, D. R., & Grant, A. M. (2010). *Evidence based coaching handbook: Putting best practices to work for your clients.* Hoboken, NJ: Wiley.

Tai, J. H., Canny, B. J., Haines, T. P., & Molloy, E. K. (2016). The role of peer-assisted learning in building evaluative judgement: Opportunities in clinical medical education. *Advances in Health Sciences Education, 21*(3), 659–676. https://doi.org/10.1007/s10459-015-9659-0.

van Merriënboer, J. J., & Sweller, J. (2010). Cognitive load theory in health professional education: Design principles and strategies. *Medical Education, 44*(1), 85–93. https://doi.org/10.1111/j.1365-2923.2009.03498.x.

Van Nieuwerburgh, C. (2017). *An introduction to coaching skills: A practical guide* (2nd ed.). London: Sage.

Winstone, N. E., Nash, R. A., Parker, M., & Rowntree, J. (2017). Supporting learner's agentic engagement with feedback: A systematic review and a taxonomy of recipience processes. *Educational Psychologist, 2*(1), 17–37. https://doi.org/10.1080/00461520.2016.1207538.

Part IV
Visibility of Impact

12

Identifying the Impact of Feedback Over Time and at Scale: Opportunities for Learning Analytics

Tracii Ryan⍟, Dragan Gašević⍟ and Michael Henderson⍟

Introduction

In higher education, feedback information is often limited to comments or a rubric provided by the educator after submission. Indeed, learners receive little information about their performance before submission, and only limited statements post submission, which are often restricted to the form and substance of the submission, rather than the thinking, strategies

---

T. Ryan (✉)
Melbourne Centre for the Study of Higher Education, The University of Melbourne, Melbourne, VIC, Australia
e-mail: tracii.ryan@unimelb.edu.au

D. Gašević
Faculty of Information Technology, Monash University, Melbourne, VIC, Australia
e-mail: dragan.gasevic@monash.edu

M. Henderson
Faculty of Education, Monash University, Melbourne, VIC, Australia
e-mail: michael.henderson@monash.edu

© The Author(s) 2019
M. Henderson et al. (eds.), *The Impact of Feedback in Higher Education*,
https://doi.org/10.1007/978-3-030-25112-3_12

or conceptual development that led to submission. Arguably, such information offers little for learners to work with, at a time when it is often too late for action.

To enhance the possibility that feedback processes will have an impact, it is recommended that feedback information is personalised to the learner, future oriented, timely and relevant to subsequent tasks (Boud & Molloy, 2013; Winstone, Nash, Rowntree, & Parker, 2017). Learners also need opportunities to relate feedback information to their work processes, learning strategies and self-regulatory skills (Hattie & Timperley, 2007). However, higher education is becoming increasingly massified and modularised, which raises numerous challenges for impactful and effective feedback processes (Boud & Molloy, 2013; Pardo, Jovanović, Dawson, Gašević, & Mirriahi, 2019). In general, massification adds to educator workloads and hinders them from designing and creating impactful feedback information, while modularisation makes it difficult for learners to act upon feedback information across the duration of their programme.

In contemporary higher education, a large component of learners' educational experience is technologically mediated. As a result, learners create vast numbers of digital traces through use of learning management systems, student administration systems, network access, cloud technologies and educator records. Examples of such trace data include, but are not limited to, the academic records of students, socio-economic and demographic factors, page views and textual content generated in online discussions between peers, or between students and educators. It is unsurprising then that these data are increasingly being utilised to understand and augment learning. This field of research and practice, known as learning analytics, has been defined as the "measurement, collection, analysis and reporting of data about learners and their contexts, for purposes of understanding and optimizing learning and the environments in which it occurs" (Siemens & Gašević, 2012, p. 1).

Learning analytics offers the potential for data mining over time to track and represent learner actions in relation to their assessment performance (Gašević, Dawson, Rogers, & Gašević, 2016; Jovanović, Gašević, Dawson, Pardo, & Mirriahi, 2017). This information can be a valuable part of the feedback process for all stakeholders, as it may support learners' decision-making and study habits, help educators shape their instructional design in scalable ways and provide institutions with valuable insights into learning and teaching practices (Greller & Drachsler, 2012). In light of the pervasiveness of massified and modularised subjects in higher education today, such benefits are highly advantageous to learners and educators alike.

In response to these challenges, this chapter explores how learning analytics can help educators design impactful feedback processes and support learners to identify the impact of feedback information, both across time and at scale. In doing so, it offers current examples of how learning analytics could guide policy and educational designs and be usefully employed to support learners to direct their own learning and study habits. This chapter also highlights how learning analytics can help individuals understand and optimise learning, and the environments in which the learning occurs.

Opportunities for Improving Feedback Impact at Scale

Large classes are a common outcome associated with rising student enrolments in higher education. However, research confirms that large classes can cause multifarious challenges for learning and teaching (Cuseo, 2007; Exeter et al., 2010; Gibbs, Lucas, & Simonite, 1996). For example, students are often reluctant to interact in large classes, which leads educators to rely on information transmission-focused teaching methods (i.e., lectures) that are known to be disadvantageous to engagement and learning (Cuseo, 2007; Exeter et al., 2010). Furthermore, due to the high student-to-staff ratio, educators tend to use assessment methods that are time-effective to assess, but which encourage students to adopt surface learning strategies, like multiple choice quizzes (Cuseo, 2007). Labour constraints in large classes also limit opportunities for educators to personally engage with learners to gauge their thinking, strategies and skills, and provide appropriate guidance (Pardo et al., 2019).

To create impact, it is necessary that feedback information is obtained or generated by learners in time for them to use it in a subsequent piece of work (Gibbs & Simpson, 2004). However, in large-class contexts where learners are reliant upon educator feedback, it is common for feedback information to be received too late to be useful (Hartley & Chesworth, 2000). This is generally because large classes tend to increase educator workloads, particularly in relation to assessment and feedback. Another issue relates to the personalisation of feedback information; while vicarious feedback (e.g., whole-class feedback, exemplars, etc.) can be beneficial for learners who have developed some level of self-regulation (Panadero & Broadbent, 2018), the impact of feedback may be maximised when the information is highly pertinent to the individual learner (Dawson et al., 2019). Of course, this requires that educators make efforts to get to know students individually, a feat that is difficult in large classes with increasingly disproportionate staff-to-student ratios (Huxham, 2007). As a result, educators are often required to trade-off between generating feedback information that is either personalised and detailed, or scalable and timely. For example, rubrics, marking sheets and statement banks can help educators provide feedback information to large classes in more sustainable ways, but these feedback modes offer little in the way of information that relates to the context of the individual learner (such as their history and motivations), or that is specifically personalised to their own performance.

In response to these issues, researchers have begun developing learning analytics-based approaches to timely and personalised feedback provision at scale. For example, Pardo (2018) proposed a feedback model for data-rich environments in which he builds primarily on the work of Butler and Winne (1995). As such, Pardo's model is rooted in the literature of self-regulated learning, where the role of externally generated feedback is to assist learners in their decision-making, self-evaluation of the efficacy of their learning strategies and reflection on the outcomes of their learning.

Pardo's (2018) model posits that personalised feedback at scale can be achieved through a combination of computer and human agents. Human agents (i.e., educators) are responsible for defining rules that stipulate which information should be included into feedback when certain conditions are met (e.g., a student answered less than a third of questions on a formative test). Computer agents execute the rules by evaluating the conditions based on data available in the profiles of each individual student. The role of computer agents is to empower educators to incorporate their content and pedagogical knowledge into feedback at scale.

At this point, it is important to reiterate one of the key messages of this book—that is, that the feedback process is necessarily learner-centred. While the supply of feedback information by computer agents benefits educators by providing a scalable feedback solution in large classes, there is no guarantee that the learner will feel appropriately supported and motivated to enact this information. This transmission-focused conceptualisation of feedback is a limitation of Pardo's (2018) model, and much research relating to feedback and learning analytics, but it could potentially be addressed by scaffolding opportunities for learners to engage with feedback information and use it to improve their learning. With this in mind, we now present findings from several research studies in which various forms of learner impact have been observed as a result of personalised *feedback information* facilitated through the use of learning analytics.

Impact on learners' satisfaction with feedback. Pardo's (2018) feedback model for data-rich environments has so far been used to provide feedback information in large-enrolment subjects which use pedagogical strategies such as blended learning and flipped classrooms. Data in existing implementations of the model have been drawn from student interactions with online resources (e.g., video watching, reading materials, and formative and summative tests) and student records (e.g., previous grades). The model has been used to provide feedback information relating to work processes with different frequency. Pardo et al. (2019) used the model to offer weekly personalised process feedback in the first half of a 12-week computer engineering undergraduate subject. The results showed a significant increase in feedback satisfaction (Cohen's $d = .49$) in comparison with the previous two offerings of the same subject. While these are certainly promising results, additional research is now needed to measure behavioural impact rather than relying on self-report data alone.

Impact on learners' reflective processes, during the course and beyond. Learning analytics borrows analytic methods and techniques from different disciplines that can be used to evaluate the effect of feedback in large classes. Gašević, Dawson, and Siemens (2015) recommend that learning analytics should not only use data about operations used by students while studying, but also the products of learning (e.g., textual content from student reflections) and contextual information (e.g., types of instruction received or personal levels of motivation). Together, these offer a useful set of information about the effects of different pedagogical interventions, including external feedback. For example, the use of assessment feedback to promote reflection was assessed with learning analytics in a study of performing arts students at a Canadian university, over two academic terms and across three different subjects (Gašević, Mirriahi, Dawson, & Joksimović, 2017). The study showed feedback played an important role in the increased use of reflection, even in follow-on subjects when there was no assessment of, or feedback on, student reflections. In spite of the comparable number of reflections produced when students were provided with feedback information, qualitative differences were observed through the use of manual content analysis and automated text analysis techniques (Joksimovićet al., 2019; Mirriahi, Joksimović, Gašević, & Dawson, 2018). That is, even if they previously received feedback information, students in a no-feedback condition articulated less specific goals for the improvement of their performance in follow-on subjects than their peers who had continued to receive feedback information.

The research studies discussed above show how learning analytics is currently providing opportunities to assist educators who are dealing with large classes. In the future, the affordances of learning analytics may further assist educators to facilitate feedback impact by drawing on other sources, such as automated feedback, peer feedback and self-feedback. Aside from reducing educator workloads, automated feedback can be extremely timely and is consistent across learners (Debuse, Lawley, & Shibl, 2008), while peer feedback opens up the learner to a range of perspectives rather than the educators' alone and can foster critical thinking and self-regulatory skills (Ciftci & Kocoglu, 2012; Moore & Teather, 2012; Wu, Petit, & Chen, 2015). In addition, self-feedback can support the development of metacognition and evaluative judgement (Boud, 1995; Huang, 2016).

Building on the work of Pardo et al. (2019), discussed earlier, learning analytics could allow learners to benefit from targeted and sophisticated automated feedback information using digital traces from various sources (e.g., engagement with learning materials, attempts at online quizzes, etc.). Learning analytics may also encourage learners to produce self-feedback based on analytics derived from any relevant indicators. These indicators could include information relating to learning behaviours, such as class attendance, off-task internet use during class, downloading course materials at the most appropriate times (e.g., not right before exams), engagement in online discussion, and the tone of discussion, for example. Educators may also be able to use textual analysis to efficiently monitor the quality and appropriateness of peer feedback.

Learning analytics could also help identify feedback impact in large classes by providing educators with information that helps them more regularly evaluate the value of feedback and assessment to learners. In large classes, educators often do not get useful instructional feedback until after the subject has been completed (e.g., through course evaluation surveys or student satisfaction scores) (Ali, Hatala, Gašević, & Jovanović, 2012). However, receiving learner evaluations of the relevance of feedback and assessment design during a course is critical to be able to identify where limitations and problems are arising and work towards addressing them quickly. To overcome this issue, learning analytics could provide additional information to give institutions, educators and learners insight into work behaviours, learning strategies or engagements leading up to assessment or across a programme. These include digital traces from activities on the learning management system (e.g., engaging with readings, forums, etc.), network traffic, class attendance and engagement and performance in formative tasks (e.g., quizzes, polls, discussion tasks, etc.).

Opportunities for Improving Feedback Impact Over Time

Institutions are increasingly offering degree programmes in the form of suites of modularised subjects—that is, subjects that are designed to not require a particular programme sequence. Such subjects allow students to customise their learning progression to suit their own interests and needs (Bridges, 2000). While modularisation of subjects may offer flexibility for students, it presents significant challenges for impactful feedback processes (Carless, Salter, Yang, & Lam, 2011), which require that learners obtain information relating to their performance or learning strategies early and often (Gibbs & Simpson, 2004). Ideally, suggestions for improvement on a task should be given to learners before they submit that task, so that they can immediately improve their work (Boud & Molloy, 2013). However, in modularised subjects, students may not have prior knowledge in the relevant content area, so it is common for educators to assess learning outcomes as late in the subject as possible (Carless et al., 2011; Deepwell & Benfield, 2012). Unfortunately, when multiple assessment tasks are clustered towards the end of the teaching period, feedback information generally arrives too late to have an impact on learners' subsequent work in that subject.

Learning analytics can provide opportunities to increase the frequency of feedback information to learners. Some of the early approaches to learning analytics have primarily been dedicated to the detection of students at risk of failing, and subsequent provision of early warning alerts to students and educators. Although significant improvements in student retention are reported thanks to such early warning systems (Arnold & Pistilli, 2012), the quality of feedback information provided to students is lacking (Tanes, Arnold, King, & Remnet, 2011). For example, while the frequency of messaging from educators to students increased rapidly with the introduction of early warning systems, the information was restricted in usefulness. This is because early warning systems generally only provide limited insights about the potential reasons why some students were at risk and what type of support they needed (Gašević et al., 2015). Similarly, while students received early warnings about potential risks to successfully completing ongoing subjects, they did not receive much actionable advice about how exactly they could enhance their learning and minimise the predicted risks.

The limitations associated with the early approaches to providing effective feedback information using learning analytics are currently being addressed through research and development of learning analytics dashboards. Learning analytics dashboards can be considered a source of feedback information for both learners and educators (Teasley, 2017), providing insights into the progression of individual learners, and the effectiveness of learning designs (Bakharia et al., 2016; Bodily & Verbert, 2017). They present analytical results of data collected from several relevant sources, such as learning management systems and student information systems. The dashboards allow students and educators to inspect patterns in learning activities and explore associations with assessment scores. Given that dashboards have access to live data sources, students and educators can therefore be offered insights in real-time and observe

12 Identifying the Impact of Feedback Over Time ...

patterns over time. State-of-the-art learning analytics dashboards use a combination of visualisations and text that incorporates pedagogical knowledge to suggest possible next steps to educators and students in order to optimise learning experiences (Broos, Verbert, Langie, Van Soom, & De Laet, 2017; Herder et al., 2018). For example, Broos et al. (2017) present a dashboard that is used at the programme level to offer students insight into the learning strategies they follow and to give advice about how those strategies can be improved. Such methods are likely to benefit students by helping them receive timely feedback information across a subject, or indeed, an entire programme of study; however, there is still a need to ensure that the information has an impact on learners.

Beyond timeliness, modularisation also stymies the potential for feedback to address work processes and self-regulated learning skills (Hattie & Timperley, 2007). This is because improvements relating to learners' work strategies and metacognition tend to be small and incremental, and take place over a long duration—such as a year or an entire programme of study. Therefore, an important requirement for impactful feedback is that learners have opportunities to take feedback information that relates to work strategies and enact them across subjects (Boud, 2015). This is difficult for educators to achieve in modularised subjects, as the cohort is likely to be enrolled in diverse programmes (Timmerman & Dijkstra, 2017; van der Vleuten et al., 2012; Winstone et al., 2017), and to experience multiple assessments with varied and complex criteria, tailored to evaluate disparate learning outcomes, over the course of their degree (Price, Handley, Millar, & O'Donovan, 2010).

Assuming that actionable feedback information is regularly obtained, learning analytics offers a way for educators and students to track learning improvements over time. However, this can only occur if the relevant competencies are being assessed through subsequent activities within a programme. Of particular importance are approaches proposed for automated detection of learning improvements using learner data. These can be based on relatively simple descriptive statistics of interaction patterns with course resources or other learners, or on sophisticated data analysis techniques, using unsupervised machine learning (e.g., latent class analysis), process mining and sequence mining. Either way, interpretation of learning strategies is typically done vis-à-vis the theoretical frameworks of deep learning, achievement goal orientation and self-regulated learning (Lust, Elen, & Clarebout, 2013; Wise, Speer, Marbouti, & Hsiao, 2013).

A study reported by Fincham, Gašević, Jovanović, and Pardo (2018) applied a combination of analytical techniques to extract learning strategies followed by undergraduate students in a computer engineering subject to evaluate the effects of personalised feedback. The extraction of learning strategies was achieved through the analysis of digital trace data about students' completion of activities, navigation through the content and completion of formative and summative assessments. The study included three offerings of the course where, in year one, students received no data-rich process feedback. In year two, students received personalised process feedback weekly in the first half of the course, as reported by Pardo et al. (2019). Finally, in year three, students received personalised process feedback throughout the entire semester. The results showed that, with the introduction and increased provision of data-rich personalised process feedback information, there was a significant decline in the proportion of students who followed the least effective learning strategy and who had the lowest academic performance. As this example shows, learning analytics may assist students to improve their learning strategies and work processes.

In the future, learning analytics may help educators and learners to identify the impact of feedback over time by offering a permanent longitudinal record of the feedback information obtained across the duration of a course. Sometimes the relevance of feedback information (especially that relating to work strategies) may be lost, particularly where there is no obvious follow-on task. This can dissatisfy and demotivate learners (Price et al., 2010), as they may feel that the feedback information was valueless. Even in cases where learners are able to recognise and value future-orientated feedback information, they may forget new strategies and fall back into old habits if they are not given repeated opportunities to practice these strategies. Having a way for learners to keep track of suggestions and recommendations over time would address both of these issues. This could be achieved by using systems to support the identification of key characteristics or themes within assessment criteria and received feedback information. For instance, by analysing rubric data and comparing it across assessments, the system could help learners to make sense of, or connect, the performances across assessments.

12 Identifying the Impact of Feedback Over Time ... 217

Leveraging learning analytics for longitudinal tracking could also enable educators to identify feedback impact by mapping the relevance of feedback information to future learning outcomes in subsequent subjects. This is important for task-related feedback information, along with information focused on work strategies and self-regulated learning skills. Such an approach would allow educators to obtain visibility of where learners need support to develop strategies and skills, which would arguably improve educators' teaching and instructional design of the same unit in future years. It would also help shape others' teaching of the student cohort as they progress through their degree. To achieve this, there is a need for subject coordinators to collaborate in order to determine the learning outcomes needed for a programme of study. This would allow for the development of programmatic assessment and feedback strategies to meet these learning outcomes. As a result, the impact of feedback would be enhanced through better alignment between assessment tasks, feedback that encouraged incremental skill development over the course of a programme and consistency of feedback practices across subjects.

Conclusion

Learning analytics allows various stakeholders to identify relevant patterns in learning and use those patterns to inform or measure the effect of feedback practices. In this chapter, we have described how learning analytics is currently supporting feedback impact by providing real-time progress updates to learners using dashboards, allowing educators to evaluate learners' use of feedback to assess new study strategies and learning processes and facilitating the provision of timely and personalised feedback information at scale. In an increasingly modularised and massified higher education system, learning analytics also offers the potential for students and teachers to monitor learner improvements across a programme (especially improvements to learning strategies and self-regulated learning skills), their interaction with feedback, as well as the actual text of the feedback information. Learners have a vehicle to track their own improvements over time, by storing information and analysing improvements on learning outcomes cross-referenced or linked to their feedback across a programme.

Although learning analytics offers much promise for the advancement of existing feedback practices, there are still certain challenges that warrant future research. First and foremost, there is a tendency for most learning analytics research to be focused on the transmission of feedback information, rather than actively supporting learners to gain impact through effective feedback processes. As such, future research should aim to develop analytic techniques that can assist with tracking learner sense-making, uptake and enactment of feedback information, both within and across subjects. Such approaches should allow for the evaluation of the effects of feedback, while providing evidence about the validity of analytic results as established in measurement science (Messick, 1995). Yet another focus for future research is to analyse learning strategies and outcomes at the cohort level and highlight those strategies which most effectively supported improved task performance. This information could be fed back to individual learners so that they could make judgements about their own learning strategies and create impact by modelling the successful strategies of others.

Another issue associated with learning analytics research is that the quality of data collected by the prevalent learning technologies is too coarse-grained and is often ungrounded in relevant theories of human learning and feedback, such as self-regulated learning (for more on this, see Gašević et al., 2015). Future research on the interplay between learning design, technology design and analytics is needed to enable the creation of learning tasks and technologies that warrant collection of granular and theoretically informed data about learners and learning contexts. Finally, further research is needed to develop techniques that can evaluate the effects of personalised feedback. In such cases, existing data analysis techniques for deriving inferences about the effects of feedback on the population level are insufficient, due to the difference in the feedback intervention each learner receives, and individual differences among learners, such as knowledge of cues provided in the feedback or knowledge of relevant learning strategies recommended in feedback (Winne, 2017).

References

Ali, L., Hatala, M., Gašević, D., & Jovanović, J. (2012). A qualitative evaluation of evolution of a learning analytics tool. *Computers & Education, 58*(1), 470–489. https://doi.org/10.1016/j.compedu.2011.08.030.

Arnold, K. E., & Pistilli, M. D. (2012, April). Course signals at Purdue: Using learning analytics to increase student success. In *Proceedings of the 2nd International Conference on Learning Analytics and Knowledge* (pp. 267–270). ACM.

Bakharia, A., Corrin, L., de Barba, P., Kennedy, G., Gašević, D., Mulder, R., ... Lockyer, L. (2016, April). A conceptual framework linking learning design with learning analytics. In *Proceedings of the Sixth International Conference on Learning Analytics & Knowledge* (pp. 329–338). ACM.

Bodily, R., & Verbert, K. (2017). Review of research on student-facing learning analytics dashboards and educational recommender systems. *IEEE Transactions on Learning Technologies, 10*(4), 405–418. https://doi.org/10.1109/TLT.2017.2740172.

Boud, D. (1995). *Enhancing learning through self assessment.* Oxon: Routledge.

Boud, D. (2015). Feedback: Ensuring that it leads to enhanced learning. *The Clinical Teacher, 12*, 3–7. https://doi.org/10.1111/tct.12345.

Boud, D., & Molloy, E. (2013). Rethinking models of feedback for learning: The challenge of design. *Assessment & Evaluation in Higher Education, 38*(6), 698–712. https://doi.org/10.1080/02602938.2012.691462.

Bridges, D. (2000). Back to the future: The higher education curriculum in the 21st century. *Cambridge Journal of Education, 30*(1), 37–55. https://doi.org/10.1080/03057640050005762.

Broos, T., Verbert, K., Langie, G., Van Soom, C., & De Laet, T. (2017). Small data as a conversation starter for learning analytics: Exam results dashboard for first-year students in higher education. *Journal of Research in Innovative Teaching & Learning, 10*(2), 94–106. https://doi.org/10.1108/JRIT-05-2017-0010.

Butler, D. L., & Winne, P. H. (1995). Feedback and self-regulated learning: A theoretical synthesis. *Review of Educational Research, 65*(3), 245–281. https://doi.org/10.3102/00346543065003245.

Carless, D., Salter, D., Yang, M., & Lam, J. (2011). Developing sustainable feedback practices. *Studies in Higher Education, 36*(4), 395–407. https://doi.org/10.1080/03075071003642449.

Ciftci, H., & Kocoglu, Z. (2012). Effects of peer E-feedback on Turkish EFL students' writing performance. *Journal of Educational Computing Research, 46*(1), 61–84.

Cuseo, J. (2007). The empirical case against large class size: Adverse effects on the teaching, learning, and retention of first-year students. *Journal of Faculty Development, 21*(1), 5–21.

Dawson, P., Henderson, M., Mahoney, P., Phillips, M., Ryan, T., Boud, D., & Molloy, E. (2019). What makes for effective feedback: Staff and student perspectives. *Assessment and Evaluation in Higher Education, 44*(1), 25–36. https://doi.org/10.1080/02602938.2018.1467877.

Debuse, J. C. W., Lawley, M., & Shibl, R. (2008). Educators' perceptions of automated feedback systems. *Australasian Journal of Educational Technology, 24*(4), 374–386. https://doi.org/10.14742/ajet.1198.

Deepwell, F., & Benfield, G. (2012). Evaluating assessment practices: The academic staff perspective. In L. Clouder, C. Brougham, S. Jewell, & G. Steventon (Eds.), *Improving student engagement and development through assessment: Theory and practice in higher education* (pp. 59–72). New York: Routledge.

Exeter, D. J., Ameratunga, S., Ratima, M., Morton, S., Dickson, M., Hsu, D., & Jackson, R. (2010). Student engagement in very large classes: The teachers' perspective. *Studies in Higher Education, 35*(7), 761–775. https://doi.org/10.1080/03075070903545058.

Fincham, O. E., Gašević, D., Jovanović, J., & Pardo, A. (2018). From study tactics to learning strategies: An analytical method for extracting interpretable representations. *IEEE Transactions on Learning Technologies, 12*(1), 59–72. https://doi.org/10.1109/TLT.2018.2823317.

Gašević, D., Dawson, S., & Siemens, G. (2015). Let's not forget: Learning analytics are about learning. *TechTrends, 59*(1), 64–71. https://doi.org/10.1007/s11528-014-0822-x.

Gašević, D., Dawson, S., Rogers, T., & Gašević, D. (2016). Learning analytics should not promote one size fits all: The effects of instructional conditions in predicting learning success. *The Internet and Higher Education, 28*, 68–84. https://doi.org/10.1016/j.iheduc.2015.10.002.

Gašević, D., Mirriahi, N., Dawson, S., & Joksimović, S. (2017). Effects of instructional conditions and experience on the adoption of a learning tool. *Computers in Human Behavior, 67*, 207–220. https://doi.org/10.1016/j.chb.2016.10.026.

Gibbs, G., & Simpson, C. (2004). Conditions under which assessment supports students' learning. *Learning and Teaching in Higher Education, 1*(1), 3–31.

Gibbs, G., Lucas, L., & Simonite, V. (1996). Class size and student performance: 1984–94. *Studies in Higher Education, 21*(3), 261–273. https://doi.org/10.1080/03075079612331381201.

Greller, W., & Drachsler, H. (2012). Translating learning into numbers: A generic framework for learning analytics. *Journal of Educational Technology & Society, 15*(3), 42–57. Retrieved from https://www.jstor.org/stable/jeductechsoci.15.3.42.

Hartley, J., & Chesworth, K. (2000). Qualitative and quantitative methods in research on essay writing: No one way. *Journal of Further and Higher Education, 24*(1), 15–24. https://doi.org/10.1080/030987700112282.

Hattie, J., & Timperley, H. (2007). The power of feedback. *Review of Educational Research, 77*(1), 81–112. https://doi.org/10.3102/003465430298487.

Herder, T., Swiecki, Z., Fougt, S. S., Tamborg, A. L., Allsopp, B. B., Shaffer, D. W., & Misfeldt, M. (2018, March). Supporting teachers' intervention in students' virtual collaboration using a network based model. In *Proceedings of the 8th International Conference on Learning Analytics and Knowledge* (pp. 21–25). ACM.

Huang, S.-C. (2016). Understanding learners' self-assessment and self-feedback on their foreign language speaking performance. *Assessment & Evaluation in Higher Education, 41*(6), 803–820. https://doi.org/10.1080/02602938.2015.1042426.

Huxham, M. (2007). Fast and effective feedback: Are model answers the answer? *Assessment & Evaluation in Higher Education, 32*(6), 601–611. https://doi.org/10.1080/02602930601116946.

Joksimović, S., Dowell, N., Gašević, D., Mirriahi, N., Dawson, S., & Graesser, A. C. (2019). Linguistic characteristics of reflective states in video annotations under different instructional conditions. *Computers in Human Behavior, 96,* 211–222. https://doi.org/10.1016/j.chb.2018.03.003.

Jovanović, J., Gašević, D., Dawson, S., Pardo, A., & Mirriahi, N. (2017). Learning analytics to unveil learning strategies in a flipped classroom. *The Internet and Higher Education, 33,* 74–85. https://doi.org/10.1016/j.iheduc.2017.02.001.

Lust, G., Elen, J., & Clarebout, G. (2013). Students' tool-use within a web enhanced course: Explanatory mechanisms of students' tool-use pattern. *Computers in Human Behavior, 29*(5), 2013–2021. https://doi.org/10.1016/j.chb.2013.03.014.

Messick, S. (1995). Standards of validity and the validity of standards in performance assessment. *Educational Measurement: Issues and Practice, 14*(4), 5–8. https://doi.org/10.1111/j.1745-3992.1995.tb00881.x.

Mirriahi, N., Joksimović, S., Gašević, D., & Dawson, S. (2018). Effects of instructional conditions and experience on student reflection: A video annotation study. *Higher Education Research & Development, 37*(6), 1245–1259. https://doi.org/10.1080/07294360.2018.1473845.

Moore, C., & Teather, S. (2012). Engaging students in peer review: Feedback as learning. *eCULTURE, 5,* 27–36.

Panadero, E., & Broadbent, J. (2018). Developing evaluative judgement: A self-regulated learning perspective. In D. Boud, R. Ajjawi, P. Dawson, & J. Tai (Eds.), *Developing evaluative judgement in higher education: Assessment for knowing and producing quality work* (pp. 81–89). Oxon: Routledge.

Pardo, A. (2018). A feedback model for data-rich learning experiences. *Assessment & Evaluation in Higher Education, 43*(3), 428–438. https://doi.org/10.1080/02602938.2017.1356905.

Pardo, A., Jovanović, J., Dawson, S., Gašević, D., & Mirriahi, N. (2019). Using learning analytics to scale the provision of personalised feedback. *British Journal of Educational Technology, 50*(1), 128–138. https://doi.org/10.1111/bjet.12592.

Price, M., Handley, K., Millar, J., & O'Donovan, B. (2010). Feedback: All that effort, but what is the effect? *Assessment & Evaluation in Higher Education, 35*(3), 277–289. https://doi.org/10.1080/02602930903541007.

Siemens, G., & Gašević, D. (2012). Guest editorial-learning and knowledge analytics. *Journal of Educational Technology & Society, 15*(3), 1–2.

Tanes, Z., Arnold, K. E., King, A. S., & Remnet, M. A. (2011). Using Signals for appropriate feedback: Perceptions and practices. *Computers & Education, 57*(4), 2414–2422. https://doi.org/10.1016/j.compedu.2011.05.016.

Teasley, S. D. (2017). Student facing dashboards: One size fits all? *Technology, Knowledge and Learning, 22*(3), 377–384. https://doi.org/10.1007/s10758-017-9314-3.

Timmerman, A. A., & Dijkstra, J. (2017). A practice approach to programmatic assessment design. *Advances in Health Sciences Education, 22*(5), 1169–1182. https://doi.org/10.1007.s10459-017-9756-3.

van der Vleuten, C. P. M., Schuwirth, L. W. T., Driessen, E. W., Dijkstra, J., Tigelaar, D., Baartman, L. K. J., & van Tartwijk, J. (2012). A model for programmatic assessment fit for purpose. *Medical Teacher, 34*(3), 205–214. https://doi.org/10.3109/0142159X.2012.652239.

Winne, P. H. (2017). Leveraging big data to help each learner and accelerate learning science. *Teachers College Record, 119*(3), 1–24.

Winstone, N. E., Nash, R. A., Rowntree, J., & Parker, M. (2017). 'It'd be useful, but I wouldn't use it': Barriers to university students' feedback seeking and recipience. *Studies in Higher Education, 42*(11), 2026–2041. https://doi.org/10.1080/03075079.2015.1130032.

Wise, A. F., Speer, J., Marbouti, F., & Hsiao, Y.-T. (2013). Broadening the notion of participation in online discussions: Examining patterns in learners' online listening behaviors. *Instructional Science, 41*(2), 323–343. https://doi.org/10.1007/s11251-012-9230-9.

Wu, W. C. V., Petit, E., & Chen, C. H. (2015). EFL writing revision with blind expert and peer review using a CMC open forum. *Computer Assisted Language Learning, 28*(1), 58–80. https://doi.org/10.1080/09588221.2014.937442.

13

Facilitating Students' Use of Feedback: Capturing and Tracking Impact Using Digital Tools

Naomi Winstone

In contemporary higher education, much emphasis is placed on student satisfaction with the feedback they *receive*. However, insight into what students actually *do* with feedback is difficult to obtain; there is a notable paucity of behavioural data in the research literature. As has been argued by key scholars (e.g. Boud & Molloy, 2013; Carless, 2015), the most important question to ask is not how feedback comments should be constructed, but whether the feedback process leads to discernible impact on students. In theory, students could be very satisfied with the detail of comments (the input) as measured by surveys such as the UK National Student Survey (NSS) or the Australian Course Experience Questionnaire (CEQ), but see little impact in terms of their learning or skills (the output).

In this chapter, I explore the role of digital tools in the feedback process, with a particular focus on how and where such tools might facilitate visualisation of the impact of these feedback processes. I first outline a series of challenges inherent to tracking the impact of feedback, and I then introduce and discuss the development of a specific digital tool for

---

N. Winstone (✉)
University of Surrey, Guildford, UK
e-mail: n.winstone@surrey.ac.uk

© The Author(s) 2019
M. Henderson et al. (eds.), *The Impact of Feedback in Higher Education*,
https://doi.org/10.1007/978-3-030-25112-3_13

tracking the impact of feedback, the *Feedback Engagement and Tracking System (FEATS)*. FEATS focuses on students' self-regulation of their learning through synthesising and tracking the impact of their feedback. Thus, I adopt a social constructivist approach to feedback (see Ajjawi & Boud, 2017), conceptualising the impact of feedback as being mediated by students' sense-making of comments, dialogic exchanges, and actions.

Conceptualising Feedback Impact

Perhaps the first step to considering how to track the impact of feedback is to consider what we might take as evidence of such impact. In a recent study (Winstone & Boud, 2019), we asked academics from the UK and Australia to describe how they would know whether their feedback had been effective; in other words, what they would see as evidence of the impact of their feedback. Of our 682 respondents, 1 in 5 reported that it was not possible to know whether feedback had been effective due to the common modular nature of courses, whereby they would not have access to what students did next. Half of the respondents from the UK conceptualised impact in terms of student satisfaction; review by peers or external examiners were also prominent responses from our UK sample. Over 60% of the Australian sample did speak of impact in terms of seeing some change in students' behaviours, knowledge, or skills. At first glance, this stark difference was somewhat perplexing. Both the UK and Australian Higher Education systems place heavy emphasis on student satisfaction; the findings of both NSS in the UK and the CEQ in Australia reveal that students are less satisfied with assessment and feedback than any other dimension of their university experience. A clue to the reasons behind these findings comes from our participants' responses to another question that we asked them. Our Australian respondents reported that they were significantly more likely than our UK respondents to design assessments with student implementation of feedback in mind. Thus, the mindset of our Australian respondents appeared to be more attuned to the potential for feedback impact than their counterparts in the UK. Putting the national differences aside, what these findings do reveal is that for many higher education staff, seeking impact of feedback is an alien and unspecified concept.

This conclusion is also mirrored in the research literature. Recent reviews of the literature on student engagement with feedback (e.g. Jönsson, 2013; Winstone, Nash, Parker, & Rowntree, 2017) report that the majority of research studies in this area assess students' self-reported behaviours in response to feedback. In contrast, there are very few examples where researchers explore the use of feedback on a behavioural level and even fewer examples where researchers collect data to follow up and see how students' engagement influences them later in time.

The data I have outlined here represent the impact of feedback from the point of view of educators; that is, do they know whether their feedback has been effective? The focus of this chapter is on students recognising and tracking impact of their use of feedback, in line with a social constructivist approach where it is the actions of the student, not of the educator, which are of primary focus. There are many challenges inherent to exactly *how* students might recognise the impact of their engagement with feedback information. First, in order to engage with feedback in ways that are likely to facilitate impact, students need to engage in mindful processing of the developmental information it may contain. Students also need to create an internal representation of the areas of their skill base that require improvement, if they are to take full advantage of opportunities to develop these skills when they arise. This is immediately challenging when we consider that feedback is sometimes poorly designed and offers students limited opportunities to improve, alongside evidence that students typically read their feedback once and do not revisit it further (e.g. Winstone, Nash, Rowntree, & Parker, 2017) and that students' subsequent recall of feedback information is weak (Nash, Winstone, Gregory, & Papps, 2018).

Second, whilst we may conceive of feedback impact as resulting from the synthesis of multiple feedback processes, not a single feedback event, students typically receive feedback information in modular chunks, and synthesising feedback is reported as a challenge that causes students frustration (e.g. Orsmond, Merry, & Reiling, 2005; Price, Handley, & Millar, 2011; Winstone, Nash, Rowntree, et al., 2017). There are also many informal elements to feedback processes which extend beyond typical assessment patterns, such as information gleaned from discussions with tutors, peers, learning advisors, and other professionals that facilitate student learning (e.g. Gravett & Winstone, 2019). As a result, the impact of feedback is unlikely to be strictly linear, whereby the effect of one feedback event feeds exclusively into immediate change in that domain; it is more likely that paths to the impact of engaging with feedback are complex and nuanced. Equally, whilst students may find it relatively simple to recognise the impact of engagement with feedback on easily quantifiable outcomes such as grades, recognising changes in their knowledge, skills, motivation, and self-concept is much more challenging.

Finally, the impact of engagement with feedback may not be realised immediately. The result of students' engagement with and use of feedback information may filter into the development of knowledge, skills, and attributes over a longer period of time. The challenge in recognising impact then becomes one of remembering the nature of feedback information, and the steps one took in response to feedback over the short term (e.g. a semester or trimester), the medium term (e.g. an academic year), and the longer term (e.g. an entire programme). Given these challenges, we now look to the potential affordances of technology to offer solutions.

The Role of Digital Tools in Capturing the Impact of Feedback

Within the literature, there are many examples of the use of digital tools to facilitate the feedback process (e.g. Donia, O'Neill, & Brutus, 2018; Pardo, Jovanovic, Dawson, Gašević, & Mirriahi, 2019). Zimbardi et al. (2017) argue that:

> Feedback is known to have a large influence on student learning gains, and the emergence of online tools has greatly enhanced the opportunity for delivering timely, expressive, digital feedback and for investigating its learning impacts. (p. 625)

Yet of the many and varied uses of technology to facilitate feedback processes, there are very few that facilitate tracking of impact (Winstone, Nash, Parker, et al., 2017); most focus on using technology to facilitate

13 Facilitating Students' Use of Feedback: Capturing and Tracking ...

feedback delivery, which is arguably just a different medium within a transmission-focused approach (Mahoney, Macfarlane, & Ajjawi, 2019; Pitt & Winstone, 2019). Yet in their conceptualisation of feedback literacy, Carless and Boud (2018) argue that feedback literate students "*use technology to access, store and revisit feedback*" (p. 5), thus recognising the potential for digital tools to facilitate students' proactive uptake of feedback.

It is often argued that students' engagement with feedback is largely invisible (Price, Handley, Millar, & O'Donovan, 2010); one significant area of potential for technology to facilitate tracking of the impact of feedback is via the digital footprint left by learners as they engage with feedback through technology-enhanced systems. Wang, Chen, and Worthy (2017) use the term "feedback analytics" (as a specific example of learning analytics) to represent measures of student engagement with feedback information; for example, in the case of video feedback, such analytics include the number of video views and students' pausing/rewinding behaviour. Similarly, Ada and Stansfield (2017) describe a system called MyFeedBack which presents to tutors information regarding their students' engagement with feedback comments, as measured by whether or not students open their feedback files and how many times they access the file. Ada and Stansfield (2017) reported that the majority of students only accessed their feedback information once. This is potentially problematic, as it is challenging to assimilate all the learning potential from a single read, and it also precludes the synthesis of feedback from multiple assignments, modules, and markers. Whilst these data undoubtedly go some way to countering the problem of the "invisibility" of students' active engagement with feedback (Handley, Price, & Millar, 2011), whether students open their feedback is necessary but not sufficient for feedback to have an impact.

A different approach to the use of technology to quantify and track the impact of feedback is reported by Zimbardi et al. (2017). They utilised a feedback analytics system to measure when and for how long students engaged with feedback on a course with multiple research report assessments. Their data provide some indication that students who showed limited engagement with their feedback did not improve as much, and as quickly, as students who engaged in depth with their feedback.

All three of these examples explore the "digital footprint" of students' interactions with feedback, but the analytics that have the potential to track the impact of feedback are staff-facing, rather than representing student-facing information that can inform their own academic development and their future engagement with feedback. This is a crucial point because students often report that they find it difficult, and in some cases unproductive, to engage with feedback information because they do not see that their efforts in this regard have "paid off" (Winstone, Nash, Rowntree, et al., 2017). In order for students' engagement with feedback to support the development of self-regulation, it is not just "closing the gap" that is important, but being able to recognise how one achieved this and whether the chosen behaviours were successful. I illustrate this point by repurposing an analogy that is commonly represented in contemporary discourse around the "student-as-consumer" in higher education. It is often argued that students should conceptualise their financial investment in relation to their own engagement with education as akin to engaging the services of a personal trainer (e.g. Emerson & Mansvelt, 2014). When one employs the services of a personal trainer, they are not paying for demanding exercise to be done for them. One would not expect to see changes in fitness just because a trainer has been employed; rather, the financial investment provides the support of an expert facilitator and motivator to guide engagement with exercise.

Taking this fitness analogy one step further, one of the most common analytics dashboards in everyday use is that representing the output from fitness and activity trackers. These data representing one's activity levels and other related health behaviours are purposefully designed to enable the individual to view and track their own engagement with exercise. In turn, the individual can see how their behaviours have changed over time and the impact of these behaviours. This promotes a self-regulatory approach where, as a result, the individual might endeavour to increase their activity levels, get more sleep, or increase their intake of water, for example.

The approach I have taken to the use of digital tools to support students' engagement with feedback draws strongly on this fitness analogy. I wanted to find a way through which students could synthesise multiple pieces of information that represented their engagement with feedback and to track where and how the steps they had taken had influenced not only their academic performance, but their broader skill development. Thus, just as with activity tracker dashboards that are arguably familiar to many students and educators alike, central to our endeavours was the fundamental principle that, if they are to support self-regulatory learning, feedback analytics should be student-facing.

The Feedback Engagement and Tracking System (FEATS)

As part of the *Developing Engagement with Feedback Toolkit* (Winstone & Nash, 2016), we developed a feedback portfolio to enable students to synthesise and reflect upon feedback from multiple sources and to set and monitor their progress towards self-identified targets for improvement. With the move to electronic management of assessment, we saw an opportunity to combine the synthesis function of the basic portfolio concept with digital tools to track engagement with, and the impact of, feedback, via a student-facing analytics dashboard within a feedback e-portfolio. Students often find it hard to interpret the data presented to them in many dashboards; as a result, the potential for the dashboard information to impact learning is minimised (Corrin & de Barba, 2015). Through a co-design process (Spinuzzi, 2005), we worked with students to design a dashboard presenting the information they wanted to see and in the way that felt most authentic to them. Simple analytics were of importance because our aim was for the dashboard to influence student action.

FEATS has three functions (see Table 13.1): a feedback review and synthesis tool (section A); a skill development tool consisting of a large resource bank (section B); and an action-planning and dialogue tool (section C). The outputs of students' activities within the portfolio are represented via a dashboard representing a simplified digital trace of their engagement with feedback and the resultant impact on their skills development and attainment (https://tinyurl.com/FEATSPortfolio; see also Fig. 13.1).

232   N. Winstone

Table 13.1 Features of FEATS and intended purpose with regard to the impact of engagement with feedback

Section	Features	Design for impact
A	Feedback review tool	Encourages mindful processing and internalisation of feedback. Students can enter formal assessment feedback, self-appraisal, peer feedback, or verbal feedback. Students "tag" each element of the review according to the skills to which it refers
	Visual synthesis of feedback	The dashboard is itself a form of feedback; students see a visual summary of the most common three strengths identified through the feedback they have entered and the most common three areas for development
	Feedback summary tool	When students are working on another assignment, they can look back at a summary of all previous feedback relating to a particular skill they might be using
	Grade tracker	Students have the option to record grades obtained for assessments and view a chart displaying grades over time. Students are encouraged to use this information to see how and where their use of feedback has had an impact on their attainment
B	Resource bank	FEATS contains a large resource bank aligned with each of the skills categories used to "tag" feedback in Section A. Students can access resources such as videos, podcasts, books, articles, workshops, and websites to support their development in this area

(continued)

13 Facilitating Students' Use of Feedback: Capturing and Tracking ...   233

Table 13.1 (continued)

Section	Features	Design for impact
C	Action planning log	Students can set specific targets for implementation of their feedback and engagement with resources to develop their skills
	Completed action record	Students can mark actions as "complete", after which these actions are transferred to a log of completed actions. This enables students to look back at actions they have taken to implement feedback and the resulting impact
	Stimulus for dialogue	Students are encouraged to share their dashboard and action plan with a personal tutor or academic advisor, such that staff also gain insight into student engagement and the resulting impact

Illustrations of Potential Impact

Both qualitative and quantitative methods have been used to evaluate FEATS. We began the project with a series of focus groups to understand students' experiences of receiving feedback information in the VLE and their perceptions of learning analytics dashboards. We then ran a series of co-design workshops with students to create design briefs which were used to develop a prototype portfolio. We collected students' perceptions of the prototype through interviews and think-aloud protocols and also interviewed academic staff about the portfolio. Once the final version of the portfolio had been launched, over the course of an academic year we tracked students' use of the tool and the impact on their approaches to feedback, self-regulation, and attainment.

Whilst presenting these data in detail is beyond the scope of this chapter, I now present two illustrations of the potential of this feedback design; the first draws upon insights gleaned during the design process that illustrate how the tool has the potential to enhance the impact of feedback from

234　N. Winstone

Fig. 13.1 FEATS dashboard

the students' perspectives. The second presents two student case studies illustrating the potential of FEATS on an individual level.

During their involvement in the design and testing of FEATS, students showed insight into its potential impact. They recognised the importance of mindful feedback processing, identified ways in which FEATS would encourage them to take meaningful action upon feedback, and saw the benefit of tracking their engagement with feedback (pseudonyms or participant numbers are used to preserve anonymity):

> This is actually making an imprint on my memory like about what the feedback was and how I can go about using it in my work.
> (Kay, Focus Group 4, discussing Section A of FEATS)

> It might even be useful for a kind of revision plan, so say after you get your feedback you could write 'before next exam I need to go over x'.
> (Think Aloud, Participant 7, discussing Section C of FEATS)

> It helps you see what you've done and yeah just kind of track yourself.
> (Stephen, Focus Group 3, discussing Section C of FEATS)

In order to illustrate the potential for the use of FEATS to support students to use feedback productively, we now turn to two student case studies, representing different disciplines and different levels of engagement with FEATS over the course of an academic year (see Table 13.2). These two students have been selected as they illustrate different outcomes of using FEATS; thus, they provide a glimpse of the *potential* for digital tools such as FEATS to strengthen the impact of feedback. As part of our evaluation, we asked students to complete the Feedback Orientation Scale (FOS; Linderbaum & Levy, 2010) at the beginning and end of the academic year, which assesses students' general beliefs and orientations regarding feedback. The FOS Utility subscale ($\alpha = .88$) measures the extent to which an individual believes that using feedback processes have beneficial outcomes; the Accountability subscale ($\alpha = .73$) represents a belief that it is one's responsibility to act upon feedback information; and the Self-efficacy subscale ($\alpha = .78$) measures an individual's perception of their ability to act upon feedback information. We also measured students' self-reported skills in using feedback (mindful reading, understanding, knowing how to act, feeling able to act, being willing to act; $\alpha = .71$).

Table 13.2 Changes in perceptions of feedback use

	Student A	Student B
Age	18	18
Programme	Psychology	Criminology
FEATS use (hours)	8	40
RCI[a]: feedback utility	2.36*	4.71*
RCI: feedback accountability	0	3.56*
RCI: feedback self-efficacy	4.16*	0
RCI: feedback skills	2.87*	1.91

[a]RCI = Reliable Change Index, a measure of intra-individual change over time, taking into account the reliability of the measurement instrument (Zahra, Hedge, Pesola, & Burr, 2016)
*RCI significant at $p < .05$

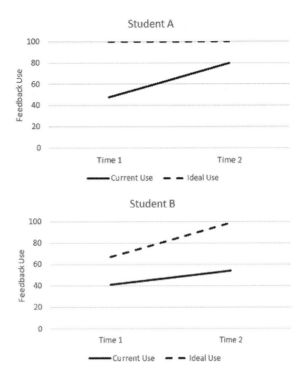

Fig. 13.2 Self-reported current and ideal feedback use

These data demonstrate that Student A showed significant gains in three out of the four measures and Student B in two out of the four measures. We also asked students to rate, on a scale from 1 to 100, the extent to which they currently act upon feedback and the ideal level of action on feedback (see Fig. 13.2).

These data demonstrate two different profiles of potential impact. Student A started the year with a strong expectation of what the ideal level of feedback use should be, which she maintained for the academic year. Her own use of feedback at the beginning of the year fell far short of this ideal, but over the course of the academic year, she narrowed this differential. She also showed a large gain in her feedback self-efficacy (Table 13.2), which aligns with this profile. In contrast, the most notable change for Student B is an increase in her perception of what the ideal level of feed-

13 Facilitating Students' Use of Feedback: Capturing and Tracking ...

back use should be, which aligns with the large change in her scores on the FOS Utility subscale. It is important to acknowledge that these profiles rely on self-report data and that it is not possible to rule out the influence of other factors on changes in students' feedback orientations. However, these two cases illustrate the potential for FEATS to support students in understanding the importance of mindful engagement with feedback and in developing students' ability and confidence to use feedback.

What Impact and for Whom?

One of the most significant challenges to realising the impact of feedback is enabling students and educators to see this impact. Given the complexity and ubiquity of much of the information shared during the feedback process, the possible levels upon which such information might conceivably have impact, and the temporal space over which the impact might be actualised, we might conceive of the impact of feedback as being somewhat elusive (e.g. Winstone & Boud, 2019). It is also important to acknowledge that students' ability to work with feedback and realise improvement on this basis is also dependent on the quality of the feedback information they are provided by their educators.

Realising the impact of feedback is complicated by the common modular structure of many degree programmes in contemporary higher education. During the design of FEATS, students saw value to a tool that would synthesise their feedback at a programme level using a skills focus, rather than maintaining feedback in modular "chunks". The digital "tagging" against key skills and immediate visual representation in FEATS facilitates this process. FEATS also serves as a permanent and interactive repository that facilitates tracking of impact. Crucially, the dashboard is designed to support the development of students' self-regulation by enabling them to visualise and monitor the outcomes of their engagement with feedback.

A system such as FEATS cannot solve all of the problems inherent to tracking the impact of feedback; rather, I have used this example as a vehicle for surfacing and exploring the potential for digital tools to support the feedback process. Crucially, as has been argued elsewhere (Pitt & Winstone, 2019), technology is not best deployed within the assessment process if it merely replicates existing processes in a digital format; instead, the focus should be on the specific affordances of technology to facilitate student learning in a dialogic feedback environment. Following my exploration of the impact of feedback in higher education, I end by proposing three key factors pertaining to the impact of feedback, highlighting the potential for FEATS to facilitate feedback tracking and impact.

1. *Impact does not come from a single feedback event, but from the synthesis of multiple feedback processes*

Modularised curricula can lead to a "pigeon-holing" approach to feedback, whereby students (and educators) can be unaware of the potential transfer of feedback information from one area to feed into another. This necessarily limits the impact of feedback because feedback information is relegated to piecemeal comments rather than a holistic and ongoing process. It is through the synthesis of information gained through multiple feedback processes, both formal and informal, that impact is strengthened and realised. Even if an assignment in one module or unit is very different to that in another module or unit, there are likely to be skills utilised in one that are of relevance to the other, and FEATS gives students the opportunity to connect their skill development across multiple assignments.

2. *Impact needs to be visible and accessible to both educators and students*

Feedback is a process, not a product. Both educators and students are invested in the process, but without dialogue, each party rarely gains insight into the process from the others' point of view. The analytics in FEATS provide students with a visual representation of common strengths and areas for improvement as identified through feedback information and can serve as a stimulus for dialogue with their educators. However, the primary purpose of FEATS is that this information is student-facing, to inform the development of their own feedback literacy.

3. *Impact can be cognitive (the student thinks differently), behavioural (the student acts differently), or motivational (the student adopts a different goal pursuit, for example)*

Perhaps the simplest way of conceptualising the impact of feedback is that students' grades increase. This is indeed a desirable outcome, but in many cases, feedback processes may have effects that are not captured by grades. As illustrated by students' perceptions of the FEATS tool, feedback can have impact on the way students think about feedback information, the behaviours they choose to adopt in response to feedback, or their approaches to learning more broadly. Conceptualising impact in a broader sense, extending beyond individual tasks, is likely to be beneficial to both educators and students.

Realising a paradigm shift from transmission-focused to learning-focused approaches to feedback requires educators and students alike to reposition feedback away from a teacher-delivered product and towards a student-driven process, where student engagement with feedback and the impact of feedback on students' learning behaviours and outcomes are of primary focus. Whilst this notion is well represented within the literature on assessment and feedback, practice continues to be dominated by cognitivist models of monologic transmission (Carless, 2015). One potential reason for the stubborn maintenance of this model is that tracking the impact of feedback is fraught with challenges, some of which have been explored in this chapter. Whilst learning analytics offer one potential solution to these challenges, if such information is directed towards educators, and not visible to students, then this approach is not supporting a learning-focused approach to feedback. Student-facing dashboards offer one promising direction of travel, whereby students view information about their engagement with feedback information and the resultant outcomes, as a way of self-regulating their behaviour. In the domain of feedback processes, impact is nuanced, multifaceted, and often intangible. Digital tools such as e-portfolios, in conjunction with student-facing analytics dashboards, hold promise in supporting students and educators to maximise the impact of a feedback process where the whole is more than the sum of its parts.

References

Ada, M. B., & Stansfield, M. (2017). The potential of learning analytics in understanding students' engagement with their assessment feedback. In *Proceedings of the 17th IEEE International Conference on Advanced Learning Technologies-ICALT2017*. Timisoara, Romania.

Ajjawi, R., & Boud, D. (2017). Researching feedback dialogue: An interactional analysis approach. *Assessment and Evaluation in Higher Education, 42*(2), 252–265. https://doi.org/10.1080/02602938.2015.1102863.

Boud, D., & Molloy, E. (2013). Rethinking models of feedback for learning: The challenge of design. *Assessment & Evaluation in Higher Education, 38*(6), 698–712. https://doi.org/10.1080/02602938.2012.691462.

Carless, D. (2015). *Excellence in university assessment.* London: Routledge.

Carless, D., & Boud, D. (2018). The development of student feedback literacy: Enabling uptake of feedback. *Assessment & Evaluation in Higher Education, 43*(8), 1315–1325. https://doi.org/10.1080/02602938.2018.1463354.

Corrin, L., & de Barba, P. (2015, March). How do students interpret feedback delivered via dashboards? In *Proceedings of the Fifth International Conference on Learning Analytics and Knowledge* (pp. 430–431).

Donia, M. B., O'Neill, T. A., & Brutus, S. (2018). The longitudinal effects of peer feedback in the development and transfer of student teamwork skills. *Learning and Individual Differences, 61,* 87–98. https://doi.org/10.1016/j.lindif.2017.11.012.

Emerson, L., & Mansvelt, J. (2014). 'If they're the customer, I'm the meat in the sandwich': An exploration of tertiary teachers' metaphorical constructions of teaching. *Higher Education Research & Development, 33*(3), 469–482. https://doi.org/10.1080/07294360.2013.841653.

Gravett, K., & Winstone, N. (2019). 'Feedback interpreters': The role of learning development professionals in facilitating university students' engagement with feedback. *Teaching in Higher Education, 24,* 723–738. https://doi.org/10.1080/13562517.2018.1498076.

Handley, K., Price, M., & Millar, J. (2011). Beyond 'doing time': Investigating the concept of student engagement with feedback. *Oxford Review of Education, 37*(4), 543–560. https://doi.org/10.1080/03054985.2011.604951.

Jönsson, A. (2013). Facilitating productive use of feedback in higher education. *Active Learning in Higher Education, 14*(1), 63–76. https://doi.org/10.1177/1469787412467125.

Linderbaum, B. A., & Levy, P. E. (2010). The development and validation of the Feedback Orientation Scale (FOS). *Journal of Management, 36* (6), 1372–1405. https://doi.org/10.1177/0149206310373145.

Mahoney, P., Macfarlane, S., & Ajjawi, R. (2019). A qualitative synthesis of video feedback in higher education. *Teaching in Higher Education, 24* (2), 157–179. https://doi.org/10.1080/13562517.2018.1471457.

Nash, R. A., Winstone, N. E., Gregory, S. E. A., & Papps, E. (2018). A memory advantage for past-oriented over future-oriented performance feedback. *Journal of Experimental Psychology. Learning, Memory, and Cognition, 44* (12), 1864–1879. https://doi.org/10.1037/xlm0000549.

Orsmond, P., Merry, S., & Reiling, K. (2005). Biology students' utilization of tutors' formative feedback: A qualitative interview study. *Assessment & Evaluation in Higher Education, 30* (4), 369–386. https://doi.org/10.1080/02602930500099177.

Pardo, A., Jovanovic, J., Dawson, S., Gašević, D., & Mirriahi, N. (2019). Using learning analytics to scale the provision of personalised feedback. *British Journal of Educational Technology, 50* (1), 128–138. https://doi.org/10.1111/bjet.12592.

Pitt, E., & Winstone, N. (2019). Dialogic feedback in a digital world. In M. Bearman, P. Dawson, J. Tai, R. Ajjawi, & D. Boud (Eds.), *Re-imagining university assessment in a digital world.* New York: Springer.

Price, M., Handley, K., & Millar, J. (2011). Feedback: Focusing attention on engagement. *Studies in Higher Education, 36* (8), 879–896. https://doi.org/10.1080/03075079.2010.483513.

Price, M., Handley, K., Millar, J., & O'Donovan, B. (2010). Feedback: All that effort, but what is the effect? *Assessment & Evaluation in Higher Education, 35* (3), 277–289. https://doi.org/10.1080/02602930903541007.

Spinuzzi, C. (2005). The methodology of participatory design. *Technical Communication, 52* (2), 163–174.

Wang, J. T. H., Chen, R., & Worthy, P. (2017, August). Feedback analytics-measuring the impact of video feedback on student learning. In *Proceedings of the Australian Conference on Science and Mathematics Education (formerly UniServe Science Conference)* (p. 135).

Winstone, N. E., & Boud, D. (2019). Exploring cultures of feedback practice: The adoption of learning-focused feedback practices in the UK and Australia. *Higher Education Research and Development, 38,* 411–425. https://doi.org/10.1080/07294360.2018.1532985.

Winstone, N. E., & Nash, R. A. (2016). *The developing engagement with feedback toolkit.* York, UK: Higher Education Academy.

Winstone, N. E., Nash, R. A., Parker, M., & Rowntree, J. (2017). Supporting learners' agentic engagement with feedback: A systematic review and a taxonomy of recipience processes. *Educational Psychologist, 52*(1), 17–37. https://doi.org/10.1080/00461520.2016.1207538.

Winstone, N. E., Nash, R. A., Rowntree, J., & Parker, M. (2017). 'It'd be useful, but I wouldn't use it': Barriers to university students' feedback seeking and recipience. *Studies in Higher Education, 42*(11), 2026–2041. https://doi.org/10.1080/03075079.2015.1130032.

Zahra, D., Hedge, C., Pesola, F., & Burr, S. (2016). Accounting for test reliability in student progression: The reliable change index. *Medical Education, 50*(7), 738–745. https://doi.org/10.1111/medu.13059.

Zimbardi, K., Colthorpe, K., Dekker, A., Engstrom, C., Bugarcic, A., Worthy, P., … Long, P. (2017). Are they using my feedback? The extent of students' feedback use has a large impact on subsequent academic performance. *Assessment & Evaluation in Higher Education, 42*(4), 625–644. https://doi.org/10.1080/02602938.2016.1174187.

Part V

Implications for Research and Practice

14

Improving Feedback Research in Naturalistic Settings

Rola Ajjawi, David Boud, Michael Henderson and Elizabeth Molloy

Introduction

This book has sought to advance a view that feedback should make a difference to students' learning. Unfortunately, feedback practices in higher education too often treat feedback as an input model (Bing-You et al., 2018; Boud & Molloy, 2013), where at best, time, effort and care are

---

R. Ajjawi (✉) · D. Boud
Centre for Research in Assessment and Digital Learning (CRADLE),
Deakin University, Geelong, VIC, Australia
e-mail: rola.ajjawi@deakin.edu.au

D. Boud
University of Technology Sydney, Ultimo, NSW, Australia
e-mail: david.boud@deakin.edu.au

Middlesex University, London, UK

M. Henderson
Faculty of Education, Monash University, Melbourne, VIC, Australia
e-mail: michael.henderson@monash.edu

© The Author(s) 2019
M. Henderson et al. (eds.), *The Impact of Feedback in Higher Education*,
https://doi.org/10.1007/978-3-030-25112-3_14

injected into the crafting of feedback information in the *hope* that it will lead to learning. This can be deeply unsatisfying for staff and is particularly inefficient as efforts are potentially wasted because effects on learning are unknown (Price, Handley, Millar, & O'Donovan, 2010). And, from the student perspective, it may not address their concerns for improving performance and it can often be unhelpful for the next phase of their learning. In keeping with the emphasis of this book, we now focus attention on designing research that can be used to investigate the influence of feedback on learners. In the higher education context, we rarely have the opportunity to undertake fully controlled studies, so our focus here is on undertaking research in naturalistic settings in which assessment tasks and feedback processes commonly have real consequences for students.

The relative proliferation of reviews and meta-analyses of feedback in higher education (Bing-You et al., 2018; Evans, 2013; Hattie & Timperley, 2007; Jonsson, 2013; Kluger & DeNisi, 1996; Winstone, Nash, Parker, & Rowntree, 2017) would suggest that in fact researchers have explored the effects of feedback on learners. Arguably, such research within the psychological tradition has a richer history in exploring the effects of feedback than other approaches to educational research (Wiliam, 2018). Limitations of existing research include a focus on student satisfaction rather than learning, the use of aggregated grades at the end of a unit of study and/or the self-reported use of feedback information (Shute, 2008). However, satisfaction does not equal learning, grades do not inform how students make sense of and utilise performance-relevant information, and cognitive sense-making does not equal contextualised action. In a comprehensive review of feedback research in higher education, Evans (2013) argued that findings of existing research were often limited through the use of self-report data, collected at a single moment in time and without sufficient attention to context. While these research approaches have been valuable in prompting researchers to pursue feedback as a worthwhile topic of investigation, they do not address the problem of the effects of feedback

---

E. Molloy
Department of Medical Education, School of Medicine, The University of Melbourne, Parkville, VIC, Australia
e-mail: elizabeth.molloy@unimelb.edu.au

14 Improving Feedback Research in Naturalistic Settings 247

in a sufficiently detailed manner for particular feedback processes to be illuminated in normal university contexts.

Importantly, findings from the existing body of research are confusing when it comes to identifying the influence of feedback because effect sizes vary widely between studies and examples of negative and/or unintended effects abound (Wiliam, 2018). Overall, we have come to a position where we can support the statement that there is no "one size fits all" type of feedback intervention, but we "know little about what kinds of feedback are likely to be helpful in a given situation" (Wiliam, 2018, p. 15). We use this statement to orient the research endeavours that we discuss in this chapter. Specifically, we seek to promote a research agenda that contributes to an understanding of how feedback works, for particular learners, in particular circumstances. What makes this chapter different to others that have looked recently at methods for researching feedback (e.g. Brown & Harris, 2018) is that we explore research designs that occur in naturalistic settings, take account of theory and focus on students' sense-making and actions in relation to this sense-making. As such, we do not discuss experimental approaches that sanitise and narrow the range of variables at play, instead focusing on better understanding of how feedback works in naturalistic settings.

Conceptual Framing for Feedback Research

If we are to better understand how feedback works, then it is not sufficient to only research the effects of a particular feedback intervention. Rather what is also required is to make sense of the ways that inputs, processes and outputs interplay within a particular context. In learning and teaching, impact is not based on a linear, direct, causal relationship between action and outcomes (Ahmad et al., 2018). Therefore, a clear rationale for the research design is necessary, which is not often the case in higher education research (Ahmad et al., 2018). By having a clear conceptual framework and rationale, we open up the possibility of relating effects with relevant inputs and processes rather than other factors. Being clear about conceptual and theoretical frameworks strengthens explanatory power and methodological rigour—both of which having been critiqued as being limited within the existing body of literature (Evans, 2013; Wiliam, 2018).

Conceptions of feedback have shifted as we have seen greater sophistication in conceptions of learning that have impacted on educational practice and research. In this book, we conceptualise feedback within a socio-constructivist frame as *processes where learners make sense of performance-relevant information to promote their learning*. This shift from behaviourist and cognitive perspectives can be conceptualised on three dimensions—a move away (1) from what the teacher does to what the student does with performance-relevant information; (2) from feedback as input (i.e. information) to a process in which students take an active part as agentic and responsible learners; and (3) from context being absent to recognition of the fundamental influence of disciplinary contexts and cultures. In this chapter, we adopt a situated, process-centred and student-centred perspective on making sense of and using performance-relevant information, choosing to foreground the effects of feedback particularly on the learner and their actions and accomplishments.

What does such a definition demand of us if we are interested in researching the effects of feedback practices on students and their learning? First, it prompts consideration of wider boundaries of feedback processes than content, delivery, timing and mode towards a more holistic focus which includes what the student does. Second, the definition prompts us to view feedback not as a primarily one-off single intervention like a flu shot, but as an iterative process that is cyclical and continuing. This leads to a focus of research not primarily on what teachers do, but to trace the enactment of performance-relevant information through the activities of learners, and to start thinking about "feedback regimes" in supportive learning environments. This leads to exploring how students engage in feedback behaviours such as feedback seeking, judging and calibrating and how they then put these into action in situated ways that vary by professional, disciplinary or local context. In other words, feedback research should explore inputs, processes, contexts and effects.

Inputs of feedback may include, but are not limited to, teacher comments. Indeed, performance-relevant information may come in different forms from many sources, such as conversations with peers, computerised responses on quizzes, haptic information generated through a hands-on procedural task, self-judgements of work against a rubric or exemplar and comments in class about another student's work. This broader perspective on performance-relevant information shifts the onus away from the teacher for "input" towards information-rich learning environments and the design of tasks the completion of which may elicit useful information. Monitoring feedback processes is thus important to track the various ways in which students make sense of the multiple sources of performance-relevant information, how knowledge inputs might be ascertained, (re)constructed and/or the problem reframed. Feedback processes again should be considered in terms broader than one-way transmission. Thoughtful nesting and sequencing of tasks can prompt feedback loops to occur. Activities that elicit students' judgements or enable reflection on and use of performance-relevant information should also be tracked to understand how each influences individual students in particular ways. Otherwise, if we assume an intervention such as feedback is homogenous and delivered context-free, we continue to obscure why feedback might be detrimental for some learners and not others, or why particular conceptions of feedback or even environment conditions might have different effects. It also opens up the research agenda to explore what sorts of performance-relevance information students make sense of and use naturally within their university curricula to influence their learning.

Categories of Effects on Students

Feedback inputs and processes can influence learning in many different ways and over different time spans. These range from immediate effects on completing tasks more effectively in the current unit of study to longer-term influences on how students approach learning throughout their enrolment. We can divide these into three broad categories: (a) task-related performance/work; (b) meta-learning processes such as self-regulation; and (c) identity effects such as orienting students to the sorts of careers they may embark on or professionals they wish to become. These categories are not exhaustive, but they help to focus on the kinds of indicators that might be pursued in feedback research.

Task-Related Effects

As learning is a key outcome of feedback, indicators of this are central to any research study. Learning can be considered in terms of the short term, contained within the current course unit; medium term, across units within a course; and the long term, beyond the course. When we are looking at learning though, we should consider not generalised measures of performance averaged across many outcomes, but learning related to the particular learning outcomes on which feedback was focused, and related learning processes. Effects may be collected from different sources, using different methods and include qualitative and quantitative data. Effects can be observed through indicators that come in different forms and are proxies for learning, for example, changes in student work as indicated through artefacts of student assessments, improvements in judgements of the work or personal accounts of how performance-relevant information has been made sense of and used.

When it comes to task-related performance or work, these have been typical of previous feedback research that looked at improvements in grades as a result of feedback as a proxy for learning. However, the trouble with relying on improvement in marks/grades is that it reveals little about the quality of the learning or the sense-making/action taken by the students as a result of the feedback regime. The relationship between performance and learning is not a straight forward one with improvements in learning not necessarily leading to changes in performance and vice versa (Soderstrom & Bjork, 2015). Furthermore, grades are typically aggregates of marks awarded for the entire task and they obscure improvements in meeting required learning outcomes or specific competencies. Grades are also focused on the immediate task and so do not shed light on broader meta-learning processes that we might deem useful for sustainable assessment, that is, extending beyond the immediate task (Boud & Soler, 2016). Medium- and long-term effects of learning require longitudinal research to span change across multiple tasks, units or programmatically. Portfolios or programmatic feedback journals may form an interesting repository of evidence of students' development where the artefacts themselves may be analysed.

Meta-Learning Processes

The second category of effects relates to meta-learning processes, such as self-regulation of learning, making evaluative judgements, emotional regulation, digital literacy, assessment literacy or feedback literacy. Collectively, these refer to meta-learning processes that extend beyond the task, and the unit, and may theoretically be transferable. Nicol and Macfarlane-Dick (2006) posited that feedback should develop students' ability to regulate their learning through setting goals, monitoring performance in relation to these goals and taking action. Others have called for the purpose of feedback to be reoriented towards developing students' evaluative judgement, that is, the capability to make judgements about the quality of work of self and others (Tai, Ajjawi, Boud, Dawson, & Panadero, 2018). Research would seek to make visible the judgements about work and learning which might typically occur in students' heads.

Assessment literacy refers to understanding of the rules, expectations and purposes of assessment. Similarly, feedback literacy refers to "understandings, capacities and dispositions needed to make sense of information and use it to enhance work or learning strategies" (Carless & Boud, 2018, p. 1315). Research might then explore specific feedback behaviours in situ, students' attitudes and positioning in relation to others to access roles and agency, as well as aspects of emotion and emotional regulation. If feedback is a function of the student, then greater sophistication and awareness as a learner should enhance take up and utilisation of feedback information. The role of trust (Carless, 2013) and effective relationships (Farrell, Bourgeois-Law, Ajjawi, & Regehr, 2017; Telio, Regehr, & Ajjawi, 2016) is increasingly being researched as these are precursors to the uptake of information and influence students' sense-making, behaviours and outcomes.

Identity Effects

The third category of effects is less immediately discernible, but equally important as feedback processes inculcate in students the practices of the discipline or profession (Molloy et al., 2019). Feedback can play an important role in orienting students to disciplinary knowledge, practices, values and expectations and what it means to be a practitioner in a given field. Through feedback conversations, educators model ways of speaking, thinking and doing within a particular profession (Ajjawi & Higgs, 2008; Molloy, 2009), thus inducting students into a profession. Analysing feedback conversations can illuminate standards of quality for work as sanctioned by that landscape of practice. Eraut wrote of students,

> we need to know much more about how their learning, indeed their very sense of professional identity, is shaped by the nature of the feedback they receive. We need more feedback on feedback. (2006, p. 118)

There is still very limited research that naturalistically explores how students make sense of performance-relevant information (or feedback inputs both intentional and unintentional) across their degree programs which inform their identities. We might consider that one of the reasons learners might get defensive when "receiving" feedback is because the self is represented in the work; that is, we invest ourselves or some aspect of our identity into the work making criticism difficult to engage with. However, much less is known about how feedback processes come to shape our personal and professional identities across a program of study.

As mentioned, we do not conceive of these categories of effects as being exhaustive. They do, however, orient us when considering research designs. The effects that we seek to explore through research are likely to influence other decisions in the research process, including the theoretical framing of feedback and learning as well as methods of data collection and analysis, which we now turn to.

Theoretical Framing for Feedback Research

Theoretical frameworks help to guide the assumptions that underpin research, about the nature of knowledge and knowing, and about learning and how it is constituted. The theoretical framework chosen should relate to the purpose of the research and the phenomenon under study, thus influencing the chosen research methods. The theoretical framework

14 Improving Feedback Research in Naturalistic Settings 253

adopted will enable the assumptions that are inevitably made in any study to be made more explicit, should direct attention to issues and features that are germane, enable appropriate research questions to be formulated and assist with the interpretation of what is uncovered. Theory may also be applied post hoc to inform the analytical process. Theory privileges particular ways of viewing the problem and obscures others. In any particular case, developing the theoretical framework and research questions to be addressed is often an iterative back and forth process. For the purposes of clarity, we start with thinking about the influence of theory when researching effects and the different levels of abstraction to which they apply.

The importance of theory for feedback research is evident. Brookhart (2018) refers to two eras in feedback research in her review of summative and formative feedback: the shift from behaviourist views of learning towards cognitive and constructivist. Remarkably, if the question of conceptual framing is still niggling, she identified that studies conducted in the behaviourist tradition showed small effects on learning, while those in the constructivist tradition identified large effects on learning. This is why understanding how feedback works is such an important endeavour. Further, we now see a greater push towards understanding feedback within a sociocultural frame (Ajjawi & Boud, 2018; Esterhazy, 2018; Sutton, 2012) which opens up new avenues for research as we describe below.

At a macro-level, we need to consider our fundamental assumptions of what constitutes knowledge and reality (or research paradigms). This chapter is too short for a comprehensive explanation of paradigms; for this, we recommend Lincoln, Lynham, and Guba (2018). However, assumptions about knowledge (dualist/objectivist versus subjectivist) and reality (being singular, real and "out there" versus multiple and constructed) matter in the ways that the researcher is positioned within the research, how quality is judged and how the research is conducted. Research in naturalistic settings may be conducted within a number of paradigms such as post-positivism, constructivism or participatory (for a fuller description of these paradigms and their implications, see Lincoln et al., 2018).

At a meso-level, we might approach learning through a variety of lenses which should relate to the purpose of the research. For example, approaching learning with a socio-constructivist lens, where individuals construct new knowledge socially in relation to previous knowledge (Packer & Goicoechea, 2000), might prompt us to explore how students interact with pedagogical and other activities and how they make sense of performance-relevant information in order to take action. While a sociocultural perspective, where knowledge is fundamentally situated within the social, cultural and historical traditions of the practice (Packer & Goicoechea, 2000), might prompt us to consider what individual students (and staff) bring to the process (e.g. personal dispositions, expectations, motivation) and the sociocultural dimensions of practice (e.g. curriculum design, disciplinary norms, institutional expectations) that influence learning. As Esterhazy (2018, p. 1304) argues:

> From a sociocultural perspective, productive feedback can be seen as a collective achievement that is enacted in situ and is shaped by the established conventions and tools of the disciplinary practices. This calls for an analytical approach that allows us to account for both the structural and enactment layers of the practices at play.

At a micro-level, we might also utilise more individualistic theories such as self-regulation of learning (Butler & Winne, 1995) or self-determination theory (Ryan & Deci, 2000). These sorts of theories help us to focus on aspects of learning which act as indicators of effects; for example, the first is about how students set goals, monitor their work and then plan actions to meet their learning goals, while the latter is a theory of motivation. Working with these theories informs the particular processes and effects being researched whether it be the types of learning goals set and how they are followed up, or about perceptions of relatedness and how these influence motivation to engage with feedback. It is beyond the scope of this chapter to consider the wide range of current learning theories and their research implications, but the point is that what is chosen influences what effects are considered worthy of investigation and so a clear theoretical framework is necessary. It is also important to seek alignment between conceptions of feedback and learning, and measurement approaches (and we mean measurement here in the broadest sense to include qualitative exploration).

Research Approaches

So far, we have highlighted issues of theory (macro, meso, micro), inputs (who, what, format, mode), process (how, when, where) and categories of effects (task, meta-learning, identity). In this section, we consider these in relation to research approaches in naturalistic and interventional research. We focus first on methodological considerations of making visible students' sense-making, then on connecting interventional inputs and processes (including innovative feedback designs) with effects.

Researching Naturalistic Sense-Making Processes

Research might overcome the limitations of analyses focused only on formal teacher-driven feedback through widening the unit of analysis to any encounter that contributes to students' learning trajectory, that is shifting the focus beyond the formal curriculum. The challenge is how to make visible the essentially internal processes of sense-making. Learners perceive information from a variety of sources, make sense of it and relate this to their prior knowledge and experience in order to inform subsequent work, for example, through a later assignment. Sense-making is thus an interpretive activity undertaken by the individual in relation to the sociocultural—where individuals bring their frames of reference to bear on the materials (Tummons, 2014). Sense-making may occur in the moment, when students seek or receive performance-relevant information, but also as they approach future-related tasks where information might be re-interpreted in light of the learner's further work.

Methodological approaches to exploring sense-making in situ can include ethnography and narrative utilising methods such as observation, artefact analysis and interview. Observation (in person, audio or video recording) of feedback encounters provides insight into behaviours such as feedback seeking as well as bodily manifestations and/or considerations of the social, cultural and design contexts at play. For example, through observation in the clinical environment, Molloy (2009) identified that although educators had well-placed intentions to promote feedback dialogue, social and contextual factors interplayed to result in typical one-way monologues. The use of ethnographic methods of observation to understand how feedback works in practice highlights that feedback processes are inextricably linked to the contexts in which they are enacted (Esterhazy & Damşa, 2019; Urquhart, Ker, & Rees, 2018). In each of these examples, the use of observation/recording of the actual feedback encounters enabled analysis of the distinctive *relational dynamics*, "collective ways of doing", and their influence on the effects of feedback processes on students (Esterhazy, 2018). These approaches open up avenues for "feedback practice" as the unit of analysis which attunes us to wider influences on what's going on such as the human-material, sociopolitical, and cultural-discursive arrangements (e.g. Jørgensen, 2019). Therefore, naturalistic research contributes to understanding of the broader learning environment and the practices present within where productive feedback is embedded in social and disciplinary practices (Esterhazy, 2018; Esterhazy & Damşa, 2019).

Depending on the category of effect being considered, we might elicit internal thinking using techniques such as think aloud (where the participants talk through their thinking as they do the task or read feedback comments) or stimulated recall (where the participants "reconstruct" their thinking during an event or where artefacts or audio clips of feedback dialogue are used to stimulate conversation about the underlying sense-making) (Henderson, Henderson, Grant, & Huang, 2010). Both of these methods are constructions constrained by what can be explicated and what always remains tacit, not to mention our inherent desire for sense-making and creating explanations (Henderson et al., 2010). Longitudinal audio-diaries can also be used where learners record their feedback experiences include how they are making sense of and enacting different sources of information during their learning journey. These diaries can then be shared with the researchers on a regular basis.

These methods of rendering sense-making visible offer rich data collection opportunities to understand the effects of feedback, but by their very nature they will also influence the phenomenon we are interested in. There is no escaping this in naturalistic research: the intrusion of research changes the outcome (Lincoln et al., 2018). In naturalistic research, the researchers' actions, preferences and predispositions are inextricable from the research processes and products. That the researcher's subjectivity informs scholarly efforts through the entire research process is unavoidable and therefore neither inherently good nor bad. The challenge is to benefit from this effect so that pedagogic interventions without accompanying research can realise similar outcomes. An example of this is in making the process explicit. This can be done for research ends as we have been discussing here, but the making of a process visible to those in the learning milieu may have similar consequences. Rather than attempting to neutralise the researcher's subjective influence, naturalistic research encourages reflection on this influence and appreciation of the ways knowledge (and data) is co-produced through interactions between researchers and participants. Our job as researchers is to be reflexive, to pay attention to the influence of the researcher on the research design (Varpio, Ajjawi, Monrouxe, O'Brien, & Rees, 2017). Effects are not decontextualized, they are influenced through interactions between learners and the learning environment and so to fully understand the effects we need to also explore how they come about through the research processes.

Interventional Research

A number of methodological approaches could be brought to bear to investigate the effects of feedback innovations. The argument here is that feedback processes may be designed to promote opportunities for students to apply the outcomes of their sense-making. It follows that any research that seeks to determine whether feedback makes a difference should engage with feedback regimes designed for this end and which reveal effects such as the use of nested assignments or iterative tasks. Careful design can enable students to produce artefacts that can be analysed with regard to student sense-making and enactment. Alignment between the conceptual and theoretical framework and the pedagogical and research designs is critical, for example choosing data collection methods that are coherent with the purposes of the educational design rather than only those that are simple to measure.

The timing of data collection in relation to feedback processes, the forms of learning and forms of effects to be measured need to be considered carefully. How distant from a feedback event might we expect to see an effect, and can we attribute the effect to a feedback process? Sagasser, Kramer, and van der Vleuten (2012) identified short loop learning which was focused on problems that were easy to resolve and needed minor learning activities, while long loop learning required a longer period of time and was focused on "complex or recurring problems needing multiple and planned longitudinal learning activities" (p. 67). An effect may take longer than expected to occur, as in the case of developing evaluative judgement where learners may come to know their disciplines over time through immersion and observation of "good work" and therefore engage more fully with notions of quality. These prolonged effects align most with categories two and three of effects mentioned earlier—meta-learning and identity effects.

In the case of long loop learning, where assessment is typically situated, Sagasser et al. (2012) found that learners regulated their learning through making sense of multiple sources of performance-relevant information as well as multiple learning activities. Therefore, only tracking comments from a teacher and assuming that learning is only a result of this is problematic. Students might make use of feedback comments to discuss with their peers, or they may learn from comments their peers obtained, or they may learn and improve in a subsequent assessment because they changed their study approach, and this had nothing to do with the feedback intervention per se.

Research might seek to "track" intermediary indicators of effects. For example, in our work (Ajjawi & Boud, 2018) on the effects of feedback dialogue on self-regulation of learning, we observed intermediary indicators such as self-evaluation of learning, monitoring of performance and reframing of thinking during the feedback conversation. It is not known whether these self-regulatory behaviours are then manifest in other learning encounters as this would require a more longitudinal form of research with follow-up, which tends to be more challenging. Capturing enactments beyond sense-making is worthwhile as mental representations cannot capture the complexity and tacit aspects of practice, plus the relationship between thinking and action is far from simple (Dohn, 2011). That is, we need to consider intermediary indicators that might help us to achieve longer-term effects. Potential emerging methodological approaches, we address here, include participatory research and learning analytics research.

Participatory Research

Given the importance of learner agency in all feedback processes that seek to make a difference, one approach is to move beyond research designs that treat students as an object acted upon to ones that assume that they are necessarily active players. Central to feedback Mark 2 (Boud & Molloy, 2013) is that students are afforded opportunities to exercise agency, to actively seek, judge and use performance-relevant information rather than be subjected to unilateral judgements. Therefore, our research processes could encourage student agency as that is basic to what we are talking about here. Students are agentic in making sense of information and taking action about it. That does not mean they do it alone or unaided, indeed many might be involved in this journey, but we must capture the individual student's learning trajectory. We need to be careful not to deny the student agency in practice or research so that they feel there is a correct answer, or they need to tell us what we want to hear. Participatory research approaches such as action research (Carr & Kemmis, 1986) is a collaborative research approach that seeks to change practices (i.e. action) in particular through a critical edge that has an emancipatory intent which seeks to reduce inequality among the players. There might be cycles of planning, action and reflection around a particular feedback intervention, where students are collaborators and participants in the research informing each aspect of the research. Design-based research (Barab & Squire, 2004) also affords iterative co-design, participation with students and a focus on design.

Learning Analytics

What information is needed on an ongoing basis to enable both learners and those who facilitate their learning to monitor feedback? This is the realm of learning analytics. While most learning analytics to date have utilised existing information to predict adverse outcomes for students on the basis of what they do (e.g. start late, do not access the learning management system, spend insufficient time on tasks), we need to consider what else might be needed for analytics to be useful for feedback research purposes. Learning analytics can enable students and teachers to do their own research on feedback through the provision of information in useful forms. For example, this might include data on: time from submission to receipt of information, time before next relevant task, accessing of rubrics, records of information sought, received and acted upon, improvements in task performance by learning outcome and criteria. These may also be used to triangulate other forms of data mentioned above.

The field of learning analytics continues to develop quickly and along with it more sophisticated and algorithmic forms of data analysis. An example may be the automatic analysis of discussion forum posts about assessment tasks to reveal the kinds of sentiment, complexity of language, frequency of patterns such as questioning, etc. However, interpretation of this analysis can be varied and misleading, for instance a high volume of questions (e.g. how, why, etc.) could be interpreted as demonstrating positive engagement and student participation in a dialogue around assessment (a possible indicator of feedback literacy), but it could simply mean that students have no agency, and are left asking questions without further clarification. Clearly, in learning analytics, like all the other methods, we need to be concerned with the nature of the effect, the theoretical frame and the validity of the data itself. In an example of case study research, Pardo, Jovanovic, Dawson, Gašević, and Mirriahi (2019) use learning analytics to inform the feedback intervention design as well as being data in the research.

Conclusion

This chapter has sought to open up conversations about researching feedback processes to examine effects rather than to provide a blueprint for doing so. It has done so from the perspective of understanding how feedback works through naturalistic studies. We have drawn attention to potential categories of research on effects of feedback: on direct learning, short, medium and long term; on students' learning processes, such as developing students' evaluative judgement over time; and on students' identity formation as scholars and/or professionals. We have also emphasised the difficulties in attributing effects on learners to particular feedback practices and the importance of exploring how effects are achieved and at what points in time, rather than simply looking for outcomes.

The greatest challenge for research on feedback is in doing research *with* rather than *on* students. This is necessary because we are exploring a phenomenon in which students not only have a stake, but one which is influenced by how students engage with it and what they do. Research designs which deny learner agency are likely to obscure the very factors which students call to action. We hope the next generation of research into feedback that makes a difference will be inspired by the need to recognise the volition of students and how they can contribute to, and benefit from, excellent feedback practices.

Acknowledgements The authors would like to thank Associate Professor Phillip Dawson for comments on an earlier version of this chapter.

References

Ahmad, A., Fenton, N., Graystone, L., Acai, A., Matthews, K. E., & Chalmers, D. (2018). *Are we making a difference?* HERDSA Guide. Hammondville, Australia: Higher Education Research and Development Society of Australasia.

Ajjawi, R., & Boud, D. (2018). Examining the nature and effects of feedback dialogue. *Assessment & Evaluation in Higher Education, 43*(7), 1106–1119. https://doi.org/10.1080/02602938.2018.1434128.

Ajjawi, R., & Higgs, J. (2008). Learning to reason: A journey of professional socialisation. *Advances in Health Sciences Education, 13*(2), 133–150. https://doi.org/10.1007/s10459-006-9032-4.

Barab, S., & Squire, K. (2004). Design-based research: Putting a stake in the ground. *The Journal of the Learning Sciences, 13*(1), 1–14. https://doi.org/10.1207/s15327809jls1301_1.

Bing-You, R., Varaklis, K., Hayes, V., Trowbridge, R., Kemp, H., & McKelvy, D. (2018). The feedback tango: An integrative review and analysis of the content of the teacher-learner feedback exchange. *Academic Medicine, 93*(4), 657–663. https://doi.org/10.1097/acm.0000000000001927.

Boud, D., & Molloy, E. K. (2013). Rethinking models of feedback for learning: The challenge of design. *Assessment & Evaluation in Higher Education, 38*(6), 698–712. https://doi.org/10.1080/02602938.2012.691462.

Boud, D., & Soler, R. (2016). Sustainable assessment revisited. *Assessment & Evaluation in Higher Education, 41*(3), 400–413. https://doi.org/10.1080/02602938.2015.1018133.

Brookhart, S. M. (2018). Summative and formative feedback. In A. A. Lipnevich & J. K. Smith (Eds.), *The Cambridge handbook of instructional feedback* (pp. 52–78). Cambridge, UK: Cambridge University Press.

Brown, G. T. L., & Harris, L. R. (2018). Methods in feedback research. In A. A. Lipnevich & J. K. Smith (Eds.), *The Cambridge handbook of instructional feedback* (pp. 97–120). Cambridge, UK: Cambridge University Press.

Butler, D. L., & Winne, P. H. (1995). Feedback and self-regulated learning: A theoretical synthesis. *Review of Educational Research, 65*(3), 245–281. https://doi.org/10.2307/1170684.

Carless, D. (2013). Trust and its role in facilitating dialogic feedback. In D. Boud & E. Molloy (Eds.), *Feedback in higher and professional education* (pp. 90–103). Abingdon: Routledge.

Carless, D., & Boud, D. (2018). The development of student feedback literacy: Enabling uptake of feedback. *Assessment & Evaluation in Higher Education, 43*(8), 1315–1325. https://doi.org/10.1080/02602938.2018.1463354.

Carr, W., & Kemmis, S. (1986). *Becoming critical: Education, knowledge, and action research.* Lewes: Falmer Press.

Dohn, N. B. (2011). On the epistemological presuppositions of reflective activities. *Educational Theory, 61*(6), 671–708. https://doi.org/10.1111/j.1741-5446.2011.00428.x.

Eraut, M. (2006). Feedback. *Learning in Health and Social Care, 5*(3), 111–118. https://doi.org/10.1111/j.1473-6861.2006.00129.x.

Esterhazy, R. (2018). What matters for productive feedback? Disciplinary practices and their relational dynamics. *Assessment & Evaluation in Higher Education, 43*(8), 1302–1314. https://doi.org/10.1080/02602938.2018.1463353.

Esterhazy, R., & Damşa, C. (2019). Unpacking the feedback process: An analysis of undergraduate students' interactional meaning-making of feedback comments. *Studies in Higher Education, 44*(2), 260–274. https://doi.org/10.1080/03075079.2017.1359249.

Evans, C. (2013). Making sense of assessment feedback in higher education. *Review of Educational Research, 83*(1), 70–120. https://doi.org/10.3102/0034654312474350.

Farrell, L., Bourgeois-Law, G., Ajjawi, R., & Regehr, G. (2017). An autoethnographic exploration of the use of goal oriented feedback to enhance brief clinical teaching encounters. *Advances in Health Sciences Education, 22*(1), 91–104. https://doi.org/10.1007/s10459-016-9686-5.

Hattie, J., & Timperley, H. (2007). The power of feedback. *Review of Educational Research, 77*(1), 81–112. https://doi.org/10.3102/003465430298487.

Henderson, L., Henderson, M., Grant, S., & Huang, H. (2010). What are users thinking in a virtual world lesson? Using stimulated recall interviews to report student cognition, and its triggers. *Journal of Virtual Worlds Research, 3*(1), 1–20.

Jonsson, A. (2013). Facilitating productive use of feedback in higher education. *Active Learning in Higher Education, 14*(1), 63–76. https://doi.org/10.1177/1469787412467125.

Jørgensen, B. M. (2019). Investigating non-engagement with feedback in higher education as a social practice. *Assessment & Evaluation in Higher Education, 44*(4), 623–635. https://doi.org/10.1080/02602938.2018.1525691.

Kluger, A. N., & DeNisi, A. (1996). The effects of feedback interventions on performance: A historical review, a meta-analysis, and a preliminary feedback intervention theory. *Psychological Bulletin, 119*(2), 254–284.

Lincoln, Y. S., Lynham, S. A., & Guba, E. G. (2018). Paradigmatic controversies, contradictions, and emerging confluences, revisited. In N. K. Denzin & Y. S. Lincoln (Eds.), *The SAGE handbook of qualitative research* (5th ed., pp. 108–150). Thousand Oaks: Sage.

Molloy, E. (2009). Time to pause: Giving and receiving feedback in clinical education. In C. Delaney & E. Molloy (Eds.), *Clinical education in the health professions: An educator's guide.* Chatswood, NSW: Elsevier Australia.

Molloy, E., Ajjawi, R., Bearman, M., Noble, C., Rudland, J., & Ryan, A. (2019). Challenging feedback myths: Values, learner involvement and promoting effects beyond the immediate task. *Medical Education.* https://doi.org/10.1111/medu.13802.

Nicol, D. J., & Macfarlane-Dick, D. (2006). Formative assessment and self-regulated learning: A model and seven principles of good feedback practice. *Studies in Higher Education, 31*(2), 199–218. https://doi.org/10.1080/03075070600572090.

Packer, M. J., & Goicoechea, J. (2000). Sociocultural and constructivist theories of learning: Ontology, not just epistemology. *Educational Psychologist, 35*(4), 227–241. https://doi.org/10.1207/S15326985EP3504_02.

Pardo, A., Jovanovic, J., Dawson, S., Gašević, D., & Mirriahi, N. (2019). Using learning analytics to scale the provision of personalised feedback. *British Jour-*

nal of Educational Technology, 50(1), 128–138. https://doi.org/10.1111/bjet.12592.

Price, M., Handley, K., Millar, J., & O'Donovan, B. (2010). Feedback: All that effort, but what is the effect? *Assessment & Evaluation in Higher Education, 35*(3), 277–289. https://doi.org/10.1080/02602930903541007.

Ryan, R. M., & Deci, E. L. (2000). Regular article: Intrinsic and extrinsic motivations: Classic definitions and new directions. *Contemporary Educational Psychology, 25*, 54–67. https://doi.org/10.1006/ceps.1999.1020.

Sagasser, M. H., Kramer, A. W., & van der Vleuten, C. P. (2012). How do postgraduate GP trainees regulate their learning and what helps and hinders them? A qualitative study. *BMC Medical Education, 12*(1), 67. https://doi.org/10.1186/1472-6920-12-67.

Shute, V. J. (2008). Focus on formative feedback. *Review of Educational Research, 78*(1), 153–189. https://doi.org/10.3102/0034654307313795.

Soderstrom, N. C., & Bjork, R. A. (2015). Learning versus performance: An integrative review. *Perspectives on Psychological Science, 10*(2), 176–199. https://doi.org/10.1177/1745691615569000.

Sutton, P. (2012). Conceptualizing feedback literacy: Knowing, being, and acting. *Innovations in Education and Teaching International, 49*(1), 31–40. https://doi.org/10.1080/14703297.2012.647781.

Tai, J., Ajjawi, R., Boud, D., Dawson, P., & Panadero, E. (2018). Developing evaluative judgement: Enabling students to make decisions about the quality of work. *Higher Education, 76*(3), 467–481. https://doi.org/10.1007/s10734-017-0220-3.

Telio, S., Regehr, G., & Ajjawi, R. (2016). Feedback and the educational alliance: Examining credibility judgements and their consequences. *Medical Education, 50*(9), 933–942. https://doi.org/10.1111/medu.13063.

Tummons, J. (2014). The textual representation of professionalism: Problematising professional standards for teachers in the UK lifelong learning sector. *Research in Post-Compulsory Education, 19*(1), 33–44. https://doi.org/10.1080/13596748.2014.872918.

Urquhart, L. M., Ker, J. S., & Rees, C. E. (2018). Exploring the influence of context on feedback at medical school: A video-ethnography study. *Advances in Health Sciences Education, 23*(1), 159–186. https://doi.org/10.1007/s10459-017-9781-2.

Varpio, L., Ajjawi, R., Monrouxe, L. V., O'Brien, B. C., & Rees, C. E. (2017). Shedding the cobra effect: Problematising thematic emergence, triangulation, saturation and member checking. *Medical Education, 51*(1), 40–50. https://doi.org/10.1111/medu.13124.

14 Improving Feedback Research in Naturalistic Settings 265

Wiliam, D. (2018). Feedback at the heart of—But definitely not all of—Formative assessment. In A. A. Lipnevich & J. K. Smith (Eds.), *The Cambridge handbook of instructional feedback* (pp. 3–28). Cambridge, UK: Cambridge University Press.

Winstone, N. E., Nash, R. A., Parker, M., & Rowntree, J. (2017). Supporting learners' agentic engagement with feedback: A systematic review and a taxonomy of recipience processes. *Educational Psychologist, 52*(1), 17–37. https://doi.org/10.1080/00461520.2016.1207538.

15

Designing Feedback for Impact

Michael Henderson⑩, Elizabeth Molloy⑩, Rola Ajjawi⑩ and David Boud⑩

Introduction

The potential for feedback processes to make a difference to learners and learners' work is widely accepted. What is also acknowledged is that we are often wasting the potential of feedback in learning through a lack of shared understanding of what feedback is (and can do). The limited view of feedback as "teacher comments on students' work" is manifest in, and perpetuated through, the enactment of feedback processes in universities. One of the compelling reasons to rethink feedback is that it is one of the few mechanisms available in higher education that recognises students as individuals with individual needs. University graduate outcomes, course outcomes and unit outcomes are set and fixed, and so too are the assessment

---

M. Henderson (✉)
Faculty of Education, Monash University, Melbourne, VIC, Australia
e-mail: michael.henderson@monash.edu

E. Molloy
Department of Medical Education, School of Medicine, The University of Melbourne, Parkville, VIC, Australia
e-mail: elizabeth.molloy@unimelb.edu.au

© The Author(s) 2019
M. Henderson et al. (eds.), *The Impact of Feedback in Higher Education,*
https://doi.org/10.1007/978-3-030-25112-3_15

tasks that align with these goals. In contrast, feedback processes can be attuned to the individual, to respond to and work for them.

This chapter highlights key considerations in building feedback processes within programmes that meet the varying needs of learners and position them with an active part to play. As Rust (2002) noted almost two decades ago, "sadly research evidence... suggest that just giving feedback to students without requiring them to actively engage with it is likely to have only limited effect" (p.153). Rust goes on to describe a study by Fritz Morris, Bjork, Gelman, and Wickens, (2000) that reveals that the passive receipt of feedback information appeared to have little impact on students who were likely to go on to replicate the same mistakes. Rust's conclusion, and one that many now subscribe to, is that students need to be actively engaged with feedback information, if not actually be a part of the information generation process itself.

Research over the past five years in particular has focussed on the agency of the learner in feedback. This work suggests that learners' uptake of feedback is improved if they have a role in seeking information that is relevant or meaningful to them. In anchoring ourselves to the definition of feedback as *processes where learners make sense of performance-relevant information to promote their learning*, and in building off recent research on feedback designs where learner agency is at the centre, we suggest in this chapter some key questions and pedagogical designs that can help inform feedback processes that make a difference.

R. Ajjawi · D. Boud
Centre for Research in Assessment and Digital Learning (CRADLE),
Deakin University, Geelong, VIC, Australia
e-mail: rola.ajjawi@deakin.edu.au

D. Boud
University of Technology Sydney, Ultimo, NSW, Australia
e-mail: david.boud@deakin.edu.au

Middlesex University, London, UK

Key Questions for Feedback Design

We suggest that there are four key questions that need to be asked when designing for feedback that makes a difference. These questions are directed to educators, educational designers and leaders, but their main implications are ultimately for learners.

Do Learners Know the Purpose of Feedback and Their Role(s) in It?

Students are likely to believe that feedback is an act of information delivery from a teacher to student, and that it largely serves the purpose of explaining a grade and is perhaps corrective in nature (Dawson et al., 2018). However, as this book has argued, feedback that makes a difference to learners must be directed to particular learners' needs. It is not just an act of giving information, but is a process in which learners make sense of, and act upon, information about their performance. Feedback cannot make a difference without learner agency. This means feedback processes are likely to be most effective when students know and understand their role in the process and can act accordingly. Therefore, efforts need to be made early in a course unit, and reinforced across a programme, to develop a common understanding of feedback—its purpose, who might be involved in different contexts and what should be expected as a result. Carless and Boud (2018) articulated the idea of learner feedback literacy as the "understandings, capacities and dispositions needed to make sense of information and use it to enhance work or learning strategies" (p. 2). A key part of learners' feedback literacy is their understanding of the purpose and processes of feedback and their own role within these processes.

However, it is not enough to simply tell students, or expect that they can indeed engage in feedback processes effectively. Their expectations of feedback are built on many years of being the recipient of information giving and their often passive responses to it. For example, Bloxham and Campbell (2010) noted that despite opportunity to do so, students were limited in their ability to initiate meaningful dialogue with their tutors to clarify or question assessment standards. Students do not have the same power as educators when negotiating meaning, they do not have the same access to academic and disciplinary language and discourse. Nor do they necessarily have well developed metacognitive skills early in their courses to identify and regulate their own thinking processes. We therefore need to ask when and how feedback literacy (Carless & Boud, 2018) and evaluative judgement (Tai, Ajjawi, Boud, Dawson, & Panadero, 2018) can be developed. For instance, when are students exposed to modelling, or scaffolded opportunities to seek and make sense of feedback information, make judgements about their work and to notice the effects of this engagement in their next iteration of work?

Can Learners Make Sense of the Information?

Learners need to be able to make sense of information available to them from multiple sources. This means we need to consider what kind of information and in what form, will be more readily usable and efficacious for learners. Too much information, which may create overload, may be just as ineffectual as the wrong kind of information. Good information from a source that lacks credibility in the students' eyes may also have little effect when it comes to translation of information into new behaviours or learning approaches. That is, information needs to not only be in a form that can be made sense of, but also is presented in ways likely to be attended to. Therefore, feedback needs to be designed in recognition of learner capacity, motivation and opportunity. As Nicol (2010) points out "the meaning of feedback comments is not transmitted from the teacher to the student; rather meaning comes into being through interaction and dialogue" (p. 507). Clearly, we need to find ways to empower learners to orchestrate ongoing conversations that help them to build confidence and skills in sense-making and planning.

Can Learners Take Action?

Teachers may provide performance-relevant information to learners, or they may create circumstances that encourage the generation of performance-relevant information from other sources including learners

15 Designing Feedback for Impact 271

themselves. Learners can also be involved in the negotiation of the kind of performance information to be generated. In addition, learners can engage in a rich process of constructing meaning, or making sense of the information, with their teachers or with others. However, regardless of the source or whether students can make sense of the information, it needs to be actionable. We argue that a key litmus test is to consider if there are any identifiable opportunities for students to utilise and test their new understanding.

In our view of feedback, the sense-making process needs to promote learning. It follows then that there is a need to find ways to evidence or reveal if and how learning has occurred. The implication is that the learner needs to have the opportunity to use feedback information in some way within the timescale of the relevant course units. A further implication is that when the information is lacking in useful detail or in a form that is not sensitive to learner needs (such as inaccessible language), it does not provide a strong basis for students to effectively make sense and act upon it to promote their future learning. It is here that we can see why grades alone are a particularly poor form of feedback information—they convey very little information that can be used.

What Effects Should We Be Looking for?

As a feedback process necessarily needs to have some kind of impact, when designing and engaging in feedback, a central activity is to look for what changes. If there is no effect (e.g. sense-making, action, motivation, development of evaluative judgement), then the process cannot be described as feedback. That is not to say that the student must comply with the feedback information, indeed, they may choose to act in different ways or even not at all. The key point is that students are engaging in acts of sense-making with respect to the information provided. As we highlight in Chapters 2 and 14, the impact of feedback can be complex and difficult to identify. It is therefore critically important from the outset not only to try to identify what effects are desirable, but also how they will be recognised by the learner and teacher.

Feedback also needs to be understood as activities, enacted over time, not once off delivery of information. Effects may be small and incremental or be something that cannot be observed for some time, for instance, when there are no relevant tasks available through which to enact the new understanding. This means that learners and educators need actively pursue ways to look for and create occasions for noticing the impact of feedback over time. The problem of course is that the further away the "effect" is from the "feedback instance", the harder it might be for any of the players to attribute the effect (e.g. changed approach to task) to any specific feedback process.

If the impact of feedback is important, we need to find ways for both teachers and students to notice effects of feedback as a normal everyday part of teaching and learning, not just in special or one-off evaluation activities. Indeed, tracking effects is important for the teacher or "source" (i.e. peer or patient or client or industry partner) as a way to calibrate their provision of feedback information. If it works, use the same approach, if it doesn't, modification is warranted.

Equally, tracking effects is important for learners to help them further hone their feedback literacy. For example, if a learner is able to articulate their needs to a teacher, such as what they would like comments to focus on, and this strategy helps them get useful information that makes a difference to their subsequent work, they are more likely to employ a similar strategy again—in their course, or afterwards as part of their commitment to ongoing learning in the workplace.

Mechanisms that help learners and teachers to chase down the effects of engaging in feedback processes could usefully be built into programmes. These scaffolds, or built-in reminders, would encourage both parties to see this "closing of the loop" as a standard, and necessary part of the feedback process. Over time, with the establishment of these habits, assessment requirements that explicitly encourage the tracing and recording of feedback effects may no longer be required.

Practices That Support Effects

Leading researchers have proposed a number of models or designs of feedback. For example, Hattie and Timperley (2007) proposed a model of reducing students' understanding of the discrepancy between their current and desired performance. Carless, Salter, Yang, and Lam (2011) advocated for a framework of sustainable feedback drawing heavily on Nicol and Macfarlane-Dick's (2006) significant work on formative and self-regulated learning, in which they devised seven principles of feedback design. More recently Boud and Molloy (2013a) proposed two models; Feedback Mark 1 and Feedback Mark 2 with an emphasis on learner engagement, sense-making and learner effects. In addition many other researchers have developed their own principles of feedback. For example, Evans' (2013) extensive literature review of assessment feedback in higher education synthesised 23 general principles of effective feedback while more recently, and Ossenberg, Henderson, and Mitchell (2019) synthesised 11 attributes to guide effective feedback. Evidently, "there are many strategies that can considerably enhance the positive impact of feedback … and there are many options for what we can usefully do" (Boud & Molloy, 2013b, p. 1). However, these models and principles do not make explicit the connection between the strategy and effects on learners and learning.

In addition, there is clearly a wide range of complex and interdependent design issues. There is no single "one-size-fits-all" option. Every learning context has its own ecology in which there are differences, often quite subtle, across students, teachers, discipline, institution, time, place and space. These differences interact and can significantly influence, challenge or subvert, what might otherwise be regarded as effective feedback strategies. For this reason, feedback designs often resist replication from one context to another. And therein lies a significant problem for the higher education sector. Which options work—and when? Just as importantly—why do some options not work?

In this section, we do not attempt to capture all possible pedagogical approaches, but rather, offer a series of strategies or considerations that have been shown to be valuable in designing feedback that makes a difference. These have been organised according to three important consider-

Designing Opportunities for Feedback

There is a call in the literature for an increasing focus on the role of active design of feedback to ensure that it does what it claims to do (Boud & Molloy, 2013a; Estahazy & Damsa, 2019). A learner-centred process, where dialogue is viewed as a necessary feature for ongoing meaning-making, is unlikely to occur without careful planning and facilitation within courses. Thoughtful design encourages ongoing dialogue between parties (teacher–student, student–student, etc., as needed) and enables learners to access resources that help their sense-making, planning and acting (and further sense-making) (Ajjawi & Boud, 2018). The design needs to account for multiple influences, processes and context.

- *Provide opportunities for action*. Since learners need to be able to act upon information received and observe the effect in subsequent performance, then it makes sense that educators deliberately design tasks so information about performance in one task can directly influence students in the following one. One way to establish these links is to explicitly design a sequence of connected assessment tasks. While this should occur within course units, it is also needed at a programmatic level—for outcomes that cross subjects and years. Generating assessment that is meaningful is important, with enough granularity of detail so that learners can see clearly what is being communicated and use these information points, linked to learning outcomes, to enhance their reflexivity and to guide their learning and studying approaches.
- *Build early feedback opportunities*. Feedback influences subsequent work and learning strategies, therefore, learners would benefit from feedback opportunities early in a course unit. In other words, feedback should tend to be front-end loaded both within units and within programmes of study. Information received at the end of a unit or course is generally of lesser value in terms of being able to act on it, than receiving useful information at a time when it can be utilised while study on

the topic is still active. It is common for institutional policies to stipulate that feedback comments must be returned to students within a set period of time after the task submission. However, it is arguably more important to consider the timing of feedback comments in relation to subsequent tasks. Feedback comments need to be provided at a time that learners are best able to use them.

- ⁕ ***Establish feedback-rich environments.*** There are severe limitations on feedback that requires continual effort by teachers to generate information for every task. A feedback-rich environment sets up all the learning tasks in ways that reflect the common practices of giving and receiving feedback that might occur in a normal working environment. Students work together and individually, sharing work, getting ideas from each other and whoever else is available. Feedback and peer learning are constructed in this way as everyday features of how people learn. Through their empirical work, Esterhazy and Damsa (2019) coined the notion of "creating feedback rich environments" and argue that feedback is a phenomenon that exists and works as a natural part of the environment. Context matters and will influence the way in which students interact with feedback information and processes (Ajjawi & Boud, 2018; Esterhazy & Damsa, 2019).
- ⁕ ***Facilitate co-construction of understanding between learners and others.*** Dialogue encouraged in verbal and written exchanges occurs within a relationship, and the properties of the relationship, including trust, have been shown to influence what is said, what is not said, and to what effect (Ajjawi & Boud, 2018). Co-construction is a way to reduce power asymmetry as both parties have to be prepared to "come to a new understanding" and potentially let go of a pre-conceived idea. Co-construction of knowledge takes trust and can also build trust between people (Molloy & Bearman, 2019). Designing opportunities for learners and teachers to have an ongoing relationship within a programme, such as that experienced in a formal "mentoring program" could encourage these conditions where both parties are prepared to be open to different ways of seeing and knowing, for the sake of learning.
- ⁕ ***Encourage multi-source feedback.*** Feedback information does not need to be generated by the teacher only—learners, peers, consumers (industry) and others (non-human) can be the source of information

that is used to make sense of performance or calibrate the learner's own judgement. Learners need opportunities and encouragement to engage in feedback cycles with a variety of sources. Through engagement, and looking for effects, students can learn over time that the value of multiple sources of feedback information is not necessarily to allow for triangulation of perspectives (arrival at "the truth" of performance), but rather that different stakeholders have different and potentially useful perspectives to offer on the production of work.

- *Explicitly prepare learners to acknowledge and work with* **affect in feedback**. Feedback is an emotional and relational process for both learners and teachers. A commonly held idea in some disciplines is that feedback should be packaged like a sandwich, with critical and potentially emotionally charged comments offered between positive comments. This process has a number of problems, not least that it can undermine student confidence in the teacher, and can result in a confusing set of messages. The use of the feedback sandwich represents a key problem here in that teachers often set out to negate or side-step emotion, treating it as an unwanted side effect that prohibits learning. However, emotion is a natural part of the feedback process and can mobilise many productive outcomes (Rowe 2017). Rather than teachers trying to bypass emotion, students may be explicitly taught early in their programmes how to recognise, plan for, reflect and act on affective states. Written assignments may include a section that asks learners to consider their affective engagement with the work and associated feedback processes. It is also useful to consider how we might support trusting relationships in high stakes assessment situations, where learners may be pre-occupied by grades and may avoid dialogic exchanges that they may believe threaten their grades (even if the dialogues may prove helpful for learning). If resourcing permits, there may be advantages in separating roles of "teacher as assessor" and "teacher as coach", so that learners feel at ease to engage in candid discussions about their learning and performance with the latter.

These principles stem from a stance that feedback is not something that simply clips onto the curriculum or is an artefact or afterthought of marking. Throughout this book, we argue that curriculum design is pivotal in helping create opportunities for students to seek performance rich information and co-produce knowledge that helps them learn. The very nature of such design that encourages learners to seek the effects of feedback should also afford students agency to operate over time as skilled evaluators and curators of their own learning.

There are two overarching points of caution we propose that may demand consideration when it comes to designing feedback processes. Firstly, there is no "one-size-fits-all" design for effective feedback processes. Different learners in different learning contexts, learning different things need differing feedback designs. We need to account for this in our designs—anticipating the need to be flexible and agile to student needs but at the same time, learners may benefit from understanding and "knowing" a set of principles that can inform manifestations of feedback in different settings and circumstances. The second point for consideration, which may trip up passionate teachers, relates to the sustainability of the feedback designs. Does the design require a heroic investment from teachers or learners that renders the process unsustainable beyond the initial enthusiasm of the instigator? Are there alternative modes of engagement that we haven't yet considered that cost both parties less, but can produce equivalent or better outcomes for learners?

Developing Learner and Teacher Capacities for Feedback

If we hope to achieve impact through feedback processes, then the capacity of the students and teachers to engage in those processes is paramount. Consequently, we propose the following pedagogical considerations as useful starting points to build feedback capability for students and teachers:

- **Embed opportunities for *learners to develop feedback literacy*.** Learners need not only to be able to use particular feedback information on any occasion, but they must also learn to understand and use feedback for themselves. This could occur, for example, through early activities that sensitise learners to the opportunities for seeking and generating and using feedback information in their courses. Another approach is to take students "back stage" and explaining rationales for why certain tasks have been designed, and what the expectations are of students, student peers, teachers and others within these processes. A key element of feedback literacy is the ability of learners to identify what information they need and then to seek that information. These skills need to be developed from the start and students in the early stages of their course are likely to need scaffolding. One strategy may be to ask students at the time of submission (such as on their assignment cover page or rubric) to state what feedback information they would most like to receive. Another successful strategy may be to set up an activity in which students are asked to analyse information that they have received, and to identify what action they can take, what they don't understand or feel they cannot action, and what is missing (Barton, Schofield, McAleer, & Ajjawi, 2016).

- **Embed opportunities for *learners to develop evaluative judgement*.** Learners should be encouraged to evaluate their own performance. Evaluative judgement is an important part of learning, in which learners develop self-regulation through the ability to make judgements about their own performance. One strategy is that of getting students to generate feedback information. However, generating feedback information is only one part of the process. Students also need to calibrate with other sources to develop deeper understanding of quality. Another strategy is for every marked assignment get students to commit to recording their own detailed judgements of their work prior to receiving feedback from others, and then use this outside input to refine their own judgements through comparisons.

- **Develop processes that *support the feedback literacy of educators*.** The construction of rich and actionable feedback information is something that is learned. Importantly, a distinction needs to be made between learning how to provide feedback information in efficient ways, and how to do it to have an effect. The best way of tracking whether comments on student work makes a difference is to actively check to see whether students show in subsequent work that they have taken note. This of course requires that subsequent tasks be available and designed in such a way that enables this to be revealed. If students persist in repeating the problems identified in the first task, this is a sign that they

15 Designing Feedback for Impact 279

have either not read or understood the information provided or that they have failed to act on it. In both cases, this demands educators elicit which of these is the problem. Each one of these is an indicator that the educator needs to fix the feedback process in one way or another. Another valuable strategy has been shown to be helpful is the moderation of feedback information (Broadbent, Panadero, & Boud, 2018). It is a common practice for teaching teams to moderate assessment grading. However, the same idea can be applied to feedback. Educators with leadership roles can set up processes in which they, or the whole teaching team, review and provide comments about the feedback provision by their colleagues. They pose the question to themselves: Will comments of this kind likely lead students to improve their work?

If enacted well, this is a synergistic situation in which designs that purposefully set out to strengthen such capacities are likely to result in long term benefits by setting up a situation in which students can more effectively engage in, and manage, their own feedback experiences.

Looking for Effects

Even though engagement with feedback is a precursor to effect, it cannot be taken to mean that effect will occur. Designing rich feedback opportunities and developing capacities such as feedback literacy are critically important, but unless the teacher and the learner can monitor the effect, their future endeavours will continue to hold a degree of uncertainty. Chapter 14 discusses this issue from a research perspective, but we also need to track effects for everyday teaching and learning purposes.

* *Enable systems that record effects.* We need to approach feedback pedagogy in the same way as longitudinal research. That is, not only design for feedback that has short, medium and long terms effect, but also look for those effects and find ways to support learners to notice the presence or absence of those effects. If learners find "the proof in the pudding", they are more likely to engage proactively in feedback processes. There are a number of pedagogical design suggestions throughout the book

that can alert learners themselves to the impact of feedback processes. These include ideas such as portfolios, feedback journaling, coaching and performance plans, and learning analytic dashboards to create, or make accessible, traces of feedback and action that are persistent over time. These can support the identification of impact and help inform future practice for both learners and educators. Utilising digital technologies is important to generate and store performance-relevant information for learners (alongside interpretations and action plans) that can be accessed by the learner over their different course units. This can help make visible the impact of feedback, and allow students and educators, to better understand and engage in feedback over time (see, e.g., Barton et al., 2016).

* ***Imagine (and capture) multiple effects.*** The problem then for teachers and educational designers is to find strategies to reveal possible impacts on the desired outcomes, such as on knowledge, skills, meta-learning, emotion and motivation. For example, if a supervisor and student on a placement engage in a feedback conversation, they hopefully co-devise strategies for the student's development and check in at a subsequent date to trace the effect on performance. At this juncture, they may discuss the perceived effectiveness or lack thereof regarding "the feedback information" and think about the influences on sense-making "uptake" including affect, motivation, opportunity and the context of the classroom on re-observation. A simple teacher prompt such as "how did our initial discussion sit with you over time?" may prompt the learner to think about and share the ways they made further sense of the inputs, which may include, for example, seeking advice from a third party such as a peer, or going back to the literature to further inform their placement strategies that align with the "directions for improvement". Of course, we should also stay alert for outcomes that are not desirable or expected, which may interfere with improved learning or well-being. An example might be an unintended negative impact on learner self-esteem or an over-reliance on the teacher as source of feedback comments.

We have described a need to not only plan for opportunities for feedback but also to develop both learner and teacher capacities, while also seeking to make effects traceable. The final section explores how the alignment of goals and activities within a programme can influence feedback, along with the impact of the institutional culture in which the programme is nested.

Thinking About Feedback at Programme and Institutional Levels

Most institutional discussions of feedback focus on what can be done in an individual course unit by individual educators. However, students experience a course as a whole and many of the skills that support effective feedback, such as self-regulation and feedback literacy, develops across a whole programme, rather than a specific unit. It is therefore necessary to consider feedback as part of the total student experience.

Programmatic Approach to Feedback

Having tasks and feedback which connect across course units and which respond to programme rather than unit learning outcomes is likely to be an important feature in generating feedback processes with effects. One of the most difficult, and yet most important, design concepts in feedback is that the information that is sought, engaged with, and acted upon needs some future context in which to be meaningful. That future context may be a related task in class, or something that will occur at a later date, perhaps in the same semester, the following year or even after graduation.

A significant challenge in higher education is modularisation of degrees. That is, other than in professional courses, individual course units are not explicitly linked or only loosely build on each other. This makes it difficult for any kind of programmatic or even consistent approach to feedback. Logically, programmatic approaches should be dependent on a continuity of vision and commitment from leaders and educators. This includes building stability within teaching teams to enhance capability to iteratively improve feedback practices through to being able to make evident the connections between tasks and learning outcomes across the programme. In addition, since it is the student who is the constant through a program, their input and role through the process need to be considered.

Developing a Feedback Culture Within the Institution

Feedback is a complex process. If we want to change the feedback designs of educators, we need to recognise that practices are situated, and linked to educator identities, past experiences, future goals, student engagement and effects, and influenced by institutional and disciplinary expectations. Indeed, institutional and disciplinary learning and teaching cultures have a significant and wide-reaching impact on the day-to-day practices of educators (Bearman et al., 2016). Effective feedback practices within and across programmes are more likely when feedback is a valued and visible enterprise at all levels. For instance, many institutions might showcase feedback practices and innovation through staff workshops and other learner and teacher events. But "good feedback institutions" might also embed meaningful feedback (not just student satisfaction) within policy and support effective practices through mentorship, induction processes and financially supported moderation processes.

Conclusion

This chapter has described a number of principles and strategies that should be considered in designing feedback processes that make a difference. An important theme throughout is that such outcomes are unlikely to happen without purposeful design. One of our most significant, and yet obvious, conclusions, is that we cannot afford to be reactive or to privilege transmission focused feedback information. Instead, feedback processes need to be carefully designed from the outset—at the course unit as well as degree levels, and we need to watch for both intended and unintended consequences in making changes.

Feedback is a core part of the teaching and learning process. It needs to be seen as another learning activity, which occurs as part of the normal instructional activities, and not conceived as an artefact that is tacked on to assessment tasks. It needs to be seen as a core activity in teaching and learning, deliberately designed, given time to be done well, and importantly, becoming more sophisticated as students become more feedback literate. When planning the learning outcomes, curriculum content, learning activities and assessments, we need to also consciously plan for feedback.

Looking for effect is the key focus of this book as a whole, as it has been the most neglected aspect of feedback. This chapter challenges us to consider where to look for effects and how this closing of the loop can be designed into the learning tasks and/or assessments. For instance, how might subsequent tasks include criteria that elicit the acting upon, and evidencing of, previous feedback information? It is important to not just assume that if we plan for an effect that it will happen. As educators, we would be served well to think about when and how we will know what the effect of the feedback has been. Both learners and teachers can assume stronger roles in tracing effects and planning changes to future activities that better support learners.

The successful and sustained improvement of feedback designs is influenced by teachers' ongoing commitment to evaluating the success of their designs and willingness to keep modifying and improving. Every design adopted needs a degree of re-invention for context. Even when a design has been found to be successful, it will need "redesign" to cater for evolving circumstances. In finding what works we need to identify indicators of success or improvement and seek to monitor for these outcomes.

References

Ajjawi, R., & Boud, D. (2018). Examining the nature and effects of feedback dialogue. *Assessment & Evaluation in Higher Education, 43*(7), 1106–1119. https://doi.org/10.1080/02602938.2018.1434128.

Barton, K., Schofield, S., McALeer, S., & Ajjawi, R. (2016). Translating evidence-based guidelines to improve feedback practices: The interACT case study. *BMC Medical Education, 16*(53), 1–12. https://doi.org/10.1186/s12909-016-0562-z.

Bearman, M., Dawson, P., Boud, D., Bennett, S., Hall, M., & Molloy, E. (2016). Support for assessment practice: Developing the Assessment Design Decisions Framework. *Teaching in Higher Education, 21*(5), 545–556. https://doi.org/10.1080/13562517.2016.1160217.

Bloxham, S., & Campbell, L. (2010). Generating dialogue in assessment feedback: Exploring the use of interactive cover sheets. *Assessment & Evaluation in Higher Education, 35*(3), 291–300.

Boud, D., & Molloy, E. (2013a). Rethinking models of feedback for learning: The challenge of design. *Assessment & Evaluation in Higher Education, 38*(6), 698–712. https://doi.org/10.1080/02602938.2012.691462.

Boud, D., & Molloy, E. (Eds.). (2013b). *Feedback in higher and professional education*. London: Routledge.

Broadbent, J., Panadero, E., & Boud, D. (2018). Implementing summative assessment with a formative flavour: A case study in a large class. *Assessment & Evaluation in Higher Education, 43*(2), 307–322. https://doi.org/10.1080/02602938.2017.1343455.

Carless, D., & Boud, D. (2018). The development of student feedback literacy: Enabling uptake of feedback. *Assessment & Evaluation in Higher Education, 43*(8), 1315–1325. https://doi.org/10.1080/02602938.2018.1463354.

Carless, D., Salter, D., Yang, M., & Lam, J. (2011). Developing sustainable feedback practices. *Studies in Higher Education, 36*(4), 395–407.

Dawson, P., Boud, D., Henderson, M., Phillips, M., Molloy, E., & Ryan, T. (2018). What makes for effective feedback: Staff and student perspectives. *Assessment and Evaluation in Higher Education*. https://doi.org/10.1080/02602938.2018.1467877.

Esterhazy, R., & Damşa, C. (2019). Unpacking the feedback process: An analysis of undergraduate students' interactional meaning-making of feedback comments. *Studies in Higher Education, 44*(2), 260–274. https://doi.org/10.1080/03075079.2017.1359249.

Evans, C. (2013). Making sense of assessment feedback in higher education. *Review of Educational Research, 83*(1), 70–120.

Fritz, C. O., Morris, P. E., Bjork, R. A., Gelman, R., & Wickens, T. D. (2000). When further learning fails: Stability and change following repeated presentation of text. *British Journal of Psychology, 91*, 493–511.

Hattie, J., & Timperley, H. (2007). The power of feedback. *Review of Educational Research, 77*(1), 81–112.

Molloy, E., & Bearman, M. (2019). Embracing the tension between vulnerability and credibility: 'Intellectual candour' in health professions education. *Medical Education, 53*(1), 32–41. https://doi.org/10.1111/medu.13649.

Nicol, D. (2010). From monologue to dialogue: Improving written feedback processes in mass higher education. *Assessment & Evaluation in Higher Education, 35*(5), 501–517.

Nicol, D., & Macfarlane-Dick, D. (2006). Formative assessment and self-regulated learning: A model and seven principles of good feedback practice. *Studies in Higher Education, 31*(2), 199–218.

Ossenberg, C., Henderson, A., & Mitchell, M. (2019). What attributes guide best practice for effective feedback? A scoping review. *Advances in Health Sciences Education, 24*(2), 383–401. https://doi.org/10.1007/s10459-018-9854-x.

Rowe, A. D. (2017). Feelings about feedback: The role of emotions in assessment for learning. In D. Carless, S. M. Bridges, C. K. Y. Chan, & R. Glofcheski (Eds.), *Scaling up assessment for learning in higher education* (pp. 159–172). Singapore: Springer.

Rust, C. (2002). The impact of assessment on student learning: How can the research literature practically help to inform the development of departmental assessment strategies and learner-centred assessment practices? *Active Learning in Higher Education, 3*(2), 145–158.

Tai, J., Ajjawi, R., Boud, D., Dawson, P., & Panadero, E. (2018). Developing evaluative judgement: Enabling students to make decisions about the quality of work. *Higher Education, 76*(3), 467–481. https://doi.org/10.1007/s10734-017-0220-3.

Index

A

Abbasi, N. 195
Abbey, C. 167
Abella, B.S. 166, 168
Acai, A. 247
accountability 20
accreditation standards 191
action research 259
active engagement 268
Ada, M.B. 229
affective processes 150
Ahmad, A. 247
Ahmed, M. 177
Ajjawi, R. 20, 27–29, 39, 42, 45, 61, 84, 86, 89, 92, 96, 107, 108, 113, 120, 129, 133, 136, 138, 158, 166, 170, 174, 226, 229, 251–253, 257, 258, 270, 274, 275, 278, 280
Akin, J. 113

Alexiadis Brown, P. 95
Ali, L. 213
Alinier, G. 169
Alken, A. 196
Allsopp, B.B. 215
Alonso-Tapia, J. 155
Alqassab, M. 138
Ameratunga, S. 209
Andrade, H. 148, 149, 151, 152
anxiety 91, 99
Armit, L. 84, 94, 96
Armson, H. 174, 190–193, 195–199
Arnold, K.E. 214
Arora, S. 177
Ashkanasy, N.M. 86
assessment 191, 199
assessment criteria 72, 133
assessment, design 226
assessment, diagnostic 18
assessment, formative 18

© The Editor(s) (if applicable) and The Author(s),
under exclusive licence to Springer Nature Switzerland AG 2019
M. Henderson et al. (eds.), *The Impact of Feedback in Higher Education*,
https://doi.org/10.1007/978-3-030-25112-3

288 Index

assessment literacy 251
assessment, summative 18
Atif, A. 43
audio/visual diaries 144
automated feedback 118, 119
Azevedo, R. 40, 43

B

Baartman, L.K.J. 31, 215
Baker, K. 199
Baker, K.H. 196, 197
Bakharia, A. 214
Bandura, A. 110
Barab, S. 259
Barnlund, D.C. 110, 113
Barrington, K. 196–198
Barton, K. 61, 92, 278, 280
Bauer, K.N. 147–149, 155, 156
Bearman, M. 39, 42, 84, 90, 92, 108, 166–168, 170, 174, 251, 275
Begaz, T. 168
behavioral processes 150
Bellini, L.M. 166, 168
Benfield, G. 214
Berg, D.A.G. 156
Bergmark, U. 40
Bernabeo, E. 191
Beuthin, R. 191–193, 199
Biggs, J. 53
Billett, S. 94–96
Bing-You, R. 190, 245, 246
Bjork, R.A. 250, 268
Black, P. 108–110, 115
Bloxham, S. 61, 269
Blumenfeld, P.C. 41
Bodily, R. 214
Boekaerts, M. 129
Boet, S. 166

Bok, H.G.J. 95
Bolhuis, S. 90
Bond, C.M. 190
Borello, F. 28, 84, 86, 88, 90
Borrell-Carrió, F. 28
Botella, J. 147, 148, 155, 157
Boud, D. 17, 20–22, 27–29, 39, 45, 55, 58–61, 88, 92, 94, 107, 113, 120, 129, 130, 133, 136, 138, 147, 149–151, 153, 156, 166, 170, 208, 212, 213, 215, 225, 226, 229, 237, 245, 250, 251, 253, 258, 259, 269, 270, 273–275, 279
Boudreau, M. 192, 193, 196, 198
Bould, M.D. 166
Bourgeois-Law, G. 28, 45, 89
Bowker, J.C. 109
Braudaway, C.A. 174
Braun & Clarke 130
Brehaut, J.C. 189, 191
Brett-Fleegler, M. 177
Bridges, D. 213
briefing 169, 170, 173, 178–180
Broadbent, J. 210, 279
Brookhart, S.M. 253
Broos, T. 215
Brown, G.T.L. 147–149, 152–154, 158, 247
Brown, K.G. 147–149, 155, 156
Bruppacher, H.R. 166
Brutus, S. 228
Buckingham, M. 199
Bugarcic, A. 55, 61, 229
Bukowski, W.M. 109
Burgess, G. 177
Burjorjee, J.E. 170
Burns, S.M. 199
Bustos Gómez, M.C. 89

Index   289

Butler, D.L. 110, 115, 150, 155, 210, 254

C

Caffarella, E.P. 196, 198
Caffarella, R.S. 196, 198
Cain, M. 94
Campbell, L. 61, 269
candour 136
Canny, B.J. 134, 200
Carless, D. 17, 22, 28, 39, 45, 54–61, 88, 92, 94, 107, 121, 130, 133–135, 213, 214, 225, 229, 239, 251, 269, 270, 273
Carr, W. 259
Carroll, K. 189, 191
Cassar, K. 88
Cerasoli, C.P. 166–168
Chalmers, D. 247
Chan, K.K.H. 133, 135
Chandra, D.B. 166
Charnin, J.E. 196, 197, 199
Chen, C.H. 212
Chen, F. 152
Cheng, A. 167, 168, 177
Chen, R. 229
Chesluk, B. 190, 195, 197
Chesworth, K. 210
Chunduri, P. 55, 60, 229
Ciftci, H. 212
Clarebout, G. 216
Clarke, J. 61
Cleland, J. 88
Cleland, J.A. 190
climate 131
coaching 191, 193–196, 198–200, 280
coaching for change 191

coaching, discipline differences 194
Coffey, S. 169
cognitive load 153, 197
cognitive processes 150, 155
Collier, L. 84, 94, 96
Colquhoun, H.L. 189, 191
Colthorpe, K. 55, 61, 229
community of practice 29
competence 89, 190
computer agents 210, 211
conceptual framework 247
Conforti, L.N. 191
connected assessment 274
context 68, 273, 277, 283
Control-Value Theory 84, 91–93, 100, 101
Cook, D.A. 168
Corrin, L. 214, 231
Cowan, J. 113, 120
credibility 89, 270
critical thinking 212
Crossman, J. 28
cultural tools 70, 76
culture 132, 138
culture of excellence 190
culture of kindness 190
Cuseo, J. 209
CVT. *See* Control-Value Theory
cybernetics 18

D

Damşa, C. 39, 68, 69, 72, 73, 76, 166, 173, 256, 274, 275
DASH. *See* Debriefing Assessment for Simulation in Healthcare
dashboard(s) 214, 217, 231, 237, 239
data mining 208
data-rich environments 210, 211

290 Index

Dawson et al 210
Dawson, P. 20, 21, 27, 43, 46, 113, 120, 133, 136, 138, 158, 251, 269, 270
Dawson, S. 42, 208, 209, 211, 212, 214, 216, 218, 228, 260
Dawson, S.L. 46
de Barba, P. 214, 231
De Laet, T. 215
debriefing 165–183
Debriefing Assessment for Simulation in Healthcare 177
debriefing, culture of 173
debriefing, definiton of 166
debriefing, improve performance 168
debriefing, microdebrief 166, 172, 173
debriefing, type of 168
debriefing, values-based 174
debriefing, venting 175
Debuse, J.C.W. 212
Deci, E.L. 254
decode 113, 117
Deepwell, F. 214
Dekker, A. 55, 61, 229
Delahunty, J. 40
Delaney, M.E. 197
Dellinger, N.F. 174
Delva, D. 95
Denisi, A. 44, 46, 107, 109, 166, 246
Dennis, A.A. 98
Der Sahakian, G. 169
design based research 259
design issues 273
Desjardins, F. 166
DeVelle, S. 110, 112
Dhingra-Kumar, N. 195, 196
dialogic 51, 52, 58, 107, 276
dialogic culture 137

dialogic process 52
dialogue 52, 56, 58–61, 270, 274
Dickson, M. 209
digital footprint 230
digital literacy 251
digital technologies 280
digital tool(s) 225, 228–231, 235, 237, 239
Dijkstra, J. 31, 215
Dine, C.J. 166, 168
Dingyloudi, F. 108, 116
disciplinary contexts 248
disciplinary language 270
discussion forum 80
dissatisfaction 3
Dohn, N.B. 258
domain-knowledge 110, 111
Donia, M.B. 228
Dornan, T. 172, 176, 179, 190, 195, 197
Dowell, N. 212
Drachsler, H. 209
Driessen, E. 192, 193, 195, 197–199
Driessen, E.W. 31, 215
Dubrowski, A. 168
Dudek, N.L. 190
Dünnebier, K. 116
Dunning, D. 150
Duval-Arnould, J.M. 167
dyadic interactions 107–110, 115
dyadic meta-accuracy 111
dyadic meta-perception 111
Dziedzic, K. 189, 191

Eccles, J.S. 157
educational alliance 44, 88, 89, 93, 99

Index 291

educator, role of 20
Edwards, D. 166
effects, longitudinal 279
effects, multiple 280
Eldridge, S. 189, 191
Elen, J. 216
Elmslie, T. 196–199
Ely, K. 147–149, 155, 156
Emerson, L. 230
emotion, antecedents 86
emotion, as a hinderance 86
emotion, mitigation 84
emotion, regulation 91, 92, 99, 101, 251
emotion, resentment 86
emotion(s) 83–102, 143, 280
emotions, productive tensions 175
Ende, J. 84, 87, 88
engagement 143
engagement, definitions of 40
engagement, learner 28
engagement, measurement of 41, 42
engagement, student 40
Engstrom, C. 55, 61, 229
e-portfolios 61
Eppich, W. 167, 168, 172, 176, 177, 179
Eppich, W.J. 171
Epstein, I. 193
Epstein, R. 28, 84, 86, 88, 90
Epstein, R.M. 87
Eraut, M. 252
Erickson, F. 84, 88
error tolerance 119
errors 108, 111–113
Esterhazy, R. 39, 46, 68, 69, 71–73, 76, 166, 173, 253, 254, 256, 274, 275
ethnography 255

Eva, K.W. 85, 189–191, 195, 197
evaluative information 19–21, 23, 24, 26, 32
evaluative judgement 20, 25, 27, 69, 130, 134, 136–140, 142–144, 158, 212, 251, 260, 270, 271, 278
Evans, C. 246, 248, 273
Everitt, H. 189, 191
exemplars 80, 133–136, 151, 158
Exeter, D.J. 209

failure 132
Falchikov, N. 28, 147, 149, 153
Farrell, L. 28, 45, 89
feedback, acceptance 190
feedback, access 229
feedback, actionable 271, 274
feedback, affect 276
feedback, agents 20
feedback, analytics 229, 231
feedback, as a *social* practice 44, 46
feedback, as input 88
feedback, as process 4, 18, 19
feedback, as relational co-construction 44
feedback, cause and effect 23
feedback, co-construction 275
feedback conceptions, aligning with effects 44
feedback, conceptions of 39
feedback, content 191–194, 197
feedback, cultures 248, 282
feedback, definition of 17, 268
feedback, delivery 229
feedback, design 136, 227, 269–282
feedback, design for 274–277

292 Index

feedback, detailed 210
feedback, development of strategies 194, 198, 199
feedback, dialogue 45, 129–132, 134, 140–142, 144, 258
feedback, early opportunities 274
feedback, educator capacity 196
feedback effect, longitudinal view of progress 193
feedback, effects 40, 228, 246, 249
feedback, enactment 130, 248
feedback, engagement 227–231, 234, 235, 237, 239, 254
Feedback Engagement and Tracking System (FEATS) 226, 231, 234, 235, 237, 238
feedback, evaluation of outcomes 197
feedback, evidence of effect 22
feedback, expectations of 269
feedback, follow-up 193, 194, 198
feedback, frequency 214
feedback, ignore 165
feedback, impact 18, 43, 136–139, 225–228, 230, 233, 237–239
feedback impact, affect 28
feedback impact, cognitive 27
feedback impact, delayed 30
feedback impact, metacognitive 27
feedback impact, motivation 28
feedback impact, not learning outcome 26
feedback impact, plural 30
feedback impact, relational 28
feedback impact, student satisfaction 30
feedback impact, types of 26
feedback impact, unintended 29
feedback impact, value laden 30

feedback impact, values, beliefs and identity 29
feedback impact, variables 23
feedback, implications for higher education 178
feedback, individualization 190
feedback, influence of 246
feedback, informal 18
feedback, information 227, 228, 230, 238
feedback, input 245, 248
feedback, iterative process 192
feedback, learner engagement 196
feedback, learner-centred 16, 17, 193
feedback literacy 21, 44, 45, 51, 52, 56, 58–61, 84, 92–94, 96–99, 101, 130, 134, 138, 144, 229, 238, 251, 269, 270, 272, 277–279, 281
feedback literacy, definition of 22
feedback loop 18, 26, 56, 61, 63, 249
feedback manager 121
Feedback Mark 1 56
Feedback Mark 2 94, 170, 259
feedback, mealy mouthed 88
feedback, misconception 17
feedback models 273
feedback, multi-source 275
feedback, negative 87, 92, 93
feedback, negative impacts of 44, 46
feedback, normative beliefs 190
feedback, observable changes 192
Feedback Orientation Scale 235, 237
feedback, over time 272
feedback, peer 138–140, 142–144, 199
feedback, personalised 208, 210, 211, 216–218
feedback, positive 101

feedback, process(es) 24, 225, 228, 238, 239, 249, 256
feedback, programmatic approach 281
feedback, purpose of 17, 192, 269
feedback, reactions 191, 192, 194, 199
feedback, reflective conversation 193
feedback regimes 248, 257
feedback, rejection 190
feedback, research 247
feedback, rich environments 172, 275
feedback sandwich 83, 86, 92, 276
feedback, sequence 24
feedback, softening the blow 88
feedback, sources 20, 190
feedback spirals 54
feedback, stages 24
feedback, sustainability 277
feedback, timely 217
feedback, timing of 87
feedback, traces 280
feedback, understood by students 165
feedback, unintended learning 46
feedback, uptake 229
feedback, use of 129, 191, 227
feedback, vanishing 88
feedforward 39
Fenton, N. 247
Fernando, N. 88
Fincham, O.E. 216
Finkelstein, S.R. 111
Firestone, R. 195, 196
Fishbach, A. 111
Fisher, C. 109, 110
Fitzgerald, M.L. 174
Flanagan, B. 167
Fleegler, E. 177
Fleming, M. 170

Fluit, C. 196
Fokkema, J.P.I. 95
Fong, C.J. 108
formative 131, 132, 138
formative assessment 148, 149, 152, 153, 155, 158, 159
Fougt, S.S. 215
Foy, M.J. 98
Frank, T. 196–198
Fredricks, J.A. 41
Frenzel, A.C. 97
Frese, M. 112
Fritz, C.O. 268
Froissard, J.-C. 43
Fung, D. 61
Funk, A. 116

G

Gagnon, L.H. 195
Gavin, M.B. 86
Gašević, D. 208, 209, 211–214, 216, 218, 228, 260
Gawande, A.A. 195, 196
Gelman, R. 268
generation (of feedback) 148, 152, 154, 157, 159
Gersh, R.E. 166, 168
Gibbs, G. 112, 209, 213
Gibson, E.J. 111
Gill, W. 29
Gjikali, K. 157
Gleaves, A. 90
goals, time invested 199
Goetz, T. 97
Goicoechea, J. 70, 254
Goldberg, A. 113
Gollwitzer, P.M. 196–199
Gondocz, T. 196

Goodall, A. 199
Goodyear, P. 74
Gooty, J. 86
Gorard, S. 23
Gourlay, L. 62
grade 17, 148, 149, 151–153, 276
graduate outcomes 267
Graesser, A.C. 212
Graham, L. 169
Graham, R. 191–193, 199
Grant, A.M. 194
Grant, S. 256
Grant, V. 168, 177
Gravett, K. 228
Graystone, L. 247
Greenhill, J. 168
Gregory, S.E.A. 190, 227
Greller, W. 209
Grimshaw, J.M. 189, 191
Guarino, A. 199
Guba, E.G. 253, 256
Guo, X. 110
Guo, Y. 110

Henderson et al. 256
Henderson, A. 273
Henderson, L. 256
Henderson, M. 21, 28, 86, 90, 121, 256, 269
Herder, T. 215
Higgs, J. 252
Hilder, J. 84, 94, 96
Hirschhorn, L.R. 195, 196
Hogan, D. 196
Holland, J. 95
Holmboe, E. 190–193, 195–199
Hoogland, H. 198
Hopfenbeck, T. 62
Hsiao, Y.-T. 216
Hsu, D. 209
Huang, H. 256
Huang, S.-C. 212
Huffman, J. 177
Huisman, B. 116
Hull, L. 177
Hunt, E.A. 167
Huxham, M. 210

H

Haines, T.P. 134, 200
Handley, K. 52, 87, 135, 166, 215, 216, 227, 229, 246
Harris, L.R. 147–149, 158, 247
Hartley, J. 210
Harvey, G. 175, 195
Hatala, M. 213
Hattie, J. 29, 44, 107, 112, 118, 170, 208, 215, 246, 273
Hayes, V. 190, 245, 246
Heath, C. 150
Heinze, A. 108, 115
Helmich, E. 90

I

Ibabe, I. 157
identity 84, 85, 87, 90, 95, 99, 100
identity effects 249, 258
identity formation 260
Ifenthaler, D. 40
Ilgen, D. 109, 110
impact 132, 143, 227
impact, at scale 209
impact, evidence of 226
impact of context 189, 191, 196, 199, 200
impact of feedback 37
impact, over time 209

Index   295

impact, social-affective 57
impact, tracking 225, 228, 237, 239
impact, undesirable 280
impact, unexpected 280
implications, for research 100
incompetence 86
individual needs 267
institution 282
institutional conditions 78
institutional culture 281
institutional policy 275
interpersonal factors 107–111, 110,
    113–116, 118–121
Interventional research 257
intrapersonal factors 108–110, 113,
    115–117, 120, 121
Iobst, W. 191
Ivers, N. 189, 191

J

Jaarsma, D.A.D.C. 95
Jackel, B. 166
Jackson, R. 209
Jaffrelot, M. 169
Janzen, K.J. 175
Jauregizar, J. 157
Jeske, S. 175
Johnson, A.C. 119
Johnson, M. 85
Joksimović, S. 212
Jonsson, A. 67, 138, 147, 148, 151,
    155, 157, 158, 190, 227, 246
Jørgensen, B.M. 46, 256
journaling 280
Jovanović, J. 208, 209, 211–213,
    216, 228, 260

K

Kahu, E.R. 40, 41
Kapur, M. 108
Karabenick, S.A. 119
Keith, N. 112
Kemmis, S. 259
Kemp, H. 190, 245, 246
Kennedy, A. 189, 191
Kennedy, G. 214
Kenny 110, 111
Ker, J.S. 47, 84, 87, 95, 100, 256
Kim, Y.W. 108
King, A.S. 214
Kirschner, P.A. 153
Kitson, A.L. 195
Kluger, A.N. 44, 46, 107, 109, 166,
    246
Kneebone, R. 169, 170, 172
Knight, L.V. 190
knowledge domain 71, 72, 74,
    76–78, 81
Kocoglu, Z. 212
Kodkany, B.S. 195, 196
Kogan, J.R. 191
Könings, K.D. 174, 189, 191–193,
    196, 198
Koopmans, R. 90, 198
Kramer, A.W. 258
Krogh et al. 177
Krogh, K. 167, 174
Kuh, G.D. 40
Kulaga, A. 191
Kulhavy, R. 112
Kumar, V. 195, 196

L

Laan, R. 90
Lam, J. 55, 213, 214, 273

296 Index

Langie, G. 215
large classes 209–213
Lau, R. 189, 191
Lawley, M. 212
Lawson, R. 156
Lay, D. 110, 112
Le, A.H. 94
Lean, J. 167
learner agency 52, 269
learner calibration 190
learner capacities 52
learner-centred 20, 274
learner change, attitudinal 197
learner change, behavioral 195, 197
learner commitment to improvement 194
learner difference 277
learner dispositions 52, 58
learner, feedback capacity 277–279
learner goals 192–194, 197–200
learner needs 268
learner resources 192
learner, self-diagnosis 197
learner, self-discipline 198
learners, high achieving 193
learners, low achieving 193
learning analytics 208–218, 239, 258, 259, 280
learning analytics, definition of 208
learning analytics, for student engagement 42
learning, as construction 21
learning-centred 4
learning change plans 196–198
learning contracts 196, 198
learning management systems 208, 213
learning outcomes 189, 194, 196, 197, 199, 200

learning plan 191–200
learning plan change, efficacy 197, 198
learning plan, co-development 191, 194, 200
learning plans, timelines 198
learning portfolio 196, 199
Leary, M. 166, 168
Leblanc, C. 95
LeBlanc, V. 168
Lecomte, F. 169
Leeks, D. 174
Leighton, J.P. 89
Levy, P.E. 108, 110, 235
Liao, J. 110
Lin, S. 108
Lincoln, Y.S. 253, 256
Linderbaum, B.A. 235
Lipnevich, A.A. 87, 156, 157
Lipsitz, S. 195, 196
Liu, D.Y.T. 43
Liu, J. 110
Lluka, L. 55, 60, 229
Lockyer, J.M. 174, 190–193, 195–199
Lockyer, L. 214
Loney, E. 190, 195, 197
Long, P. 55, 60, 229
longitudinal 51, 52, 54, 60, 62, 63
longitudinal audio-diaries 256
Looking for effects 279
Lovell, B. 196
Lucas, L. 209
Luctkar-Flude, M. 169
Lust, G. 216
Luursema, J.M. 196
Lynham, S.A. 253, 256

M

Macfadyen, L.P. 42
Macfarlane-Dick, D. 155, 251, 273
Macfarlane, S. 229
MacLean, H. 175
MacLeod, T. 192, 193, 195, 197–199
MacVicar, R. 196, 197, 199
Mahoney, P. 229
Mahony, M.J. 28
Mandernach, B.J. 40, 41
Mann, K. 28, 29, 95, 190, 192, 193, 195–199
Mann, K.V. 189, 191
Manos, S. 193
Mansvelt, J. 230
Marbouti, F. 216
Mark, D. 170
Marks, M.B. 190
Marx Delaney, M. 195, 196
massification 208, 209, 217
Matthews, K.E. 247
Maxwell, J. 23
Mayra, C.R. 119
Mazmanian, P.E. 196, 197
Mazmanian, P.M. 196, 197
McAleer, S. 61, 92, 278, 280
McConnell, M. 85
McKelvy, D. 190, 245, 246
McKenzie, H. 88
McLellan, H. 175
McMullen, M. 170
McNaughton, N. 85
meaning making. *See* sense-making
measurement, of feedback 37
measurement, what is easy 44
measuring learning 40
Merry, S. 28, 227
Messick, S. 218
meta-learning 258, 280

meta-learning effects 249
Meta-learning processes 251
metacognition 212, 215
Metcalfe, J. 112
Metsemakers, J. 28, 29
Michie, S. 189, 191
microfeedback 173
Millar, J. 52, 87, 166, 215, 216, 227, 229, 246
Miller, S. 95
Mirriahi, N. 208, 209, 211, 212, 216, 228, 260
Misfeldt, M. 215
Mitchell, M. 273
moderation 279, 282
modularisation 208, 209, 213–215, 217, 281
modularisation of curriculum 31
Moizer, J. 167
Molloy, E.K. 17, 21, 28, 29, 39, 55, 84, 86, 88, 90, 92, 94–96, 108, 134, 166, 170, 174, 200, 208, 213, 225, 245, 251, 252, 255, 259, 269, 273–275
Monrouxe, L.V. 98, 100, 257
Monuteaux, M. 177
Moore, C. 212
Morrison, K. 23
Morris, P.E. 268
Morton, S. 209
motivation 91, 110, 280
motivation, extrinsic 101
motivation, intrinsic 101
motivation, student 148, 153–155, 157
Moulton, C.-A. 168
Mulder, R. 214
Müller, A. 108, 109, 115, 119
Murray, E. 189, 191

298 Index

Myers, G. 113

N
Nadler, D.A. 110
Naik, V.N. 166
Narciss, S. 107, 108, 110, 116, 150, 151
Nash, R.A. 67, 108, 158, 189–191, 208, 215, 227, 228, 230, 231, 246
naturalistic research 256
naturalistic settings 247
Nelson, K. 41
Nestel, D. 167–170, 172, 174, 177
Nichols, D. 191
Nickle, P. 175
Nicol, D. 21, 27, 52, 61, 129, 131, 155, 251, 270, 273
Nicol, P. 195
Noble, C. 84, 92, 94, 96, 166, 174, 251
non-human 275
Norenna, L. 175
Norton. L. 87, 129

O
Objective Structured Assessment of Debriefing 177, 179
O'Brien, B.C. 257
observation 255
O'Donovan, B. 52, 166, 215, 216, 229, 246
Oettingen, G. 199
O'Halloran, K.C. 197
O'Keefe, M. 195
Oliver, M. 62
Olsen-Lynch, E. 169

O'Neill, T.A. 228
Ong, B.N. 189, 191
online discussion 213
open-ended questions 193
opportunities for improvement 192
origins of feedback 39
Oriot, D. 169
Orsmond, Merry and Handley 131
Orsmond, P. 28, 227
OSAD. *See* Objective Structured Assessment of Debriefing
O'Shea, S. 40
Overton, G.K. 196, 197, 199
Owen, C. 195

P
Packer, M.J. 70, 254
Padgett, M.B. 174
Paige, J. 177
Palincsar, A.S. 52
Panadero, E. 20, 27, 113, 133, 136, 138, 147–149, 151–155, 157, 158, 210, 251, 270, 279
Papps, E. 190, 227
Parboosingh, J. 196
Pardo, A. 208–212, 216, 228, 260
Paris, A.H. 41
Parker, J.G. 109
Parker, M. 67, 108, 158, 189–191, 208, 215, 227, 228, 230, 246
Park, J. 168
Participatory research 259
Patchan, M. 116
Peacock, R. 189, 191
Pearce, J. 166
peer assessment, of *feedback* 178
peer coaching 177
peer feedback 109, 111, 116, 121

peers 135, 275
Pekrun, R. 84, 91, 97
Pereles, L. 196
performance 132
Perry, R.P. 97
person-centred theory 191, 195
personality traits 110
Petit, E. 212
Phillips, M. 21, 269
Pisarski, E.E. 189, 191
Pistilli, M.D. 214
Pitt, E. 87, 129, 229, 237
Pomerantz, A. 84, 88
portfolio(s) 231, 233, 280
Poulos, A. 28
power 270
Power, M. 192, 193, 195, 197–199
prebriefing. *See* briefing
presage 53, 57, 58
Price, M. 52, 87, 166, 215, 216, 227, 229, 246
problem-solving 108

Q

quality 133, 134, 137, 140, 142, 143
Qureshi, N. 189, 191

R

R2C2 educator resources 192
R2C2 model 191–194, 199, 200
R2C2, research directions 200
Rach, S. 108, 115
Radloff, A. 166
Raemer, D.B. 169, 171, 175, 177
Ramani, S. 189, 191
Ramaprasad, A. 108
Ratima, M. 209

reactive 282
Rees, C.E. 39, 47, 84, 87, 95, 98, 100, 108, 190, 256, 257
Reflection 198
Regehr, G. 28, 45, 86, 89, 96, 191, 197, 251
Reiling, K. 28, 227
relational dynamics 256
relationship 89, 91, 93, 100
relationship, learner and teacher 191–194
Remnet, M.A. 214
research, naturalistic 246, 260
resilience 28, 132
Rethans, J.-J. 172, 176, 179
Reznick, R.K. 168
Richards, D. 43
Riegel, B.J. 166, 168
risk 95, 97
Robinson, T. 177
Roder, S. 196–199
Rogers, A. 189, 191
Rogers, C.R. 195
Rogers, T. 208
role-play 98, 167
Roscoe, R.D. 119
Ross, J.A. 151
Ross, K. 192, 193, 195–199
Ross, S. 191
Rowe, A.D. 28, 85, 87
Rowntree, J. 67, 108, 158, 189–191, 208, 215, 227, 228, 230, 246
Rubin, K.H. 109
rubric(s) 80, 207, 216
Rudland, J. 84, 92, 166, 174, 195, 251
Rudolph, J.W. 169, 171, 175, 177, 179
Rummel, N. 116

300 Index

Runnacles, J. 177
Rust, C. 52, 268
Ryan, A. 84, 92, 166, 174, 251
Ryan, R.M. 254
Ryan, T. 21, 28, 86, 90, 121, 269

S

Saab, N. 116
Saddawi-Konefka, D. 196, 197, 199
Sadler, D.R. 27, 133, 134
Sagasser, M.H 258
Sales, A. 189, 191
Säljö, R. 68–70, 76
Salter, D. 55, 213, 214, 273
Samter, J. 174
Sargeant, J. 28, 29, 95, 174, 190–193,
    195–199
satisfaction 211, 213
Saurastri, R. 195, 196
Savoldelli, G. 169
scaffold 108, 132, 144
Schallert, D.L. 108
Scharff, L.F.V. 196–198
Schofield, S. 61, 92, 278, 280
Schumacher, D.J. 196, 197
Schunn, C. 116
Schuwirth, L.W.T. 31, 215
science of behavior change 195
Scott, S.V. 67
Segers, M. 107
self-assessment 131, 132, 147–159,
    190
self-assessment, definitions of 147
self-determination 254
self-efficacy 110, 148, 154–156, 236
self-esteem 87
self-feedback 148–159
self-perception 110

self-regulated learning 148, 154–156,
    159
self-regulation 129, 131, 132, 155,
    208, 210, 212, 216, 230, 231,
    233, 237, 239, 251, 254, 258,
    281
Semrau, K.E.A. 195, 196
sense-making 17, 19, 21, 24, 25, 58,
    86, 90, 91, 100, 167, 171, 174,
    175, 182, 218, 226, 255, 270,
    274, 280
Sevdalis, N. 177
Shaffer, D.W. 215
Sharma, N. 195, 196
Shearer, C. 192, 193, 196, 198
Sherbino, J. 168
Shibl, R. 212
Shulman, L.S. 169
Shute, V.J. 68, 118, 246
Siddall, V.J. 167
side-effect 276
Siegel, D.J. 87
Siemens & Gašević 208
Siemens, G. 211, 214, 218
Silberman, J. 87
Silver, I. 192, 193, 195–199
Simon, R. 169, 171, 175, 177
Simonite, V. 209
Simpson, C. 112, 209, 213
simulation 166–183
simulation, advantages 172
Sinclair, D. 28, 29
Singh, V.P. 195, 196
Sitkin, S.B. 112
Sitzmann, T. 147–149, 155, 156
Sly, C. 84, 94, 96
Smith, J.K. 87, 156, 157
social constructivism 17, 21, 52, 54,
    61

social theory of learning 29
socio-constructivist 248, 253
socio-constructivist theory 69
sociocultural 253, 254
sociocultural perspective 68, 70, 71, 76, 77
sociocultural theory 68, 69
Soderstrom, N.C. 250
Soklaridis, S. 192, 193, 196, 198
Soler, S. 250
Spanjers, I.A.E. 198
Speer, J. 216
Spinuzzi, C. 231
Spruijt, A. 95
Squire, K. 259
standards 88, 95–97, 135
Stansfield, M. 229
statements of intent 196
Steen-Utheim, A. 61, 62, 107
Stephens, E.J. 91
Stevenson, F. 189, 191
Stewart, J. 113
stimulated recall 256
Stober, D.R. 194
Street, K. 196–198
Strijbos, J.W. 108, 109, 115, 116, 119, 147–149, 151–154
student engagement 38, 47, 227
student engagement, review of literature 42
student learning 228, 238
student-as-consumer 230
Suls, J.M. 150
summative 131
summative assessment 148, 149, 152, 153
surveys, student satisfaction 22
Sutton, P. 29, 253
Swatz, A.L. 174

Sweller, J. 197
Swiecki, Z. 215
Sydor, D. 170
Szyld, D. 177

T

Tai, J. 20, 27, 42, 113, 120, 133, 134, 136, 138, 158, 200, 251, 270
Tamborg, A.L. 215
Tan, E. 196
Tan, K.H.K. 155
Tanes, Z. 214
Tannenbaum, S.I. 166–168
task related effects 249
Taylor, S. 109, 110
teacher, feedback capacity 277–279
teacher, heroism 277
teacher-centred 19, 20, 84
teaching-centred 4
Teasley, S.D. 214
Teather, S. 212
technology 228, 229, 237
Telio, S. 28, 39, 45, 86, 89, 96, 251
Ten Haaf, J. 198
Teunissen, P.W. 95, 166, 171, 172, 176, 179
Theoretical framework 252
theory 253
theory, behavior change science 195
theory, cognitive load 197
theory, informed self-assessment 195
theory, learner centredness 197
theory, person-centred 195
theory, reflection 190, 193, 195, 197, 198
theory, self-directedness 197
think aloud 256
Thomas, J.S. 86

302   Index

Thompson, D.G. 156
Tigelaar, D. 31, 215
Tillema, H.H. 107
Timmerman, A.A. 31, 215
Timms, M. 110, 112
Timperley, H. 44, 107, 112, 118,
    170, 208, 215, 246, 273
To, J. 134
Tomlinson, M. 137
Towler, M. 167
Tracey, S. 190
tracing effects 283
tracking effects 272
tracking impact 227
Treat, R. 168
Treweek, S. 189, 191
Trowbridge, R. 190, 245, 246
Trowler, P. 71
trust 86, 88, 89, 101, 251
trustworthiness 89, 101
Tu, Y. 111
Tuller, D.E. 195, 196
Tummons, J. 255
Tunny, T. 195
Tyerman, J. 169

U

Ufer, S. 108, 115
unintended effects 247
Upshaw, H.S. 111
Urquhart, L.M. 47, 84, 87, 95, 100,
    256

V

Valtcheva, A. 151
van Berlo, J. 198
van Beukelen, P. 95

van den Broek, P. 116
van der Leeuw, R.M. 166, 171
van der Vleuten, C.P.M. 28, 29, 31,
    95, 166, 171, 189–191, 195,
    197, 198, 215, 258
van Driel, J.H. 116
Van Gennip, N. 107
van Goor, H. 196
Van Heukelom, J.N. 168
Van Merriënboer, J.J.G. 197, 198
Van Nieuwerburgh, C. 194
Van Soom, C. 215
van Stralen, M.M. 189
van Tartwijk, J. 31, 215
Vandewalle, D. 109
Varaklis, K. 190, 245, 246
Vardi, I. 166
Värlander, S. 85
Varpio, L. 257
Verbert, K. 214, 215
Victor, R. 55, 61, 229
video feedback 229
video reflexive ethnography 100
visualisations 215
vulnerability 90, 100
Vuori, J. 40
Vygotsky, L.S. 68–70

W

Wakefield, J. 196–199
Walker, C. 90
Wang, J.T.H. 229
Wang, L. 170
Warner, J.R. 108
Warren, A. 192, 193, 196, 198
Wearn, A. 195
Wenger, E. 29
Wertsch, J.V. 68–71

West, R. 189
Westman, S. 40
Wichmann, A. 116
Wickens, T.D. 268
Wiener, N. 18, 39
Wigfield, A. 157
Wiliam, D. 108, 110, 115, 246–248
Wilkinson, T. 195
Williams, J. 108, 110
Williams, K.M. 108
Williams, L. 135
Williamson, Z.H. 108
Wilson, J. 119
Wilson, R. 170
Winne, P.H. 110, 115, 150, 155, 210, 218, 254
Winstone, N. 61, 129, 228, 229, 237
Winstone, N.E. 67, 108, 158, 189–191, 208, 215, 226–228, 230, 231, 237, 246
Wise, A.F. 216
Wiseman, P.J. 42
Wittek, A. 61, 107
workload 208, 210, 212

workplace 84, 86, 87, 92–96, 98, 272
Worthy, P. 55, 61, 229
written plan 193
Wu, W.C.V. 212

X

Xeroulis, G.J. 168
Xue, X. 110

Y

Yan, Z. 149
Yang, M. 55, 107, 121, 213, 214, 273
Yau, J.Y.-K. 40
Yen, W. 192, 193, 195, 197–199

Z

Zendejas, B. 168
Zetkulic, M. 174, 191–193, 196, 198
Zhang, Y. 110
Zimbardi, K. 55, 61, 228, 229
Zimmerman, B.J. 155
zone of optimal control 90

Printed in the United States
By Bookmasters